PATIENTS
AT RISK

PATIENTS
AT RISK

*The Rise of the Nurse Practitioner and
Physician Assistant in Healthcare*

NIRAN AL-AGBA, M.D.
REBEKAH BERNARD, M.D.

Universal Publishers
Irvine • Boca Raton

Patients at Risk:
The Rise of the Nurse Practitioner and Physician Assistant in Healthcare

Universal Publishers, Inc.
Irvine • Boca Raton
USA • 2020
www.Universal-Publishers.com

ISBN: 978-1-62734-316-9 (pbk.)
ISBN: 978-1-62734-317-6 (ebk.)

Typeset by Medlar Publishing Solutions Pvt Ltd, India
Cover design by Ivan Popov

Library of Congress Cataloging-in-Publication Data

Names: Al-Agba, Niran, 1974- author. | Bernard, Rebekah, 1974- author.
Title: Patients at risk : the rise of the nurse practitioner and physician assistant in
    healthcare / Niran Al-Agba, M.D., Rebekah Bernard, M.D.
Description: Irvine : Universal-Publishers, Inc., [2020] | Includes bibliographical
    references.
Identifiers: LCCN 2020034646 (print) | LCCN 2020034647 (ebook) |
    ISBN 9781627343169 (paperback) | ISBN 9781627343176 (ebook)
Subjects: LCSH: Patients--Safety measures. | Medical errors--Prevention. |
    Physician and patient.
Classification: LCC R729.8 .A43 2020 (print) | LCC R729.8 (ebook) |
    DDC 610.28/9--dc23
LC record available at https://lccn.loc.gov/2020034646
LC ebook record available at https://lccn.loc.gov/2020034647

DEDICATION

This book is dedicated to the memory of Alexus Jamel Ochoa-Dockins and the countless others who have been harmed by a healthcare system corrupted by greed. May the telling of her story give a voice to those who have been silenced and lead to changes in healthcare policy that will ensure that all patients receive equitable, high quality medical care.

(Photo contributed by family)

TABLE OF CONTENTS

INTRODUCTION

On a sunny Tuesday in March 2015, the steps of Capitol Hill were draped in white as nurse practitioners from across the United States descended on the nation's capital. Their long white coats flapping, and stethoscopes draped around their necks, the lobbyists marched with determined steps.

The organizer of the event, the American Association of Nurse Practitioners, called it a record day. Nurse practitioners had scheduled more than 250 visits with legislators.[1] Their message to lawmakers was clear: Nurse practitioners are just as good—or better—than physicians.[2] Further, if it were legal for nurse practitioners to practice autonomously, the country would save money while also increasing access to healthcare in physician shortage areas —a promise with tremendous appeal to those in public office.[3]

The nurse practitioners had a compelling argument. The cost of the 15,000 hours of training required of physicians before being permitted to practice medicine is much higher than the minimum 500 hours required of nurse practitioners.[4] At the same time, lobbyists showed lawmakers studies that appeared to indicate that nurse practitioners were just as safe and effective as physicians, despite this difference in training and experience. So, why pay for the high cost of medical school and residency for physicians when nurses can be trained in less time and for less money?

Lawmakers listened attentively to these arguments. Representatives with large rural constituencies were particularly intrigued by the idea that nurse practitioners could increase access to healthcare in underserved areas. After all, economists were once again predicting a physician shortage, and nurse practitioners promised to fill that void.

By 2019, legislators in 23 states and Washington DC were convinced. Despite opposition from physician and patient advocacy groups, lawmakers in these states granted nurse practitioners the right to provide medical care to patients without physician supervision. Corporations and private equity markets were delighted. Instead of paying top dollar for fully trained physicians, these organizations now had the green light to hire less expensive nurse practitioners. Retail pharmacies across the nation rushed to install nurse practitioners into mini-clinics on every corner. Hospitals began to staff emergency departments and intensive care units with "doctors" of nursing. University medical centers even began to utilize nurse practitioners to teach medical students and resident physicians. Noting the success of nurse practitioners, other groups began to follow suit, with physician assistants, pharmacists, and psychologists lobbying for expanded practice rights.

With an increased demand for nurse practitioners, private, for-profit training programs rapidly emerged. These programs competed fiercely for student tuition dollars, boasting 100% acceptance rates to potential students,[5] offering flexible options for nurses to work and attend school at the same time,[6] and promising accelerated study tracks to become a nurse practitioner in just 2 years.[7] Some programs even promoted 'direct entry' programs that allowed non-nurses to become nurse practitioners—no previous nursing experience required.[8] Students flocked to attend such programs, many of which offered 100% online training.[9] Not to be left behind, physician assistant programs began to jump on the bandwagon with Yale University graduating its first online class of physician assistants in May 2020.[10]

Experienced nurse practitioners who completed their training at traditional brick-and-mortar nursing institutions complained that these programs were nothing more than 'diploma mills' offering inadequate clinical experience. However, the American Association of Nurse Practitioners did nothing to slow down the production of new graduates. Increasingly, nurse practitioners were starting their first day of work with little to no nursing experience—and corporations were ready to hire them to care for patients independently, no questions asked, due to the lower payroll costs compared to trained physicians.

Unfortunately, most Americans have remained dangerously unaware of this revolution in healthcare. Being treated by a non-physician is not on the radar of the average patient, most of whom assume that anyone in a white coat is a physician. If patients do wonder about being treated by a non-physician, they are reassured that their nurse practitioner or physician assistant is 'just as good' as a doctor, an idea reinforced by multi-million-dollar direct-to-patient advertising campaigns. But is care by nurse practitioners and physician assistants really as good as that of physicians?

Imagine this scenario: There is a looming shortage of pilots in the nation, and experts expect that there will not be enough available pilots to fly the nearly 2 million Americans who want to board a domestic flight every day. It takes about two years and 1,500 flight hours for a pilot to be certified to fly commercially by the Federal Aviation Administration (FAA).[11] Imagine that instead of training additional pilots from scratch, the FAA decided to put flight attendants in the cockpit. The attendants would take an online course on aviation with flight simulations, and then spend 500 hours in the cockpit shadowing a certified pilot before they were permitted to fly independently. Statistically speaking, there is an extremely low chance of a plane crash, and if there are no complications or mishaps, the flight attendants should do just as well as the fully trained pilots. But if your flight were being flown by a pilot with little experience, would getting onboard really be as safe?

A similar scenario is playing out in hospitals and clinics across our nation. Patients are being treated by practitioners with just a fraction of the training of physicians, and few are questioning whether this care is safe or effective. Americans should be every bit as concerned about their safety when they enter medical care as when they board an airplane. After all, more people receive medical care than fly in this country, with the Centers for Disease Control estimating that almost 85% of American adults—about 213 million people—have had contact with a healthcare professional in the past year.[12]

Like pilots, physicians have strict regulations that govern their education and training, and the requirements are standardized across the entire country. For non-physicians, however, this is not the case. Due to a lack of standardization, some non-physicians train for a relatively short time without access to experienced mentors in the clinical settings in which they will practice. Treatment by these practitioners may place patients at harm.

Consider the case of Brad Guilbeaux, a 45-year old father of two from Texas.[13] Just a few days after the March 2015 lobbying event described above, Brad initiated care with nurse practitioner Kevin G. Morgan. Although he was generally healthy, Brad was seeking an improvement in his overall sense of wellness and vitality. Nurse practitioner Morgan ordered blood tests, which showed normal thyroid and testosterone levels. Even though these labs were normal, the nurse practitioner wanted to make his patient feel better, so he prescribed Brad high doses of supplemental testosterone and thyroid medication. This treatment must have indeed given the patient an improved sense of well-being, as Brad returned to the nurse practitioner for continued prescriptions for the next year and a half. Unfortunately, Brad was unaware of the risks of taking these medications. More alarmingly, nurse practitioner Morgan was also unaware of the risks in prescribing them. As a family nurse practitioner who trained through an online program, Morgan did not have the training or experience to treat endocrine problems like thyroid disease or low testosterone. He seemed to be unaware of the increased risk of heart attacks in patients on these medications and was not being properly supervised by a physician. This lack of training and supervision was to prove fatal. On February 23, 2017, Brad Guilbeaux died of cardiac arrest caused by hormone therapy.

Even after being implicated in his death, it took nearly a year for the Texas Board of Nursing to take any action against Morgan, who continued to treat patients until his license was finally suspended on December 1, 2017. The Board also charged him with a second patient death and with harming 10 other patients by writing prescriptions for unnecessary medications.[14] Patients like Brad Guilbeaux, who are seeking an improvement in their health, are put at risk when they receive treatment from unqualified clinicians. Unfortunately, the risk is growing as non-physicians increasingly gain the right to provide medical care to patients with no supervision.

The rise of independently practicing non-physician practitioners has everything to do with money, politics, and control—and nothing to do with better patient care. The growth of these professions is the result of a systematic and coordinated effort by special interest groups to convince politicians, policymakers, and patients that non-physicians can do everything that doctors can do. Corporations have been quick to capitalize on the expansion of these practice rights. Across the country, physicians are being replaced by non-physician practitioners to save companies money. In the emergency department, for example, the chance of being treated by a non-physician instead of a medical doctor has skyrocketed over the last twenty years.[15] Most retail clinics, drugstore chains, and urgent care clinics are staffed entirely with non-physicians.[16] Large healthcare systems and even many university teaching hospitals have replaced staff physicians with non-physician practitioners.[17]

For no reason other than cost savings, physicians are being fired from their corporate jobs and replaced by nurse practitioners or physician assistants.[18] In states that still require non-physician supervision, doctors are being forced to supervise a high number of nurse practitioners and physician assistants to keep their jobs.[19] These doctors dare not speak out; physicians who express concerns about non-physician practitioners face punishment. Steven Maron, MD, a pediatrician with 31 years of experience, was fired from United Community Health Center in southern Arizona after writing a newspaper article explaining the difference in training between a physician and a nurse practitioner. As Maron pointed out in his op-ed, while there are excellent and experienced nurse practitioners and physician assistants, their education and training are not the same as that of a physician. He suggested that to make an informed decision about medical care, the public should know who is treating them and the critical differences in the training of clinicians.[20] Although Maron had worked for the community health center serving socioeconomically depressed children for 10 years without any disciplinary actions, he was terminated just days after the op-ed appeared in the *Green Valley News*. "I was told that my article stood in opposition to the principles of the organization, specifically the principle of mutual respect."[21]

Maron's firing likely stemmed not from a lack of respect, but from a vested interest in keeping patients in the dark about the difference in training between clinicians. After all, if patients begin to demand a doctor, organizations like United Community Health Center, which currently employs twice as many non-physician practitioners as physicians,[22] would be forced to restructure their entire staffing model.

THE RISE OF NON-PHYSICIAN PRACTITIONERS

Physicians created both the nurse practitioner and physician assistant professions. The roles were designed for the two to work side-by-side to provide complementary care, with physicians providing careful supervision and mentoring, and treating the most complex patients. This model works. Studies show that when physicians and non-physician practitioners work together, patients receive high-quality and cost-effective care.[23] However, this scientifically proven model began to shift in the 1970s, as nurse practitioners sought an expanded role in healthcare.

Nurse practitioners began to organize in the 1980s to advocate for increased practice rights. In 1993, they formed a coalition specifically to lobby Congress for "provider" status—a designation allowing nurse practitioners to be directly reimbursed for services, bypassing physician supervision.[24] This lobbying organization trained nurse practitioners in political activism, including how to most effectively communicate with legislators.[25] Nurse practitioners were taught how to share personal stories of patient care focusing on the needs of underserved patients. They also showed legislators studies that seemed to indicate that care by nurse practitioners was equivalent to physicians and more cost-effective.[26]

After hearing this direct testimony, many legislators were convinced. In 1997, 18 senators and 58 representatives co-sponsored the Primary Care Health Practitioner Incentive Act. The bill, which was signed into law by President Bill Clinton as the Balanced Budget Act of 1997, granted provider status and direct Medicare reimbursement to nurse practitioners.[27] The American College of Nurse Practitioners attributed their success to lobbying efforts from its members, stating that "the key to success came from the calls, the faxes, emails that applied the pressure on Congress to get the job done."[28]

The Affordable Care Act of 2010 further expanded the role of nurse practitioners by funding new community-based nurse-managed health centers. The law increased the production of nurse practitioners by authorizing millions of dollars to increase training program enrollment.[29] This expansion of funding resulted in a rapid proliferation of nurse practitioner training programs.

Historically, nurse practitioners trained at brick and mortar institutions, often associated with esteemed universities. These schools accepted only the top candidates, usually seasoned nurses with extensive clinical experience, and provided intense training. While such programs still exist, less rigorous training programs have become increasingly common. These schools, accused by critics of being nothing more than "diploma mills," boast high acceptance rates, 100% online curricula, and accelerated tracks with minimal clinical experience requirements.

For example, the nurse practitioner who was held responsible for the death of Brad Guilbeaux (as well as the death of another patient and harm to ten others) graduated from McNeese State University's Family Nurse Practitioner Program, which is only offered online.[30,31] He had just two years of experience as a nurse practitioner when he began to treat Brad Guilbeaux and was not being properly supervised by a physician despite the requirements of Texas law.[32]

Not to be outdone by nurse practitioners, physician assistants have also sought legislation to allow unsupervised practice and to be directly reimbursed for their services.[33] In 2019, physician assistants won a landmark legislative victory, and they are now permitted to practice independently for the first time in the state of North Dakota.[34]

Other professions are following suit:

- Optometrists are aggressively lobbying to expand their scope of practice to include surgical procedures. Currently, only ophthalmologists—who train for four additional years—have these privileges.[35]
- Psychologists are seeking the right to prescribe psychotropic medications—previously the domain of psychiatrists, who train for an additional four to five years after medical school.
- Pharmacists are advocating for the right to not only dispense medications, but also to make medical diagnoses, order lab tests, and prescribe medications without physician involvement.[36]
- Naturopaths, alternative practitioners who do not follow standard scientific practice, successfully lobbied to be considered primary care physicians in several states and even receive payment from insurance and Medicaid in Washington, Oregon, and Vermont.[37]
- In several states, chiropractors have won the right to perform minor surgery, do pelvic examinations, and practice obstetrics.[38]

As non-physician groups continue to push for an elevated role in healthcare, more Americans will receive treatment from non-physician practitioners without ever being informed. Patients rarely think to ask about the qualifications or experience of their healthcare practitioners. We simply assume that the person providing us with treatment in a healthcare setting is qualified, especially when we are under medical duress. But with the replacement of physicians by non-physician practitioners, it is no longer safe to assume that all care is the same. More alarmingly, patients are increasingly learning that they no longer have a choice regarding who will provide their medical care.

In 2019, there were a little over 1 million physicians actively licensed in the United States[39] and 421,000 non-physician practitioners: 290,000 nurse practitioners[40] and 131,000 physician assistants.[41] While physicians currently outnumber non-physician practitioners in the United States, the rate at which non-physicians graduate and enter the healthcare field is significantly outpacing that of physicians. For example, over a ten-year period, the number of physician assistants increased by 53.8%[42] and nurse practitioners doubled,[43] while physicians grew by only 12%.[44] An examination of the growth of these professions between 2010 and 2020 shows even more dramatic growth in nonphysician practitioners compared to physicians (see graph below). If these trends persist, it is not unreasonable to expect that the number of non-physician practitioners will eventually surpass the number of physicians.

In other words, if you aren't already being treated by a non-physician practitioner, then odds are, you soon will be.

GROWTH SINCE **2010** IN THE NUMBER OF ACTIVE
US PHYSICIANS AND NON-PHYSICIAN PROVIDERS

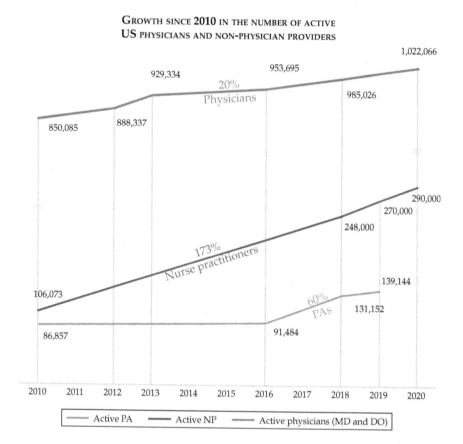

WHERE IS THE DATA?

Non-physician advocacy groups point to studies that claim that nurse practitioners and physician assistants can provide care for patients safely and effectively. Indeed, some studies have shown that non-physicians can and do provide quality care when working in teams with physicians, following clear medical protocols. *However, there are absolutely no credible scientific studies that support the safety and efficacy of non-physicians practicing without physician supervision. None.*

This is a bold statement, but it is unequivocally true. While medical literature headlines and abstracts may imply that the non-physician practitioners being studied were providing care 'independently,' the fine print reveals otherwise. A detailed reading of each article makes it clear that in every single study, physicians were available for consultation and supervision when non-physician practitioners ran into trouble. Proponents of independent non-physician practice are making a dangerous assumption: that if a non-physician can practice safely with physician supervision, as studies seem to indicate, then they should be able to practice equally as safely without physician involvement.

Patients need to know the truth. *Patients at Risk: The Rise of the Nurse Practitioner and Physician Assistant in Healthcare* will provide you with the essential background you need to understand the dangers you may face in an increasingly corporate healthcare system. More importantly, it will provide you with tools to protect yourself and your family from harm:

- Learn to identify who is providing your care.
- Gain the confidence to ask for your practitioner's credentials if they are unclear.
- Learn the differences in training and education of each type of medical practitioner.
- Know to ask if a non-physician is practicing under physician supervision.
- Be empowered to walk away from a medical practitioner if you are uncomfortable with the quality of care.
- Find out where to look for physician-led medical care.

Most importantly, this book will cause you to speak out and demand changes to our healthcare system that prioritize patient care.

CHAPTER 1

DIFFERENCES THAT CAN KILL

Alexus Ochoa-Dockins was a healthy and vibrant 19-year-old girl from Oklahoma. A straight-A student and top-notch athlete, only an unfortunate injury to her knee—a torn anterior cruciate ligament—precluded her participation in Division 1 basketball during her first year of college. In September 2015, Alexus had just begun her sophomore year at Redland College in El Reno, Oklahoma. On Thursday, September 24, she began feeling unwell, but like most healthy teenagers, Alexus ignored her symptoms and went about her regular activities.

According to court records, Alexus and her boyfriend Cortez Wright drove home for the weekend to visit family and returned to El Reno on the afternoon of Sunday, September 27, 2015. Upon arrival at her college dormitory, Alexus began to experience chest pain. She told her boyfriend that she couldn't breathe. Then, Alexus fainted.

Alarmed, her boyfriend called 9-1-1. An ambulance owned by the local hospital—Mercy El-Reno—responded to the call. The emergency paramedic who arrived on the scene immediately suspected that Alexus was suffering from a pulmonary embolism and called ahead to the emergency room to give her assessment. (A pulmonary embolism is a life-threatening medical condition, caused when a blood clot in the lungs interrupts the flow of oxygen to the rest of the body.) Without proper medication to dissolve the blood clot, patients are at high risk of death.

When Alexus arrived by ambulance at the Mercy El-Reno emergency room on September 27, nurse practitioner Antoinette Thompson met her to provide care. Thompson was an experienced health professional. She had worked for 15 years as a firefighter and paramedic before returning to school to become a nurse. She also worked for several years as an emergency room nurse before returning to school in 2012 to become a nurse practitioner. Thompson graduated from the University of South Alabama in 2014 with a master's degree in nursing, where her curriculum was completed entirely online, other than the two weeks of classes she attended on-campus. In addition to her online training, Thompson was required to complete 500 hours of clinical experience. She earned these hours working at a county health department providing medical care to healthy, stable pregnant women.

On December 30, 2014, Thompson passed her nurse practitioner certification exam and applied for a job with the Mercy Health system. Although she had no nurse practitioner experience in an emergency room or urgent care setting, Thompson was hired a month later to work in the emergency room of Mercy-El Reno Hospital. On the day that Alexus was rushed to the emergency room, Thompson had been a nurse practitioner for only eight months. Alexus Ochoa's life now rested in her hands.[45]

HISTORY OF NURSING

The first nurse practitioner program opened in 1965, and by 2019, more than 290,000 nurse practitioners were licensed to practice in the United States.[46] This number has grown exponentially in recent decades, with the total number of nurse practitioners doubling between 2005 and 2019. Meanwhile, new physician graduates have remained relatively flat. How and why has the nurse practitioner model grown so rapidly?

The origin of professional nursing is generally attributed to Florence Nightingale, a British social reformer. In 1854, Nightingale, along with a team of 38 women, succeeded in significantly reducing mortality in a Crimean War hospital barrack by establishing standards for basic sanitation, the provision of medical necessities, and close attention to the psychological needs of the soldiers. Upon her return from the war, Nightingale started a School for Nursing in London and wrote the book "Notes on Nursing: What It Is and What It Is Not" (1859).

In the United States, a female physician—Susan Dimock, MD—established the first professional nursing school. Dimock studied medicine in Switzerland after her application was rejected from Harvard University, which refused to accept women at the time. After graduating from the University of Zurich with high honors, Dimock returned to the New England Hospital for Women and Children in Boston, where she developed a training program for nurses in 1872, including lectures on the study of anatomy. Linda Richards, a graduate of Dimock's nursing program, became America's first professional nurse and went on to establish nursing schools across the country.

The number of nursing professionals rapidly increased in the early 1900s as the number of hospitals in the U.S. grew from 149 in 1873 to 4,400 in 1910. With an increased demand for hospital nurses, nursing schools began to fall under hospital authority. This change shifted nursing training from the Nightingale-Dimock model of using books and lectures to a greater emphasis on clinical experience—a development considered by some nurses to be a clever disguise for cheap labor.

Nurses were also in demand outside the hospital. The growth of inner cities and crowded living arrangements led to greater numbers of patients being afflicted with tuberculosis and other communicable diseases. Community nurses were critical in the care of these patients. The importance of public health nursing was further bolstered by the 1918 flu pandemic.

During World War II, nurse volunteers served soldiers in the field and civilians at home. The war provided nurses with experience in leadership, which they utilized upon returning home to organize and lobby for better pay and working conditions. By the 1950s, most nursing schools moved out of hospitals and into universities. Anticipating the need for more nurses, the Federal Nurse Training Act of 1964 increased funding for nurse training.

THE DEVELOPMENT OF THE NURSE PRACTITIONER MODEL

The designation of *nurse practitioner* was first described in 1964, when pediatrician Henry Silver and nursing professor Loretta Ford created a pediatric nurse practitioner program at the University of Colorado. The program opened its doors in 1965, with the goal of graduating advanced nurses who would work alongside physicians to provide well-childcare. Nurses were trained to perform well-child exams, administer immunizations, and provide education on disease prevention and health promotion.[47] The new designation caught on, growing to 65 nurse practitioner programs in 1973. Rather than focusing simply on wellness, nurse practitioner programs began to train nurses on diagnosing and treating disease states.

This created a challenge: the scope of practice for a nurse practitioner now fell outside of the American Nurses Association's 1955 definition of nursing, which emphasized that nurses did not diagnose or prescribe. To resolve this problem, the U.S. Department of Health, Education and Welfare (today's Department of Health and Human Services) established a *Committee to Study Extended Role for Nurses* in the 1970s. The group concluded that extending nursing scope of practice was "essential to providing equal access to healthcare for all Americans," and called for a national certification for nurse practitioners, as well as increased federal funding to train nurse practitioners.[48] Private philanthropy played a large role in the development of the nurse practitioner model, with the Commonwealth Fund, Robert Wood Johnson Foundation, and the Carnegie Corporation of New York all donating large sums of money towards the effort.[49]

Idaho became the first state to recognize the nurse practitioner role in 1971. In an effort to increase healthcare in underserved areas, the Rural Health Clinic Act of 1977 authorized funding for nurse practitioners working in rural health centers. The law further required that 50% of all services provided by federally funded rural health clinics be provided by nurse practitioners or physician assistants. In 1989, the Omnibus Budget Reconciliation Act added reimbursement for rural nurse practitioners working under physician supervision outside of these clinic settings.[50]

While the goal of the first nurse practitioner program was for physicians and nurse practitioners to work together collaboratively, the tide began to shift as nurse practitioners sought more autonomy and independence. Up until this point, nurse practitioners were paid through their association with a physician or hospital, except in certain rural areas. In the 1990s, nurse practitioner leaders began a concerted campaign to make direct reimbursement a "top legislative priority."[51] They did this by bringing together 125 nursing leaders in 1993 for a leadership summit, which led to the formation of the National Nurse Practitioner Coalition. This Coalition combined eleven different organizations to form a powerful lobbying group that would later become the American College of Nurse Practitioners (ACNP).[52]

Members of the ACNP received training on political activism, attending lectures on how to effectively spread their message to legislators. The College released calls-to-action with specific instructions on how to communicate with policymakers—and their hard work paid off. As policymaker support for nurse practitioner legislation grew, nursing organizations "thanked their congressional advocates with awards and recognition at local, state, and national meetings, and worked within their membership to express gratitude at the district level."[53]

Even nurse practitioner students were encouraged to participate in the political process. "Political advocacy is built into nurse practitioner programs," said Dara Grieger, MD, a former nurse practitioner-turned-physician, who attended political events during her nurse training program. "If there was an important vote pending and they needed our support, class would be canceled for the day. You needed to be there to make an impression on the legislature." In 1994, on the day of the final vote granting nurse practitioners prescribing privileges in Tennessee, Grieger recalls, "our entire class was taken by faculty to the state capital to sit in the chamber."[54]

To take their agenda to the next level, the ACNP hired a full-time lobbying firm in 1996, which would prove to be a highly strategic decision. The very next year, President Bill Clinton signed the Balanced Budget Act, recognizing nurse practitioners as "providers" by Medicare and Medicaid, and authorizing direct payment for their services in any setting.

THE ROBERT WOOD JOHNSON FOUNDATION

The increase in nurse practitioner autonomy has been influenced by major funding from advocacy groups, most importantly, the Robert Wood Johnson Foundation (RWJF). Robert Wood Johnson was the founder of the company Johnson & Johnson, one of the world's largest manufacturers of health products. Today, the RWJF is considered the United States' largest health-focused philanthropy, with $11.4 billion in assets reported in 2017.[55] The Foundation has shown a particular interest in nursing, contributing $674 million since 1972 to promote the work of nurses across the country.[56]

The RWJF has been instrumental in advocating for an expanded role for nurse practitioners. Since 1997, the organization has spent $41.2 million to fund Executive Nurse Health Policy Fellowships intended to "prepare a select cadre of outstanding nurse executives for leadership roles in clinical service, education, and public health."[57] The RWJF chose Shirley Chater, PhD, RN, FAAN, a nurse with political experience, as the fellowship's founding chair. Chater previously served as commissioner of the U.S. Social Security Administration under President Bill Clinton.[58] According to the Foundation, the fellowship offers "exclusive, hands-on policy experience with the most influential congressional and executive offices in the nation's capital."[59] Nurse fellows "spend a year in Washington, D.C., working on health-related legislative and regulatory issues with members of Congress and the executive branch. They … also engage in seminars and discussions on health policy and participate in leadership development programs.[60]

Through this program, more than a dozen RWJ nurse fellows participated in congressional committees responsible for crafting health-care legislation and formed powerful relationships with legislators.[61] Of the 300 nurse fellows produced by the RWJF, more than 30 were later appointed to health committees and task forces. Six were appointed to high-level positions in local, state, and federal government programs, including the Commission of Veterans Affairs and the National Institutes of Health. Twenty-seven RWJ fellows and alumni participated in the Institute of Medicine's influential 2010 Future of Nursing initiative.[62]

These opportunities led to politically important connections for nurses. In 1989, Congress named Nurse Carol Ann Lockhart, PhD, RN to its 13-member Physician Payment Review Commission, a group tasked with providing advice on reforming payments to physicians.[63] Based on the Commission's recommendations, the Omnibus Budget Reconciliation Act of 1989 granted reimbursement to rural nurse practitioners, established Medicaid payments for primary care nurse practitioners, and mandated a study of Medicare payments for non-physician practitioners.[64]

Another politically influential nurse, Sheila P. Burke, RN, MPA, became the chief of staff for Senate Majority Leader Robert Dole. In 2000, Burke was appointed as a member of the Medicare Payment Advisory Commission, which would ultimately recommend that nurse practitioners receive direct payment for services.[65] The plan to place nurses into positions of leadership was so successful that in 2014, nurse practitioner groups announced it as a national strategy: to put 10,000 nurses on boards by the year 2020.[66]

FUTURE OF NURSING REPORT

In 2009, the RWJF gave $4.2 million to the Institute of Medicine (now the National Academy of Medicine) to develop policy recommendations for nursing. The Institute's *Future of Nursing* committee released their report in 2010, providing "national recommendations for action on the future of nursing."[67]

The Institute of Medicine calls itself "objective, independent, and evidence-based." However, in addition to being heavily funded by the RWJF, 11 of the 18 Future of Nursing committee members had close relationships with the RWJF as board members or recipients of grants and scholarships. Several of the committee members had close ties with the American Association of Retired Persons (AARP), which receives funding from the Robert Wood Johnson Foundation.[68]

The Institute of Medicine's *Future of Nursing* committee was chaired by college-president-turned-politician Donna Shalala and members included a Chief Nursing Officer, several academic nursing professors, a nurse-midwife, the Vice Chairman of Johnson & Johnson, the CEO of the AARP, several healthcare administrators, think-tank advisors, a chief information officer, a business professor, and just three physicians. Of the physicians that participated on the committee, one worked in academia, another was the chairman and CEO of insurance giant Aetna, and the third was Vice-President of pharmacy giant CVS-Caremark.[69]

This committee, heavily weighted with nurses and industry, recommended significant changes in nursing education and payment structure. In particular, the group called for an increase in nurse practitioners with a doctorate (Doctor of Nursing) and demanded that insurance companies pay nurse practitioners directly. Ultimately, the report proclaimed that "nurses should be full partners with physicians and other healthcare professionals in redesigning healthcare in the United States."[70]

In addition to funding the *Future of Nursing* Report, the RWJF worked to implement the report's recommendations. The organization chose the AARP to lead its *Campaign for Action*, granting the organization $1.35 million in 2010.[71] The AARP received another $4.5 million per year in 2013, 2014, and 2015, and $8 million in 2019.[72] According to their website, "the *Campaign* works with policymakers, healthcare professionals, educators, and business leaders to respond to the country's increasing demand for safe, high-quality, and effective healthcare."[73] Efforts have included funding Action Coalitions in 34 states and helping to place nurses in leadership positions and board seats.

This technique worked. Government agencies and academic centers hastened to comply with the Institute of Medicine's recommendations, with a surge in the development of doctorate-degree programs and new 'residency' training programs for nurses.[74] Thousands of nurses received leadership training and were placed on boards.[75] Dashboard indicators on the *Campaign for Action* show that since these efforts began, ten states have granted nurse practitioners independent practice, and fifteen states have made incremental to substantial progress towards independent practice.[76]

Why is the Robert Wood Johnson Foundation so invested in expanding the role of nurse practitioners in the U.S? Some critics suspect that the Foundation has much to gain by funding the profession, pointing to

Johnson & Johnson's role as a drug maker and noting that an increased volume of prescribers would likely benefit the company's bottom line. For example, nurse practitioners (and physician assistants) have been found to prescribe more medications, including pain medications, than physicians.[77] Jannsen Pharmaceutics, a subsidiary of Johnson & Johnson, is a major producer of opioid pain medications and has been accused of aggressively marketing these drugs to prescribers and the public.[78]

Others note a close relationship with the mega-pharmacy chain CVS, which has collaborated closely with the Foundation in its goal to increase and expand the scope of practice of nurse practitioners. CVS has much to gain from this collaboration, as the chain has been hiring nurse practitioners to work at Minute Clinics within its drugstores since 2000, boasting more than 37 million patient visits.[79] Patients treated at Minute Clinics are likely to fill prescriptions written by their nurse practitioner at the very same CVS—perhaps even a drug produced by Johnson & Johnson. In addition to prescription medications, Johnson & Johnson manufactures a vast array of over-the-counter medications and household products. An increase in customers into CVS stores may result in more purchases of products with an even higher profit margin than prescription drugs.[80]

Another group that has maintained close ties with the Robert Wood Johnson Foundation is the AARP. While the exact nature of the relationship is unclear, critics note that the AARP receives millions of dollars from insurance companies by acting as an intermediary for seniors purchasing supplemental Medicare plans. In 2017, the AARP received $627 million from insurance giant UnitedHealthcare and its pharmacy subsidiary, OptumRx, which dispenses drugs and products made by Johnson & Johnson.[81]

STEPS TOWARD INDEPENDENT PRACTICE

Nurse practitioner leaders have lobbied for the freedom to practice without the requirement of being supervised by a physician, something they call "Full Practice Authority (FPA)." According to the American Association of Nurse Practitioners (AANP), FPA is "the authorization of nurse practitioners to evaluate patients, diagnose, order and interpret diagnostic tests and initiate and manage treatments—including prescribe medications—under the exclusive licensure authority of the state board of nursing."[82]

In the 1980s, Alaska, New Hampshire, Oregon, and Washington became the first states to grant nurse practitioners independent practice, hoping that nurse practitioners would increase access for underserved patients. Several other states with large rural areas followed in the 1990s, and by 2019, nearly half of the states in the union had legalized the practice of independent nurse practitioners.

Nurse practitioner organizations have been successful in achieving expanded practice rights not only through legislative efforts, but also through media campaigns directly to patients. The AANP has spent millions on public relations campaigns. Their goal: to gain patient trust in nurses as the leader of the clinical team. For example, in July 2016, the group launched a public relations campaign to promote an expanded scope of practice for nurse practitioners at the Veterans Administration (VA). Using TV and radio ads with the slogan "Veterans Deserve Care," the organization promised top-quality care to veterans. The ads claimed that the change in law "offers zero risk … in ensuring that veterans have zero delay to accessing necessary primary care within the VA system."[83] This campaign was successful. In September 2017, the VA granted nurse practitioners the right to treat patients without physician supervision at VA hospitals and clinics across the country, despite criticisms that the VA's own Evidence-Brief from 2014 concluded that there was insufficient evidence to make conclusions about the safety and efficacy of nurse practitioners.[84] Moreover, when some clinics asked to maintain physician supervision, the VA made it clear that physicians were no longer to supervise nurse practitioners—period.[85]

While the VA ruling has expanded practice rights for nurse practitioners, veterans are now losing the choice to see a physician. Jacob Ryan, a 38-year old veteran was unhappy about the care he received from an unsupervised nurse practitioner at the Palo Alto VA in California: "I was subjected to multiple unnecessary blood tests that had no indication, including a prostate screening test."[86] Prostate screening is not recommended for young men with no family history of prostate cancer. He also said that he felt treated "by a cookie-cutter algorithm or protocol," rather than receiving the personalized care that he believes all veterans deserve. "Our veteran population is one of the most at-risk in our nation. They deserve the highest level of physician-led care. Instead, this directive creates a 2-tier healthcare system for soldiers, sailors, airmen, and marines who fought to give and maintain our country's freedom."

Henry Travers, MD, a U.S. Navy veteran who served as a physician in the Middle East during Operation Desert Storm, observed that in granting nurse practitioner independent practice, "the VA did nothing to ameliorate the long wait times, falsified records and other failings that adversely impacted veterans over the last 3 years. Thus, the 'promise' of better care access promoted by professional nursing was, like the 'promise' of rural access, not only unfulfilled, but predictably a sham from the outset."[87]

Galvanized by their success at the VA, the AANP launched another media campaign in 2018 entitled, "We Choose NPs," which included television and radio ads, a patient-focused website, and digital advertising. The information used by the campaign implies that nurse practitioner (NP) care is better than physician care. The website claims that nurse practitioners have "98% satisfaction," with a link to a study of 200 patients in Flint, Michigan who ostensibly preferred nurse practitioner care to that of physicians.[88] The site also claims "NPs are a healthy choice for patients" and that nurse practitioners keep patients' health "on track"—apparently unlike physicians who wait "until something is wrong."[89]

The coronavirus pandemic of 2020 offered nurse practitioners a further opportunity to advance their goal of 'full practice authority.' On March 20, 2020, Sophia Thomas, the president of the American Association of Nurse Practitioners, sent a letter to the National Governors Association asking governors of all states to waive supervisory requirements for nurse practitioners. Despite the fact that many non-frontline medical workers were being furloughed and elective medical care delayed, the letter urged an expansion of practice rights for nurses, arguing that waiving supervision requirements "would remove a significant roadblock towards ensuring states have the necessary workforce capacity our nation needs during a pandemic."[90]

Many physicians and patient advocates expressed dismay at the use of a medical crisis to promote a political agenda. Neilly Buckalew, a hospital physician, wrote that "diagnosing, triaging, and treating COVID-19 is far beyond the training or experience of a nurse practitioner," noting that she herself, a board-certified physician, was still relying on the guidance of her infectious disease and critical care colleagues to provide appropriate care for patients.[91]

Some physicians pointed out that there was no reason that nurse practitioners couldn't help out in the pandemic without independent practice, working under the guidance of a physician. Others asked why nurse practitioners were not offering to return to their roots to provide essential bedside nursing in hospitals that were desperately pleading for nursing coverage and paying nurses top dollar in hazard pay. But once again, nurse practitioners in national leadership positions focused on advancing their goal of promoting independent practice, securing several wins. Governors from Kentucky, Louisiana, New Jersey, New York, and Wisconsin agreed to suspend supervisory requirements for nurse practitioners during the pandemic.[92] At the same time, New York took steps to limit the right of patients to sue for malpractice.[93]

While nurse practitioner leaders have emphasized the importance of "full practice authority" (FPA), not all nurse practitioners welcome the idea of independent practice. So many nurse practitioners have expressed concerns about FPA that the closing ceremony of the American Association of Nurse Practitioner's 2019 conference included a lecture by Margaret Fitzgerald, a nurse practitioner educator and advocate, addressing nurse practitioner opposition. Fitzgerald encouraged nurse practitioners to avoid vocalizing opposition to independent practice. Her lecture included a slide of a smiley face with a zipper for a mouth. The caption read, "Sometimes the strongest NP voice is silent."[94] One attendee summarized Fitzgerald's message this way: "If an APRN [Advanced Practice Registered Nurse] does not support FPA and vocalizes that...especially on social media...it actually can hurt our profession. I truly believe that any APRN who states that they are against FPA ... it is usually due to a lack of understanding of FPA and it is our responsibility to explain it to them respectfully. So I encourage each of you...if you come across a post from an APRN who seems not to be in support of FPA...please send them a private message educating them about FPA in a respectful manner. If you do not feel comfortable doing that ... please just send me a screenshot of their post and I will send them a message to address it."[95] In addition to this messaging, the nurse practitioner association created a reporting link on their website encouraging members to "report negative statements made about the NP role" coming from any source, with a promise to keep informants' identities confidential.[96]

Some nurse practitioners who oppose independent practice are terrified to speak out due to fear of repercussions, writing anonymously of their concerns. For example, a post on Reddit (a popular social media site) titled "I'm about to graduate from NP school and I am utterly unprepared" garnered 152 comments, many agreeing and commiserating with the author.[97] A post on AllNurses, a social media website for nurses, also expressed concern about the quality of nurse practitioner education.[98]

Some nurse practitioners are not afraid to speak out. Stephanie Frederick, CRNP, published a letter online that she wrote to the executive director of the Commission on Collegiate Nursing Education expressing her concerns about today's nurse practitioner programs. Noting a lack of minimum requirements for entry, uncontrolled growth of graduates, and inadequate preceptorships, Frederick wrote that the cornerstone of nurse practitioner education was "crumbling."[99]

Rayne Thoman, a psychiatric registered nurse, agrees with Frederick's assessment. Thoman reported deficiencies in her psychiatric and mental health nurse practitioner program to the Commission on Collegiate Nursing Education (CCNE) and the New York State Education Department's Board of Nursing in September 2019. In her complaint, Thoman outlined a number of problems with her nurse practitioner program. She noted that while the CCNE requires that nurse practitioners receive adequate preparation to care for patients "across the lifespan," her program offered only one lecture on the care of children and adolescents and one lecture on the care of older adults, and provided no specific clinical hours in any patient population. She reported that her courses on psychopathophysiology (the study of the causes of psychiatric disorders) and psychopharmacology (the study of medications used to treat psychiatric disorders) were both offered online without any lecture material or slides, writing: "There was absolutely no instruction for these courses or test outlines. No discussion boards. These courses basically taught you how to quickly look something up in a textbook." Thoman also complained that examinations for these courses were performed online and without proctors, allowing students to work together or look up information during the exam.

In addition to problems with the educational components of her program, Thoman also reported that she was not provided with adequate clinical experience opportunities or properly trained preceptors. For example, Thoman noted that her school allowed students to complete clinical hours with physician assistants and nurse practitioners who were not yet certified, in direct violation of New York educational requirements for nurse practitioner programs. A year after her initial complaint, Thoman has had no resolution of her concerns: "The CCNE did nothing, and the New York Department of Education investigation is still open and pending."

Thoman is concerned about the safety of patients being cared for by graduates of programs like hers. "The ultimate goal of graduate nursing education is to become competent to prescribe medications, diagnose diseases, and maintain patient safety. How these types of programs can continue to exist is beyond my comprehension. Going to a school like this truly feels like you hand them your money, keep quiet, and just take your degree." While Thoman is passionate about expanding her knowledge base, she says that patient safety is her top priority. She is now considering an alternate route—instead of becoming a nurse practitioner, she is planning to apply to medical school to become a physician.[100]

Indeed, studies show that many nurses do not feel that they are being adequately prepared to provide evidence-based care. A 2017 survey published in Worldviews Evidence Based Nursing, asked over 2,300 nurses from 19 hospitals and health systems to assess their skills in 24 practice competencies. Overall, the nurses reported that they did not feel competent in meeting any of the indicators, including collecting data, communicating evidence, and implementing change to improve care. Nurses with a master's degree (nurse practitioner level) had higher scores than nurses with bachelor's degrees, but still overwhelmingly did not assess themselves as competent in evidence-based practice.[101]

While nurse practitioner leaders are concerned about the quality of nursing education, they seem to be especially troubled by social media posts that display an inadequate knowledge base. In a 2019 editorial, "Social Media is Not for Clinical References," Sophia L Thomas, DNP, the President of the American Association of Nurse Practitioners urged nurse practitioners to avoid posting clinical cases or questions online. Thomas expressed concern about anti-nurse practitioner groups "trolling" nurse practitioner private social media pages to find evidence of clinical deficiencies. She advised nurse practitioners to learn by using evidence-based clinical tools or by a "quick online search."[102] But nurse practitioner students say that until the core deficits in nurse practitioner education are resolved, they are forced to turn to sources like social media for answers and help.[103]

Despite concerns from their members, nurse practitioner groups have strategically positioned the profession as a highly capable provider of American healthcare—equal to physicians. So, how does one become a nurse practitioner?

CHAPTER 2

IS THERE A NURSE PRACTITIONER IN THE HOUSE?

By the time Alexus Ochoa arrived at the emergency department, she was already extremely ill. Her vital signs were abnormal—her heart was racing, and her blood oxygen saturation level was dangerously low.

New nurse practitioner Antoinette Thompson appeared to have no idea what to do. Records indicate that she did not formulate a differential diagnosis—a list of possible explanations for a patient's symptoms. Instead, Thompson ordered a shotgun array of tests, including a panel of blood work, a urine sample, and a CT scan—a high-resolution x-ray—of Alexus's chest.

Although the nurse practitioner did not seem to realize it at the time, she had serendipitously hit upon the right test by ordering a CT scan. This imaging test would have shown that Alexus was suffering from a blood clot in her lungs.

However, before the test could be completed, Alexus fainted in the bathroom while providing a urine sample. This second fainting spell appears to have completely derailed the nurse practitioner. Distracted by this new symptom, Thompson's thinking headed in an entirely different direction. Seemingly less concerned about Alexus's difficulty breathing, she began to wonder if Alexus had fainted because something was wrong with her brain.

Focused on this new concern, Thompson postponed the chest CT scan and ordered an immediate head CT scan instead. When the head scan came back normal, Thompson failed to re-order the chest CT to evaluate Alexus's lungs. Instead, the nurse practitioner was drawn in by on a new finding. At 8:30 that evening, Thompson received a report that Alexus's urine test showed a presumptive positive detection of the illegal drug methamphetamine.

This finding should have seemed illogical to the nurse practitioner. First, Alexus was a college athlete and an honor student. She vehemently denied taking illicit drugs. Alexus's boyfriend and mother also insisted that Alexus had never used drugs. Second, Alexus did not exhibit any behavior consistent with ingesting methamphetamine. Her pupils were not dilated. She was not speaking rapidly nor was she exhibiting twitching or other neurological changes. Most importantly, methamphetamine toxicity did not fit as a cause of Alexus's clinical signs and symptoms, in particular her low blood pressure and oxygen level.

There was another reason Thompson should have been skeptical of these results. While Alexus's urine showed a presumptive positive for methamphetamine, it was *negative* for amphetamine. This made the likelihood of methamphetamine ingestion—a chemical which is broken down into amphetamine in the body—a statistical impossibility. Indeed, a second drug test would confirm the absence of any illicit drugs in Alexus Ochoa's system.

Unfortunately, this abnormal result would turn out to be the proverbial 'red herring' that can sometimes trip up newly minted healthcare professionals. Thompson seemed to become almost fixated on this presumptively positive urine drug test, ignoring all other possible causes of Alexus's symptoms. Instead, she focused all of her attention on providing treatments for a misdiagnosis of methamphetamine toxicity.

ALL ABOUT NURSES

Understanding nurse practitioner training begins with learning about the training of a nurse. While the word *nurse* is often used colloquially to describe various healthcare roles such as a medical assistant at a doctor's office or a personal care aid at a hospital, the term has a strict legal definition, indicating that a professional license has been obtained in a field of nursing study.

The most basic form of licensure related to nursing is a *certified nursing assistant*. A certified nursing assistant is licensed to provide basic healthcare assistance under the supervision of an upper-level nurse. Certified nursing assistant programs are offered at community colleges or vocational schools and may be completed in about eight weeks.

The first level of nursing licensure is the *licensed practical nurse (LPN)*, which requires a one-year course of study and passing a certification exam. These nurses are licensed to perform a limited number of nursing duties. A higher level of responsibility can be attained by earning the degree of a *registered nurse (RN)*. There are two pathways by which to accomplish this. The first consists of a 2-year associate degree and the second requires a 4-year bachelor's degree.

The associate degree in nursing is skills focused. Most curricula include two semesters of anatomy and physiology and several courses on psychology, with most coursework focusing on bedside nursing studies. Nursing bachelor programs add more science coursework, requiring two semesters of anatomy and physiology, one semester each of human growth and development, human nutrition, microbiology, psychology or sociology, statistics, and one course in the hard sciences—either chemistry, biology, physics, or biochemistry. After this coursework is complete, Bachelor of Nursing students spend four semesters studying bedside nursing. All registered nurses must complete clinical rotations, involving hands-on experience with patients in hospital and outpatient settings. To practice as a registered nurse, students must pass a national licensing exam after graduation.

The associate degree is a shorter and less expensive route that offers more options for nursing students who work while attending school. While 60 percent of RNs enter practice with an associate degree, there has been a surge in associate level nurses who go on to earn a bachelor's degree. In fact, there are currently 747 programs that allow associate level nurses to earn a bachelor's degree.[104] It usually takes two years for an associate degree-level RN to earn a bachelor's degree (BSN). However, accelerated programs now allow nurses to complete a BSN in 12 to 18 months. Many of these programs are online, specifically designed for nurses to continue working throughout the school program.

THE NURSE PRACTITIONER DEGREE

The number of nurse practitioner programs has grown rapidly since the origin of the profession in 1965. Today, there are more than 400 nurse practitioner programs in the United States.[105] In contrast, there are just 179 medical schools across the country.[106] With such an abundance of nurse practitioner programs, schools are now fiercely competing for students to fill their classrooms. One of the downsides of the increased capacity for students is that the criteria for entry has declined. In fact, at least nine programs boast 100% acceptance rates—every student who applies is guaranteed acceptance.[107]

The ease of being accepted to a big name, online, for-profit program was described by SummitRN at the website allnurses.com. The author, a registered nurse, reported receiving multiple telephone calls from a nurse practitioner school that she had clicked on while web surfing. While on the phone with the school's representative, the nurse filled out the online application "in about 10 minutes." She says that she was told, "We don't need references, no CV, only transcripts [from nursing school], no essay, no interview, no fees." Within 36 hours, the nurse had received an acceptance email to the program.[108]

The increase in what many call nurse practitioner 'diploma mills' has drawn concern from many sources, including senior nurse practitioners. Penny Kaye Jensen, past president of the American Association of Nurse Practitioners (AANP) took to social media to deliver a message. She wrote that while the AANP was unable to "call out" specific programs due to potential liability, "I personally think those who teach in these programs should be embarrassed and ashamed … some chose to follow the almighty dollar and have no pride." She further stated that nurse practitioner schools "need to establish rigorous admission criteria into NP [nurse practitioner] programs and not admit 'every warm body'," adding, "It's a major issue that students no longer need at least 5 years' experience as a RN before applying to a NP program." Jensen bemoaned the decline in the quality of nurse practitioner programs, and wrote "these subpar programs without clinical placements should has [sic] never been accredited, additional clinical hours are needed and nursing needs to establish the BSN as an entry level into practice."[109]

Despite concerns, nurse practitioner programs continue to flourish and compete for student enrollment. To attract students, many nurse practitioner programs offer great flexibility for both nurses and non-nurses, including part-time and accelerated options. For example, registered nurses without a bachelor's degree can become a nurse practitioner by entering a special program that allows them to obtain a bachelor's and then a nurse practitioner degree in 3 years (full-time) or 4–5 years (part-time). Nurses with a bachelor's degree can become a nurse practitioner in just 15 months of full-time study or 2–4 years of part-time study. There are even programs that promise completion of a nurse practitioner master's degree in only 12 to 15-months—completely online.

In other words, registered nurses who already have a bachelor's degree in nursing can become a Family Nurse Practitioner in under two years, with coursework completed entirely online. Compare this to physician training, which requires at least 7 years of study (4 years of medical school and 3 years of residency training) after receiving a bachelor's degree. The proponents of the nurse practitioner model argue that nurse practitioner programs don't take as long as medical school because unlike most medical students, nurses have a wealth of clinical nursing experience to draw from. While this may be the case for traditional nurse practitioner programs, new, direct-entry programs now allow non-nurses to go directly to nurse practitioner school—no nursing experience required. Although these direct-entry programs take a bit longer than the accelerated 12–15-month programs available to nurses, most allow non-nurses to become nurse practitioners in about 2–3 years.[110]

DIRECT ENTRY NURSE PRACTITIONER PROGRAMS

The direct entry nurse practitioner program allows anyone with a bachelor's degree in any subject to become a nurse practitioner by earning a master's degree. The University of Virginia advertises their direct program this way: "From English majors to engineering graduates, former attorneys to biologists, UVA Nursing's CNL [direct entry] program attracts professionals united in a common purpose: the desire to be nurses."[111] What's more, the direct entry nurse practitioner degree can be completed in under two years, with Marquette University advertising a "Direct Entry MSN" program that "lets you leverage your previous, non-nursing bachelor's degree to earn a [Master's in Nursing] in as few as 18 months."[112]

Dara Grieger, MD who trained as a nurse practitioner before attending medical school, graduated from one such direct entry program. "My first three semesters were registered nurse-level classes, plus just enough clinical experience to earn the minimum required to sit for the NCLEX [nursing exam]. The second three semesters were the nurse practitioner part." Grieger, who had never worked as a nurse before attending nurse practitioner school, graduated in only six semesters.[113]

California, the state with the most direct entry programs, boasts 14 different options, including Azusa Pacific University, with a price tag of about $80,000. The University of San Francisco advertises a direct program that can be completed in 2 years of full-time study—3 days of classroom work and 2 days of clinical practice per week. The program has a tuition price of $91,120. Massachusetts hosts at least 7 direct entry programs, including a distinct program offered through the MGH Institute of Health Professionals in Boston. This program allows non-nurses to become nurse practitioners in only 3 years—completely online. Even the Ivy League schools have gotten onboard with the direct-to-nurse practitioner programs, including Columbia University, the University of Pennsylvania, and Yale.

In 1990, there were just 12 programs that offered direct entry nurse practitioner options. By 2010, there were 65 such programs.[114] With the number of non-nurses willing to pay the hefty tuition prices to become nurse practitioners, the number of programs continues to increase.

ONLINE TRAINING

Nearly half of the 400 academic institutions offering nurse practitioner training programs promote distance education—online training—ranging from 50–99% of required academic training sessions.[115] Nurse practitioner Antoinette Thompson completed her training through one of these online programs at the University of South Alabama. Ten percent of these distance education nurse practitioner programs advertise a curriculum held *completely* online, such as at Texas A&M at Corpus Christi and the University of Southern Indiana. Columbus State University in Georgia advertises that family nurse practitioner students can complete coursework "100% online … in as little as two years," for an annual tuition of $17,000.[116]

Some online programs are even more accelerated. According to the website besthealthdegrees.com, Vanderbilt University's School of Nursing offers a 1-year online program for nurses with a bachelor's degree to earn a master's degree as a nurse practitioner. The website states, "Vandy's 1-year online MSN programs prepare graduates for careers as midwives, nurse practitioners, and psychiatric nurses, to name a few."[117]

For nurses without a bachelor's degree, becoming a nurse practitioner does not take much longer. For example, MCPHS University offers a 3-year program for nurses with an associate degree to become a family nurse practitioner. The website notes that the program is part-time, "designed for working nurses." Students spend one year completing their bachelor's degree, followed by master's level work.[118]

CLINICAL HOURS

One challenge to online learning is the need to practice medical care on actual patients. It is difficult to learn about the nuances of patient care from a computer, and those who learn completely online miss out on developing the necessary skills required for human interaction. While nurse practitioners may complete all their background training through online courses, they must also complete some direct clinical patient experience. This portion of training is called preceptorship and includes a series of rotations where students practice clinical skills and gain experience under a certified nurse practitioner or physician.

To qualify for the nurse practitioner certifying exam, students must complete a minimum of 500 clinically supervised hours. Some programs require more clinical hours, with one study showing that the requirement typically ranges from 540 to 825 hours, with an average requirement of 686 clinical hours.[119] Students may work with either a certified nurse practitioner or a physician for their preceptor hours. The setting may be in a private practice medical office, a community health center, an urgent care clinic, or a long-term care facility like a nursing home.

Clinical experience can be widely variable, depending highly on both the preceptor's willingness to teach and the student's enthusiasm to learn. Depending on the setting, a student may be exposed to a high volume of patients, or the practice may be slower, with less teaching cases for the student to observe. Experience may involve simply shadowing the preceptor and absorbing whatever information is provided, or the preceptor may allow a more hands-on approach with patients.

Ultimately, a student's educational experience will be limited by the type of material that he or she is exposed to during the time allowed. For example, if a student is precepting with a Family Physician who provides mostly adult care, then the student may not receive much pediatric exposure. If a nurse practitioner preceptor has a mostly female patient practice, then a student may be limited in exposure to male health. According to her deposition testimony, nurse practitioner Antoinette Thompson's clinical hours lacked this patient diversity. She completed her clinical hours working at a county health department, providing prenatal care to healthy, pregnant women.

The variability in clinical experience is a common complaint of nurse practitioner students, as they often have little choice in where they complete their hours. Because the rapid increase in nurse practitioner schools has created a strain on willing preceptors, many students are forced to search out their own preceptors and must accept whatever they find. The internet abounds with articles advising students on how to find a clinical preceptor. Suggestions include networking, starting a year early, cold calling doctors and nurse practitioners, being willing to travel, and utilizing services and even paid headhunters to find a preceptor.[120]

CERTIFYING EXAMINATIONS

Upon completion of a nurse practitioner training program, students must take a credentialing examination through one of five certifying organizations.[121] The family nurse practitioner exam is a 3–4-hour long exam of about 200 questions. In 2015, pass rates were 75% and 81% for two different certifying exams.[122] Applicants who fail the nurse practitioner exam must take fifteen hours of continuing education in the areas of weakness and may then retake the exam. They can retake the test twice in a calendar year until they achieve a passing rate.[123]

For comparison, physicians take a series of three standardized examinations, called "step" exams before they obtain a medical license, followed by a specialty board examination at the end of residency training. Step 1 is an eight-hour, 280-question test taken after the second year of medical school to evaluate a student's mastery of science. Step 2 is a nine-hour, 318-question exam taken in the fourth year of medical school to assess a student's clinical skills. Step 3 is the final exam that graduate medical students take during their internship year to receive a license to practice medicine. The exam takes two days to complete: the first day includes 7 hours of testing and covers "Foundations of Independent Practice," while the second day includes 9 hours of multiple-choice questions and computer-based simulations.[124]

While all physicians must take these three exams to be licensed to practice medicine, most physicians will go on to take a board examination in their specialty after they complete residency training. The family medicine physician board exam is nine hours long and consists of 320 questions.[125] The internal medicine board exam is 10 hours, with an additional four hours for specialists in cardiovascular disease.[126] Some specialties like psychiatry and surgical fields also have oral board exams, in which they must answer questions from trained examiners.[127] Physician certification is not permanent. Doctors must take recertification exams periodically and comply with burdensome "maintenance of certification" programs to keep their board certification active.

In further contrast to physicians, once certified, nurse practitioners remain so—indefinitely. There is no need to re-certify by taking another exam 10 years later. Rather, simple submission of practice hours is adequate, and even volunteer hours count for continuing nursing education credit.[128]

TYPES OF NURSE PRACTITIONERS

Nurse practitioners often demand the right to practice "to the full extent of their education and training," but with 183 different types of nursing certifications, determining exactly what type of education and training a nurse practitioner has completed can be challenging (see Appendix for a partial listing).[129]

The first nurse practitioner training program was designed for nurses to gain experience in treating pediatric patients, and most early programs focused on caring for adults and children in primary care settings. Over time, additional training programs began to provide certifications for nurse practitioners to work in fields outside of primary care, with little standardization.

By 2005, the choices and pathways for nurse practitioners had become so numerous and complicated that nursing leaders gathered to develop a consensus model to standardize and simplify nurse practitioner designations. The report was published in 2008, with a goal of implementing recommended changes by 2015.[130] By 2020, many states still had not yet fully adopted the model.

The consensus model placed nurse practitioners into four major categories:

- Clinical nurse specialist (CNS)
- Certified nurse practitioner (CNP)
- Certified registered nurse anesthetist (CRNA)
- Certified nurse-midwife (CNM)

Clinical nurse specialists and certified nurse practitioners were further subdivided by population focus:

- Family/individual across the lifespan
- Adult-geriatric
- Neonatal
- Pediatric
- Women's health
- Psychiatric/mental health

While there can be some overlap, the difference between clinical nurse specialist and nurse practitioner often relates to practice setting.

Clinical nurse specialists focus on education at the patient's bedside, often in the hospital. They generally work in close collaboration with other medical professionals, often supervising nurses. They may work as educators, in research, and in nursing leadership. In contrast, nurse practitioners tend to function more as a medical provider for direct patient care.

FAMILY NURSE PRACTITIONER

Most nurse practitioners obtain their licenses as a Family Nurse Practitioner (FNP). According to the AANP, "an FNP is an advanced practice registered nurse who provides a wide range of family-focused health-care services to patients of all ages, including infants, adolescents, adults and seniors. FNPs maintain patient records; perform physical exams; order or perform diagnostic tests; prescribe medications; develop treatment plans; and treat acute and chronic illnesses, conditions and injuries that fall under primary care. FNPs practice in a variety of health care settings, including community health centers, private practice, healthcare systems and universities."[131]

Most FNP programs are completed in two to three years, with many online programs available. Georgetown University School of Nursing advertises a program to "become an FNP online in 19 months."[132] The Chamberlain University FNP program encourages nurses to "expand your nursing practice in 3 years while you work full time."[133]

In just 2–3 years, family nurse practitioners are considered to be certified to provide competent care to patients of all ages, for all primary health problems. Compare this to family physicians, who train for a total of seven years—four years of medical school and three years of residency—to receive a similar certification. Family nurse practitioners are required to complete a minimum of 500 clinical hours before they may take the certifying exam to become licensed and may practice independently in half the states in the union. By the time family physicians are permitted to treat patients independently, they have completed 15,000 clinical hours of experience.

NURSE PRACTITIONERS IN ACUTE CARE

While most nurse practitioners train in primary care where they learn to managing patients with stable medical conditions, some will go on to work in acute settings like hospitals and emergency departments. To ensure that nurse practitioners were prepared to care for acutely ill patients, the consensus model called for additional training programs for acute care and mandated that only nurse practitioners with this training should work in such settings.

According to the National College of State Boards of Licensing, employers are responsible for verifying that nurse practitioners are properly trained for the setting in which they are hired, but determining whether a nurse practitioner is certified to work in a given area has proven to be challenging for employers. Take the case of Mercy-El Reno hospital, which hired primary care nurse practitioner Antoinette Thompson to work in an acute care setting, despite a lack of certifying credentials in acute care.

Nurse practitioners can obtain a certification in acute care by completing an Adult-Gerontology Acute Care Nurse Practitioner (AG-ACNP) program or by completing a dual program as a Family NP/Adult-Gerontological Acute Care Nurse Practitioner. Nurses with a master's degree may also obtain acute care certification by attending a doctorate program. For example, the University of South Alabama offers a 100% online doctorate degree in acute care that can be completed in five to six semesters of full-time study.[134]

To be certified as an acute care nurse practitioner, students must complete a minimum of 500 supervised practice hours.[135] This certification permits nurse practitioners to provide care in emergency rooms, hospitals, and intensive care units to patients age 13 and up, including the "frail elderly."[136] For contrast, hospital and emergency room physicians must complete four years of medical school and at least three to four years of residency training in internal medicine or emergency medicine—requiring well over 20,000 hours of experience before they are permitted to treat patients independently. Critical care physicians must complete an additional two to three years of fellowship training to be certified to work in an intensive care setting.

NURSE PRACTITIONERS IN SPECIALTY CARE

While the nurse practitioner role has traditionally emphasized primary care, specialty care is on the rise. As more nurse practitioners enter into specialty practice, some nursing leaders are calling for further updates to the consensus model, arguing that specialty education and certification are often "misaligned."[137]

How many nurse practitioners work in specialty fields? It depends on who you ask. While the American Association of Nurse Practitioners reports that 78% percent of nurse practitioners practice in the field of primary care,[138] the Health Resources and Services Administration (HRSA) reports that only 48% of nurse practitioners practiced in primary care in 2012. According to HRSA, the remainder of the nurse practitioner workforce practiced in internal medicine subspecialties (13%), surgical specialties (9%), pediatric subspecialties (3%), psychiatry/mental health (5.6%), and 20% reported as "other."[139]

Nurse practitioners with basic training in primary care can easily get a job in a subspecialty setting just by spending time working in a specialty office. After working for a certain number of hours under the tutelage of a physician, nurse practitioners may apply for and be granted "certifications" in fields like orthopedics and dermatology. There is nothing to stop a nurse practitioner from taking a course or two and then hanging out their own shingle, self-identifying as a specialist. For example, a nurse practitioner in Saratoga, New York, opened her own rheumatology practice specializing in diseases of the joints and connective tissue in October 2018. This practitioner, who also offers medical marijuana certifications in her office, lists her credentials as a master's degree in adult nursing care and "the completion of 19 postgraduate Rheumatology courses offered through the American College of Rheumatology."[140]

Physicians can't do this. Doctors are required to complete a multi-year residency training program before they are permitted to advertise themselves as specialists in a field like cardiology, dermatology, or orthopedics. For physicians to change specialty, for example, to go from being a primary care physician to becoming a psychiatrist or a dermatologist, a physician would be required to complete an entire separate residency program—*another* 3–4 years. To become a rheumatologist, for example, a physician must complete a 3-year residency program in internal medicine or pediatrics, followed by a 2–3-year fellowship in rheumatology. A family physician or internist would never be permitted to self-identify as a rheumatologist without this extra training, regardless of how many courses they completed through the American College of Rheumatology.

In many states, nurse practitioners are free to open medical spas where they inject patients with fillers and Botox. Online courses and weekend 'boot camps' abound for nurse practitioners to learn these skills. According to www.nursepractitionerschools.com, aesthetic nurse practitioners are under no legal obligation to pursue specialized credentialing to practice in the field. The site notes that, "many nurses who are worn out by the intense emotional demands of a specialty such as acute care nursing can find work as an aesthetic nurse practitioner to be a welcome change."[141]

Nurse practitioners are also assuming the roles of proceduralists. A primary care physician at a Texas VA writing anonymously because he fears retribution noted that one of his patients was referred to an ear, nose, and throat (ENT) specialist within the VA system for hoarseness and voice changes. A nurse practitioner performed a laryngoscopy procedure, inserting a flexible camera tube into the patient's throat. No physician supervisor was listed as present during the examination.[142] A physician without an ENT residency training would not be permitted by a hospital to perform this procedure independently, nor would malpractice insurance cover this type of work for a non-specialist physician. Moreover, few physicians would desire to do such a procedure without the proper training, due to an understanding of the risks involved.

Primary care physicians are particularly disturbed when they refer patients to a specialist, only to have them seen by a lesser trained nurse practitioner or physician assistant. Rural family physician Kimberly Becher, MD writes, "In many states, there are independently practicing nurse practitioners who attempt to do the work of a physician with no physician collaboration." She notes that it is "insulting" that patients she refers for consultation are seen by practitioners with less training than she herself has as a primary care physician.[143] Yet this trend continues, and often with the support of subspecialist physicians and programs. In 2019, the University of California, San Diego, Moores Cancer Center expanded the role of nurse practitioners, allowing them to independently order and assess the performance of chemotherapy treatments following a protocol. The criteria for these non-physician practitioners: at least 3 years of oncology experience and the completion of 20 chemotherapy orders under the direct supervision of an oncologist.[144] The university claims that allowing non-physician practitioners to provide increased care is due to a potential shortage in oncologists. Are patients informed that their cancer treatment is being directed by a nurse practitioner and not an oncologist?

PSYCHIATRIC/MENTAL HEALTH NURSE PRACTITIONER

Mental health is a rapidly growing field for nurse practitioners. There are hundreds of training programs for this field, including many online schools. One example is the Vanderbilt School of Nursing, which allows nurses with a bachelor's degree to become a psychiatric nurse practitioner in just 3 *semesters*. Nurses without a bachelor's degree must complete an additional 2 semesters before they can start the program, and anyone with a bachelor's degree in any subject can enter the program after completing a one year "full-time baccalaureate equivalent program" and then "progress" to the psychiatric-mental health program.[145] After a minimum of 500 clinical hours of experience, psychiatric nurse practitioner students can take a certifying exam, which will permit them to treat patients "across the lifespan," including children with serious mental health problems.[146]

To become a psychiatrist, a physician must complete a four-year residency program after medical school—the equivalent of at least 15,000 hours. To treat children and adolescents, a psychiatrist must complete an additional 2 years or about 5,000 additional hours of intensive training, while mental health nurse practitioners may graduate with only 100 hours of experience working with young patients.

Child and adolescent psychiatrists are some of the most vocal critics of the short training period for mental health nurse practitioners. Despite the difference in training hours, psychiatrists report that they have been fired and replaced by less expensive—and less experienced—nurse practitioners. Alison DeLuca, MD, a child and adolescent psychiatrist, was terminated from her job in a health provider shortage area in New Mexico. DeLuca was never given a negative performance review. She was simply told that her patients were going to be transferred to a nurse practitioner because the company "had decided to consolidate services." DeLuca was deeply concerned for her patients. "This population is underserved, underprivileged, and patients are very ill with chronic disease." She contacted the New Mexico Board of Medicine to inform them of her termination. "I wanted them to know that the psychiatrist shortage in the state has nothing to do with physicians not wanting to work. It's because we are being let go." DeLuca has still received no response from the Board.[147]

Another psychiatrist, speaking anonymously because she fears reprisal, said that she was replaced from a Federally Qualified Health Center by a psychiatric nurse practitioner who received her degree from an online nursing program. "Before I was let go, the nurse practitioner would sometimes 'sit-in' on my telepsychiatry sessions, but I never had any real dialogue with her, or any teaching moments." As a psychiatrist, she noted that training included "3 years doing a general psychiatry residency, and another 2 in pediatric and adolescent psychiatry. On top of that, I spent a year in a longitudinal autism spectrum clinic, even working with preschool children. This is not the type of experience that can be gained from an online program or just 'shadowing' a psychiatrist."[148]

Rayne Thoman, RN, is a psychiatric nurse who has worked with both psychiatrists and psychiatric/mental health nurse practitioners. "After working with both professionals, I can see the vast difference," she says, noting that unlike the psychiatrists she works with, mental health nurse practitioners "can't explain how or why psychiatric drugs work." Thoman says that as a nurse, she didn't realize the difference until she started her own mental health nurse practitioner program. "I started really paying attention to the people I worked with, and it opened my eyes."[149]

Robert Duprey, MD was a psychiatry nurse practitioner for eight years before he decided to return to medical school to become a psychiatrist. "My epiphany came when I realized how much more pathophysiology the psychiatry physicians I worked with knew than I did," he said. He describes a case in which a patient was experiencing severe flu-like symptoms. "I thought the patient had the flu, but the attending physician realized that he was actually suffering a drug reaction from a combination of medications." It was at that moment that Duprey says he realized, "I want what they have," and determined to go back to school to become a physician—specifically, a psychiatrist. Duprey supports the idea of psychiatric nurse practitioners working in close contact with physicians, "in a true team."[150] In an ideal situation, psychiatrists and nurse practitioners would have day-to-day, one-on-one interaction to ensure patient safety. Unfortunately, many companies choose to use psychiatry nurse practitioners not to complement psychiatrists, but to replace them. Despite the difference in years of training, many companies see the two professions as equal to each other. For example, Aspire Psychology in Portland, Oregon, placed this advertisement on Indeed.com in March 2019: "Hiring psychiatric nurse practitioner or psychiatrist—$180,000–200,000 per year."[151]

CERTIFIED REGISTERED NURSE ANESTHETIST (CRNA)

According to the American Association of Nurse Anesthetists, a certification to become a nurse anesthetist was first implemented in 1945. Currently, the pathway to becoming a certified registered nurse anesthetist begins with a bachelor's degree in nursing and one year of full-time work experience as a registered nurse in a critical care setting. Nurse anesthesia training programs take anywhere from 2–4 years, and graduates complete 2,500 clinical hours, administering about 850 anesthetics during their training. While most nurse anesthetists provide anesthesia in hospital or out-patient settings, some have branched into other fields, including pain management and the administration of intravenous ketamine for the treatment of depression.

Physicians who wish to administer anesthesia or provide pain management injections must complete a four-year residency training after medical school. According to law professor Edward P. Richards III, JD, MPH, "more than any other specialty, anesthesiology in the United States has blurred the distinction between physicians and nurse practitioners."[152]

While the American Association of Nurse Anesthetists proudly states on their website that nurses were among the first to provide anesthesia in the United States, offering care "to wounded soldiers on the battlefields of the Civil War," Richards points out that early anesthesia was a very different matter in those days, consisting of "a paper cone and a container of ether, both held by a nurse. This created the perception that anesthesia was a nursing task."[153]

In his book, *Law and the Physician: A Practical Guide* (1993), Richards notes that allowing nurses to administer anesthesia was not problematic until the practice became "much more sophisticated and technologically oriented." At this point, the gulf in knowledge between physicians trained in anesthesiology and nurse anesthetists became significant.

Anesthesia is an area of particular acrimony between physicians and nurse practitioners. Nurse anesthetists insist that they can provide the same level of care as their physician counterparts and note that 17 states allow them to provide anesthesia without physician supervision.[154] The American Society of Anesthesiologists disagrees, pointing out that studies showing similar outcomes between nurse practitioners and anesthesiologists tend to be funded by pro-nurse groups. They also note that fully independent nurse practitioners work with low-risk patients during low-risk procedures and that it is impossible to draw conclusions about the care of higher-risk patients and surgeries.[155] In fact, in cases in which an anesthesia or surgical complication occurred, physician-directed anesthesia was associated with lower rates of morbidity, preventing 6.9 excess deaths per 1000 cases.[156]

In many outpatient surgical centers, anesthesia is provided by certified registered nurse anesthetists (CRNA) without physician supervision.

While most of these cases are low risk and will not have any adverse events, when anesthesia goes wrong, the results can be catastrophic. For example, a 45-year-old father of three died when the CRNA failed to properly intubate him following an anesthetic complication. Rather than placing the breathing tube into the patient's airway, the CRNA misplaced the tube into the patient's stomach. The CRNA "admitted that he had not performed an intubation in the five years preceding." In addition, "he never discussed the risks and complications of anesthesia with the patient because he did not want to scare him."[157]

In August 2010, 4-year old Rose Tecumseh died after receiving deep sedation for dental work. Reports said that Dallas, TX CRNA Pamela Wilson failed to properly hydrate the child after giving a medication intended to dry her oral secretions for oral surgery. Wilson also reportedly failed to check the child's temperature or vital signs and quickly discharged the patient before the child was properly aroused. A media investigation said that the CRNA paid a settlement of $500,000 despite never being investigated or sanctioned by the Texas Board of Nursing.[158]

One of the controversies in the anesthesia world is the use of the term "anesthesiologist." The term has traditionally been synonymous with a physician trained in anesthesiology, with the word physician typically omitted. In recent years, nurse anesthetists have called for a change in terminology, asking to be called "nurse anesthesiologists." In October 2019, John McDonough, a certified registered nurse anesthetist in Florida, petitioned the Board of Nursing to be permitted to refer to himself as a "nurse anesthesiologist." In a report for a National Public Radio station, McDonough stated, "I am not a technician. I am not a physician extender. I am not a mid-level provider. I am, in fact, a scientific expert on the art and science of anesthesia."[159] Despite complaints from the Florida Society of Anesthesiologists (which represents residency-trained physicians) that changing the terminology would further confuse patients, the Florida Board of Nursing voted unanimously to approve McDonough's request to call himself a nurse anesthesiologist.

When critics of nursing anesthesia speak out, they face repercussions. The Anesthesia Patient Safety Foundation reported that the American Association of Nurse Anesthetists decided to withhold financial support from the group when it published a summary of the World Health Organization's "Standards for a Safe Practice of Anesthesia." The World Health Organization policy, which was unanimously approved by countries represented in the United Nation's World Health Assembly included a recommendation that anesthesia should be "provided, led, or overseen by an anesthesiologist." According to the president of the Anesthesia Patient Safety Foundation, the Nurse Anesthetist board demanded that the article be retracted, and when the Foundation refused, citing patient safety, the nurse anesthetist group withdrew its funding.[160]

CERTIFIED NURSE-MIDWIFE (CNM)

According to the *Consensus Model for APRN Regulation* (2008), a certified nurse-midwife does not just deliver babies and provide gynecologic care. Nurse midwives can also provide primary care to women throughout their life. They are authorized to care for newborn babies in the first 28 days of life. They may also provide treatment to male partners of their patients for sexual and reproductive health issues. This care can be provided in both acute care settings as well as outpatient settings and at the patient's home.[161] Preparation for this extensive array of skills can be found at forty different nurse-midwifery programs. While the requirements for entry vary, some allow non-nurses to enter into the program, while others do not require any experience in labor and delivery prior to admission.

Frontier Nursing University offers online coursework, full- or part-time options, and requires 675 hours for a master's degree as a nurse-midwife. The program notes that graduates can obtain a doctorate by performing an additional 360 hours or can "add a Women's Health Care Nurse Practitioner Post-Graduate Certificate with only 4 credit hours and 180 clinical hours."[162] Vanderbilt School of Nursing, rated #1 by *U.S. News and World Reports* for its midwifery program, will accept students without a nursing background into a special nurse-midwife program. Students must complete a "Pre-Specialty year" with weekly "face-to-face coursework the first semester." Registered nurses with a bachelor's degree may proceed directly into the four-semester program through a "hybrid learning format" which includes a combination of face-to-face classes and clinical rotations.[163]

In comparison, obstetrician-gynecologists undergo intensive training consisting of at least four years of residency training after medical school. Most obstetricians will hand-off care of newborn babies to pediatricians or neonatologists, an entirely different discipline of medicine with its own required 3–4-year residency training.

While most nurse-midwives perform deliveries in a hospital setting with obstetrician back-up in case an emergency cesarean section is needed, some deliver babies at freestanding birth centers and even at patient homes. In its series "Failure to Deliver," *USA Today* exposed the trend of home births and cited cases of nurse-midwives who failed to identify signs of maternal-fetal distress.[164] For example, in December 2017, nurse-midwife Cynthia Denbow was supervising the birth of Athena Riley's first child at a freestanding birth center in Fort Walton Beach, FL. The nurse-midwife failed to discover that the baby was in breech position, rather than head-first, until the patient was completely dilated and ready to push. Breech position makes delivering a baby much more difficult and increases the risk of complications to mother and child. Despite this, rather than transferring the patient to the hospital for a cesarean section, the nurse midwife attempted to deliver the baby vaginally. This was the wrong decision. The baby was stuck, and after nearly 30 minutes of pushing, began to show signs of distress. Nurse-midwife Denbow finally called 911, and Riley underwent an emergency cesarean section. Baby Riley did not survive.

In September 2011, another nurse-midwife Sadie Moss Jones agreed to assist Gia McGinley with her attempt to have a vaginal delivery. McGinly, at 39-years-old, had previously delivered a baby by cesarean section. Vaginal deliveries after cesarean sections carry a higher risk to the baby and the mother because the scar where the uterus was opened can rupture. Most obstetricians will only allow a trial of a vaginal delivery with careful observation in the hospital and will perform another cesarean section if there is any sign at all of maternal-fetal distress. Aside from McGinley's previous cesarean section, her attempt at vaginal delivery was further complicated by the size of her baby, weighing over 11 pounds at birth. The accurate estimation of a baby's birth weight is one of the factors that obstetricians use to determine whether it is safe to proceed with a vaginal delivery. This nurse-midwife either did not accurately assess the baby's weight as being large or did not consider it to be a factor in the delivery. Unfortunately, this combination of factors caused McGinley's uterus to rupture during labor contractions. When she fainted, nurse-midwife Jones called paramedics and the patient was taken to the hospital for an emergency cesarean-section. Sadly, Baby McGinley did not survive.

Problems can arise not only during home deliveries but also in the hospital setting. Dr. Judy Robinson, the Chief of Obstetrics and Gynecology at Methodist Hospital, the largest hospital in Indiana, also worked at HealthNet, a clinic serving women of lower socioeconomic status. Robinson discovered that nurse-midwives at the clinic were managing complex, high-risk patients without physician involvement. According to a news report, when Robinson tried to intervene, she was told by the head midwife, "don't you physicians dare try to take care of these patients … The only time you're going to see a patient is if I tell you you're going to see a patient." Robinson learned that the facility was billing the government for physician-level care, paying the midwives a lower fee, and pocketing the difference. Concerned for patient safety when she saw several babies harmed, Robinson reported the practice for the improper billing of patients. Although they denied wrongdoing, Methodist and HealthNet were required to pay $18 million to the government for incorrect billing practices.[165]

Fortunately, most of the time, babies are born uneventfully. When everything goes right, delivering a baby seems like a straightforward process. It is when things go wrong that seconds—and years of training—really matter. An obstetrician may attend hundreds of deliveries without experiencing any complications. It is for this reason that physicians are expected to participate in many thousands of deliveries during their four-year training period, to provide the opportunity to see these occasional adverse events and to learn how to respond.

IS THERE A DOCTOR IN THE HOUSE?

In clinical settings, most patients assume that a "doctor" is a medical doctor or physician. But in recent years, an explosion of doctorates in various medical professions has made the label of "doctor" far less clear. One example of a type of doctorate degree that may confuse the public is the Doctor of Nursing Practice (DNP), or "Doctor Nurse" degree. Historically, nurses who wished to attain a level of education beyond a master's degree could earn a doctorate level degree as a Ph.D. in nursing. This degree was generally sought by nurses who wished to pursue research and teaching. In 2001, the first DNP program was created at the University of Kentucky College of Nursing. Created as a way to "establish a higher level of credibility for nurses" to provide direct patient care, nursing leaders aggressively promoted the new degree to students. The DNP degree was further bolstered by the Institute of Medicine's "Future of Nursing" report, published in 2010, which called for an increase in nurses with a doctorate.

Starting with only a handful of programs in 2006, there are now 348 DNP programs currently enrolling students at schools of nursing nationwide, and an additional 98 new DNP programs in the planning stages.[166] The question must be asked: does doctoral-level training teach nurse practitioners how to better provide patient care? Or was the creation of the DNP degree a political maneuver, designed to appropriate the title of "doctor" and create a false sense of equivalence between nurse practitioners and physicians in the minds of the public?

According to Orla Weinhold, MD, a physician who worked as a family nurse practitioner for eight years before attending medical school, the DNP degree does not significantly expand the clinical training of nurse practitioners. "Most DNP programs are completely non-clinical," says Weinhold, who runs a social media group for nurses and physician assistants who are interested in advancing their careers. "I tell anyone who wants to advance their education … to go to medical school instead."[167]

Even Mary Mundinger, DrPH (Doctor of Public Health), a public health researcher long considered to be one of the most important advocates for nurse practitioners, has expressed concern about the nurse practitioner doctorate. In a 2019 article titled "Potential Crisis in Nurse Practitioner Education in the United States," Mundinger noted that only 15% of all nurse practitioner doctorates are clinical degrees. She wrote that the increase in nonclinical doctorates is out of proportion with the "nation's growing need for primary care clinicians."[168]

Indeed, a review of the curriculum of most two-year DNP programs shows a predominance of non-clinical material. Take Duke University's five-semester program, for instance. The curriculum does include Evidence-Based Practice I and II, which relate to direct patient care, however, the remaining coursework is far less clinically oriented. Additional classes include Transforming the Nation's Health, Data-Driven Health Care, Effective Leadership, and Transformation of Health Systems.[169] Chamberlain University's curriculum seems to be mostly nonclinical as well, offering courses on health policy, informatics, population health, and organizational leadership during its two-year DNP program.[170]

According to the American Association of Colleges of Nursing, DNP programs are required to provide core competencies, including scientific foundations for practice, focusing on the need to use science in healthcare and advanced nursing practice, but most DNP programs place a heavy emphasis on healthcare policy and on learning to publish research promoting nursing practice—less on fine-tuning clinical knowledge and skills. Additional competencies required for a DNP degree include organizational leadership for quality improvement, clinical scholarship and analytical methods for evidence-based practice, information systems and patient care technology, healthcare policy advocacy, inter-professional collaboration, and clinical prevention and population health.[171] All of these skills are intended to be achieved in programs that are meant to be completed by nurses with a master's degree in just 1–2 years of full-time study, or 2–3 years of part-time study.[172] During this time frame, DNP students must also complete 1000 clinical practice hours, although 500 of those hours can be applied from their previous nursing practice.[173]

Many DNP programs were originally designed for nurses to fulfill leadership roles rather than enhance clinical practice.[174] However, some nurses are using the degree to try to demonstrate equivalence to physician training. For example, Melissa DeCapua, DNP, wrote in an article, "The DNP creates parity with other advanced healthcare providers. When nurse practitioners earn a doctorate degree, they place themselves on par with other doctorally trained professionals. Physicians … hold doctorate degrees, for example."[175] To further complicate matters, the use of the term doctor by non-physicians can be confusing for patients, who may not understand the difference between a medical doctor, who receives more than ten years of education and training, and a doctorally prepared nurse, with a minimum of 1000 hours of clinical hands-on training as a nurse practitioner. Educational parity and expertise cannot possibly be achieved in a fraction of the time it takes to become a medical expert.

RESIDENCY AND FELLOWSHIPS

The term "residency" in medical education has traditionally represented the training period immediately following medical school. The term stems from the amount of time that physicians have to spend on-duty or "in-residence" at a hospital or clinic.[176] The first year of residency, often called internship, is one of the most intense and difficult times in the life of a physician. Although recent accreditation rules have tried to limit the amount of time that physicians-in-training spend on-duty, many physicians continue to report spending 80–100 hours per week during their residency years.[177] Physician residencies begin at 3-years for general internal medicine, pediatrics, and family medicine. Medicine and surgery specialties may require many additional years of training. Residency programs are highly standardized and must comply with strict accreditation standards.[178]

For nurse practitioners, hospitals and clinics are organizing additional training programs in the form of apprenticeships, using the term residency. Nurse practitioners' residencies are typically short in duration, usually no more than a year or two, require no more than 40-hours per week of work, and are highly compensated compared to physician resident salaries.[179] Because of the demanding nature of traditional physician residencies, many physicians resent the appropriation of the term by other medical clinicians.

Specialized physician training after residency is called a "fellowship." These fellowship positions are intensely competitive, prestigious, and rigorous. Typically, fellowships last 1–3 years, although further sub specialization may require additional years of training. For example, a hepatologist, or a physician who sub-specializes in diseases of the liver, first completes 3 years of internal medicine training. He or she will then go on to another 3 years of gastroenterology fellowship training and an additional 1 year of sub-specialization fellowship in diseases of the liver.

By comparison, nurse practitioner programs that use the term nurse "fellowships" are generally a year in length and do not require any previous residency training.[180] Sometimes the term is used when describing programs that consist of just a few days or weeks of additional instruction. While these additional training periods may help provide nurse practitioners with more education, there are several concerns. First, these programs simply cannot provide the same fund of knowledge that physicians receive as the base of their education in medical school. Secondly, unlike physician residencies and fellowships, there is no current standardization for nurse practitioner programs, nor are they accredited by any central oversight agency. Without clear standards, there is no guarantee that graduates will truly have a deep understanding of a field of medicine. Instead, nurse practitioner "residency" graduates may end up with just another certificate on the wall, leading them to a false sense of security in their expertise.

CHAPTER 3

A SLIPPERY SLOPE

At 8:32 pm on September 27, 2015, nurse practitioner Antoinette Thompson received a urine drug test result showing a presumptively positive finding of methamphetamine on her patient, Alexus Ochoa.

Alexus adamantly denied any history of drug use. She had no signs or symptoms of methamphetamine use, such as dilated pupils or high blood pressure. Besides, the urine drug test showed no metabolites of methamphetamine in the young woman's system. These clues should have made any clinician suspect the drug result was falsely positive. That did not happen; once Nurse practitioner Thompson saw the test result; she began to direct all of her interventions toward treating methamphetamine toxicity. Was it her lack of knowledge that precluded questioning the test result? It appears so.

Later, when asked if she knew that methamphetamine would cause dilation in a patient's pupils, she denied this knowledge, stating "I just went by what the drug screen said." Convinced that Alexus's symptoms were caused by illicit drug use and that her diagnostic workup was complete, this nurse practitioner canceled the other tests she had ordered, including her original order for a chest CT. This imaging test would have undoubtedly diagnosed the patient's massive pulmonary embolism.

Without a thorough understanding of the cause of a symptom or clinical finding, it is impossible to provide proper medical treatment. Rather than directing care to correct Alexus's underlying problem, nurse practitioner Thompson instead turned her attention toward treating the patient's symptoms. She began to administer medications to lower Alexus's rapid heart rate. This was another mistake. Alexus's heart was beating fast to compensate for the lack of oxygen caused by the blockage in her lungs. She needed as much blood flow as she could get if she were to survive. Without an understanding of the core problem, nurse practitioner Thompson was unable to recognize this mechanism. She simply saw an excessively fast heart rate and focused on trying to slow it down. The nurse practitioner administered adenosine, an anti-arrhythmic medication that temporarily stops one of two natural electrical pacemakers in the heart.

When Alexus's heart rate failed to slow down, Thompson began to wonder if perhaps the patient's heart rate was increased because she was having a panic attack from the presumed illicit drug in her system. The nurse practitioner decided to try giving Alexus diazepam (Valium), an anti-anxiety medication. When this did not work, Thompson moved on to trying yet another drug. She ordered metoprolol (Labetalol), a medication that slows the heart by blocking electrical channels. Because this drug also acts on receptors within the blood vessels themselves, metoprolol lowers blood pressure as well as heart rate.

A normal blood pressure reading is 120/80 in a healthy young person. Alexus had a blood pressure of 86/67 when this nurse practitioner incorrectly gave her metoprolol. This dangerously low blood pressure was a sign that Alexus's heart was having trouble keeping up with her body's demand for oxygen, and a sign of impending cardiovascular collapse. Adding a medication to slow her heart and lower her blood pressure even further was the last thing that this young athlete needed.

A SLIPPERY SLOPE

The expansion of practice rights for nurse practitioners has created a slippery slope by encouraging other traditionally physician-supervised medical professions to seek practice independence for themselves. Carefully following the nurse practitioner model, physician assistants, psychologists, pharmacists, optometrists, and chiropractors are taking steps to gain increased practice rights. Using legislative efforts and public marketing campaigns, these groups have advocated for increased practice independence and expansion of services. While nurse practitioners have had the most success in taking over roles traditionally played by physicians, another group is close behind them—physician assistants.

Noting that their programs are often longer and more rigorous than some nurse practitioner programs, physician assistant advocates argue that they should have the same rights as nurse practitioners. They also point out that legal changes favoring nurse practitioner independence have taken a toll on physician assistants, who now have fewer employment opportunities since companies prefer to hire practitioners who do not require physician supervision. Modeling the efforts of nurse practitioner groups, physician assistants have lobbied for expanded rights, promising to increase access to medical care in rural and underserved areas. In 2019, North Dakota became the first state to permit physician assistants to practice without physician supervision. Legislation is pending in additional states to expand physician assistant practice throughout the country.

THE DEVELOPMENT OF THE PHYSICIAN ASSISTANT (PA) MODEL

The first physician assistant training program was opened in 1965, the same year that the first nurse practitioner program began. Eugene Stead MD, a physician at Duke University, invited four Navy veterans to attend a 2-year training program. Stead hoped to build upon the experience of military corpsmen who had served during the Vietnam War and were returning home to civilian life.

Henry Silver, MD, the same physician who founded the first pediatric nurse practitioner program also developed the first pediatric physician assistant program in 1969 at the University of Colorado. Silver hoped a predicted physician shortage could be addressed by training pediatric clinicians in only 5 years rather than the requisite 11 years required of pediatric physicians. The first cohort of graduates, called "childcare associates," entered into practice in 1972. An article in the Milwaukee Journal that year read: "Nine young Colorado women are starting to practice as childcare associates, legally practicing medicine after only five years of training after high school. Dr. Henry Silver … said the nine would be limited to practicing at hospitals, clinics, or offices of doctors."[181]

In 1971, federal funds were designated to establish additional physician assistant training programs with the goal of training healthcare providers to serve in primary care and rural and medically underserved areas. With increased funding, the model grew rapidly. In 1980 there were about 7,000 physician assistants, but only a decade and a half later, the number had quadrupled to 29,000. At the turn of the century, there were 40,000 physician assistants, and by 2018 the number had ballooned to 130,000 physician assistants and 255 training programs.[182]

Traditionally, physician assistants have worked very closely with physicians—as the name implies, as an assistant or "physician extender." However, in recent years, some physician assistants began to call for an increase in autonomy and separation from physicians. This change in ideology has much to do with increased market competition from independent nurse practitioners. It also reflects a growing desire of physician assistants to be recognized as medical professionals. Some physician assistants today decry the label of assistant, even though the word is literally in their job title—something that the profession is actively working to change.

To detach from their roots of physician supervision, physician assistant leaders have taken steps to change the name of the profession, removing the word *assistant*. They began their efforts by hiring a research group to survey physician assistants about the possibility of name change. In 2019, the American Academy of Physician Assistants presented the research company's findings. Their main conclusion: "Based on research and analysis findings, it is strongly suggested that an exploration of an alternate title should be pursued."[183] Suggestions included using only the abbreviation 'PA' or changing the name to 'physician associate.'

Might this name change be confusing to the public? One physician assistant, Laura Record-Halpern, isn't concerned, saying she has "a license to practice medicine … just like the [physicians] do."[184] If patients ask what 'PA' means, physician assistant Elizabeth Prevou suggests answering, "it means I am a medical practitioner."[185]

But will patients know that they are not being treated by a physician?

In response to the bewildering expansion of clinician titles and designations, Dr. Roland Goetz, Board Chairman of the American Academy of Family Physicians (AAFP), said the profession worries that they are losing control of the word "doctor."[186] The American Medical Association (AMA), sharing similar concerns, launched a "truth in advertising" campaign, noting that patients are having difficulty distinguishing physician and non-physician "doctors."[187]

Despite these concerns, the American Academy of Physician Assistants rebranded itself the 'American Academy of PAs'—AAPA. The group also began a marketing campaign to promote the name change, telling colleagues and patients to "Just Say PA."[188]

In addition to changing their name, the AAPA has also called for a change in ideology. In May 2017, the group called for an end to direct physician supervision, replacing it with a new structure called "Optimal Team Practice." According to their website, "Optimal Team Practice occurs when PAs, physicians, and other healthcare professionals work together to provide quality care without burdensome administrative constraints."[189] Optimal Team Practice eliminates direct physician supervision. Instead, physician assistants practice "to the full extent of their education, training, and experience," the same verbiage that nurse practitioners use when describing 'full practice authority.'[190] The group also requested their own physician assistant board, as opposed to being regulated by the Board of Medicine. Physician assistants also demanded that they be directly reimbursed for services by insurers.

Just like nurse practitioners, physician assistants are marketing themselves to the public through media campaigns. Video, print, radio, billboard, and social media ads abound with the slogan: "Your PA Can." The AAPA website proclaims: "With thousands of hours of medical training and a versatile skillset, PAs are expanding access to team-based care. When it comes to quality healthcare, your PA can handle it."[191]

Are these claims true? This is a question that deserves an answer.

PHYSICIAN ASSISTANT EDUCATIONAL PATHWAYS

It takes about 6 years to become a physician assistant. Most students have a 4-year bachelor's degree and then spend two years in physician assistant school to earn a master's degree in the discipline. To be accepted to physician assistant school, students are required to complete a core science curriculum consisting of one semester each of general biology, microbiology, chemistry, and biochemistry or organic chemistry, about three-quarters of the sciences required for medical school applicants. The average grade point average (GPA) for accepted physician assistant students is 3.49, with a science GPA of 3.36. To compare this to physician training: medical school enrollees have an average GPA of 3.72 and a science GPA of 3.65.

Most physician assistant programs require students to have spent time working in patient care, which can include experience as an EMT/paramedic, in nursing, or other clinical experience. While many physician assistant students have worked in healthcare for several years between college and starting physician assistant school, not every enrollee has healthcare experience before starting school. For example, there are accelerated direct entry educational tracks that allow high school students to proceed directly into a physician assistant program, completing a combined Bachelor of Science and Master's in physician assistant studies degree in just 5 years. Currently, there are 40 such programs across the U.S.[192]

The first year of physician assistant school includes lectures and classwork, with the second year consisting of clinical rotations in different medical specialties. Physician assistant leadership organizations are quick to point out that unlike nurse practitioners who practice under a nursing model, physician assistants train on a medical model. Dawn Morton-Rias, president and CEO of the National Commission on Certification of Physician Assistants said in an article that that "PAs are … educated like physicians,"[193] and according to Jonathan Sobel, president and chair of the Board of Directors of the American Academy of PAs, physician assistants are on "what's essentially a condensed medical school model."[194]

While physician assistants are trained using the same medical model that physicians study, medical school is twice as long. Physicians are also required to complete an additional 3–7 years of residency training before they are permitted to provide patient care independently. As Henry Travers, MD, puts it, "Medical school is like 'basic training.' Physician assistants may be kicked out of the nest to fly on their own at the end of basic training, whereas physicians must train three or more years before practicing."[195]

Physician assistant school tends to be more flexible than medical school, offering part-time and online training programs.[196] In 2015, Yale School of Medicine introduced the first online physician assistant program (2020 cost: $108,612 for the 28-month program),[197] and other schools are following suit in developing their own online programs.[198]

CLINICAL HOURS

Physician assistants are required to complete 2,000 clinical hours of experience during school, rotating through internal medicine, surgical, obstetrics, emergency medicine, and pediatric specialty areas.[199] This is more than the number of hours required of nurse practitioners (500–1500) but far less than physicians, who complete at least 15,000 hours—5,000 during medical school and another 9,000–10,000 hours during residency training.[200]

THE PHYSICIAN ASSISTANT DOCTOR OF MEDICAL SCIENCE

To compete with the nursing doctoral degree, some schools have created their own Doctor Physician Assistant degree—the "Doctor of Medical Science" (DMSc). For example, the DMSc program at Lynchburg University states on its website that the doctorate is "developed for PAs and by

PAs to advance the PA profession."[201] Most DMSc degrees are attainable in 12 months online, and like the Lynchburg program, they are convenient enough to be earned while simultaneously working full-time as a physician assistant. Like most nursing doctorate practice curricula, most of the coursework is not directly clinical. Classes include healthcare administration, global health issues, organizational behavior and leadership, healthcare law, and evidence-based research.[202]

Will the addition of this additional doctorate confuse patients? Perhaps. An article in the Knox Sentinel told readers that Lincoln Memorial University-DeBusk College of Osteopathic Medicine's new doctorate in medical science "is a Ph.D. program that will give physician assistants the same level of education as those with doctor of medicine and doctor of osteopathic medicine degrees."[203]

On April 10, 2020, a news station in New York reported this headline: "It totally prepared me for this: University of Lynchburg medical student skips graduation to treat Covid-19 patients in New York." The subheading states, "Mordechai Saks is a doctor, graduated from Doctor of Medical Science Program." Nowhere in the article does it clarify that Saks is not a physician with a medical degree, but a physician assistant.[204]

CERTIFYING EXAMINATIONS, POST-GRADUATE TRAINING, AND SPECIALIZATION

There is one certifying exam at the end of physician assistant school—the Physician Assistant National Certifying Examination, or "PANCE," a five-hour, 300-question test which must also be taken every ten years to recertify. In 2016, 93% of test-takers passed the PANCE. After graduating from school and passing the PANCE, physician assistants may apply for a license to practice. Physician assistants are licensed under the board of medicine in their state and have been required to practice under the supervision of a physician until 2019, when North Dakota became the first state to permit independent physician assistant practice.

Most physician assistants work outside of primary care—only 26.6% work in family medicine, general internal medicine, or general pediatrics. However, few physician assistants receive formal training in medical subspecialties. So how do physician assistants gain the necessary experience to work in these specialty areas? Most physician assistants gain experience through on-the-job training. As Ben Tanner, PA, says, answering an inquiry on the website Quora about how physician assistants specialize, "You simply find someone who will hire you in the specialty you want to work in."[205] The discussion site Reddit is filled with anonymous answers from physician assistants: "Basically, you just apply for the job. If you want to work in cardiology, you apply to cardiology jobs. Want to work in Neuro? Apply for neuro jobs." However, the user notes that it "certainly helps if you did a rotation or have experience in that specialty."[206]

While not required for most physician assistant jobs, additional post-graduate training programs for physician assistants have been developed, especially for those who want additional training in emergency medicine and surgical fields. Proponents of these programs, which are usually 1 year long, argue that this form of training is faster paced and more formalized than on-the-job supervised training. However, a study from 2002 showed that while most physician assistant students were aware of residency programs, only 7% planned to attend, due in part to the perception that formal training provides less value than on-the-job training.[207] In fact, Quora user Jeff Necessary, a PA with 22 years-experience, argued that he doesn't expect physician assistant residency programs to take off. "One of our selling points as a profession is that our generalized education allows flexibility that physicians [who are required to complete a residency to change specialty] lack." He goes on to describe personally changing fields multiple times over 21 years—from spine surgery to sports medicine; pain management, rehabilitation, and finally hospital medicine. "At each change, there were new things I had to learn; fortunately, my supervisors were patient and willing to teach me. And I have also had to teach myself." Ben Tanner, a physician assistant Quora user who has also switched specialties, and even worked in two different fields at once, concurs. "Mostly you learn on the job, but if you're proactive you can find resources to bone up on that field and improve your knowledge and skills."[208]

It's not surprising that physician assistants are less inclined to work in primary care where they earn less than their colleagues practicing in specialty fields. A survey of physician assistants in 2016 showed that the average family practice physician assistant earned $96,000, while emergency room physician assistants made $126,000, orthopedic physician assistants $125,000, and dermatology PAs $134,000. Other higher-earning specialty fields include radiology, where physician assistants earn about $150,000, and mental health, with an average physician assistant salary of $125,000.[209] Why be a physician when you can be a physician assistant in a fraction of the time and at far less expense? Because of the significantly higher cost of medical school compared to physician assistant school, both in terms of tuition expense and potential lost wages during additional years of study, economists have argued that physician assistant school may be a better financial decision, particularly for women.[210]

Despite the financial disincentives, there are physician assistants who decide to go back to school to become physicians themselves, like Christin Giordano, MD, who wrote about her experience.[211] "By my sixth month [working as a PA] I hit a ceiling … While I was proficient at my job, often caring for patients with little supervision, I was acutely aware of the lack of depth of my knowledge." Giordano started medical school two years after becoming a physician assistant. Within the first month of medical school, she writes, "it became clear that the depth of knowledge expected of physicians was vastly different and more intense than that of PAs."

Giordano noted that with medical school training "I process information completely differently than I had before. I no longer work just inside an algorithm but can now critically evaluate and develop unique plans for my patients in a way that my prior training did not allow. As a PA, I knew how to treat adequately most patients but [as a physician] I now know the why of the algorithms and can, hopefully, develop my own for patients who do not quite fit that algorithm." For those who argue that PA school is just an "abbreviated" version of med school, Giordano disagrees. "Having now done both, I can unequivocally say that it is not."

STEPS TOWARD UNSUPERVISED PRACTICE FOR PHYSICIAN ASSISTANTS

Physician assistants still require supervision in every state but one: North Dakota, which granted independent practice in 2019. The new law removes the requirement for physician assistants to have a written agreement with a physician for supervision, allows physician assistants to own their own practice, and "removes references to physician responsibility for care provided by physician assistants."[212] With a large rural area, the state legislature was partially influenced by promises that independent physician assistants would expand access to underserved parts of the state. As they lauded the shift towards unsupervised practice, the North Dakota Physician Assistant Association also tempered the move, insisting that physician assistants in North Dakota "will still do what they have always done and practice in the team model."[213]

Other states are contemplating expanding physician assistants' scope. Like nurse practitioners, physician assistant leaders have seen the coronavirus pandemic as an opportunity to increase practice independence. Using the hashtag #InItToPivot, physician assistants took to social media site Twitter to note that "PAs have the unique ability to move and fill gaps in the healthcare team. We are embracing our ability to 'pivot' from one field to another to meet the demands of this healthcare crisis."[214] Some states quickly responded, with governors of Maine[215] and Iowa[216] fast-tracking legislation to remove supervisory requirements from physician assistants in March 2020. An additional five states granted more autonomy and less physician supervision for physician assistants, including California, Hawaii, Illinois, Missouri, and Rhode Island.[217]

Not every physician assistant is ready to embrace independent practice. Opponents also took to social media sites like Twitter to express concerns about increased responsibility and lack of physician supervision. PA-C Life wrote, "I had no idea how many PAs out there want full practice authority. Do they not realize they can get it … by going to med school?" Later in the thread, the physician assistant added, "Almost 6 years in, all spent in ortho, and I think I want [full practice authority] even less if possible." While some physician assistants disagreed, many others wrote to support the maintenance of physician supervision.[218]

PSYCHOLOGISTS—FROM TALK THERAPY TO PRESCRIPTION AUTHORITY

According to the American Psychological Association, psychologists are trained to evaluate patients and provide psychotherapy "to help people learn to cope more effectively with life issues and mental health problems."[219] Like the term *nurse*, the word *psychologist* has a strict legal definition, indicating that a professional license has been obtained in the field of psychology. Licensed psychologists must hold a doctorate (PhD or PsyD), which usually takes seven years to earn. Psychologists complete a 1-year full time clinical internship with at least 1,500 hours of supervised practice and must pass a national exam.

To increase access to psychiatric care to military personnel, the Department of Defense began a pilot project in the 1980s to train psychologists to prescribe psychiatric medications under certain circumstances. Ten military psychologists were carefully selected for the program. After receiving over 2 years of extensive didactic and clinical psychopharmacology training, the psychologists were permitted to pre-scribe certain medications under physician supervision. Patients treated by psychologists were between the ages of 18 and 65, and most had few co-existing medical problems.[220] Despite these limitations, advocates for psychology prescribing proclaimed the pilot project a success, and the American Psychological Association began to push for expanded prac-tice rights for civilian psychologists.[221]

The first legislation to allow psychologist prescribing was introduced in Hawaii in 1985. Although the bill did not pass, advocates for psychol-ogy prescribing did not give up, introducing another 88 bills across the country in the following years.[222] By 2002, they had succeeded, with New Mexico becoming the first state to grant psychologists the right to pre-scribe medication. Psychologists have since gained prescription rights in Iowa, Idaho, Illinois, Louisiana, and the Public Health Service, Indian Health Service, and the US military.

Advocates argue that expanding prescribing rights to psychologists will increase patient access to psychiatric care. However, workforce data indicates that psychiatrist and psychologist practice locations overlap to a considerable degree in most states, and that practice expansion is unlikely to increase access in rural and underserved areas.[223]

Opponents of independent prescribing privileges for psychologists point to the potential dangers of psychiatric medications, especially among high-risk patients with health comorbidities. An April 2017 letter from the American Medical Association (AMA) to the Nebraska Department of Health and Human Services noted that more than half of the 30 most com-monly prescribed psychiatric medications carry 'Black Box Warnings' from the Food and Drug Administration.[224] These warnings indicate the risk for serious and deadly side effects, such as strokes, heart attacks, and birth defects among pregnant women. In addition, prescription claims data in Louisiana and New Mexico shows that psychologists are prescribing medications outside of those used for treating psychiatric illness, includ-ing warfarin (a powerful and potentially dangerous blood thinner), blood pressure medications, cholesterol medications, and muscle relaxers.[225]

William Robiner, PhD, a psychology professor at the University of Minnesota Medical School, is on the board of advisors of Psychologists Opposed to Prescription Privileges for Psychologists. Robiner strongly opposes prescription rights for psychologists, arguing that the force behind these efforts is the American Psychological Association rather than practicing psychologists, who he says overwhelmingly do not feel qualified to prescribe nor desire this responsibility.[226]

So, who really stands to benefit from increased rights for psychologists?

The answer: Healthcare corporations and government entities who hope to save money on the cost of professional medical labor by hiring prescribing psychologists rather than psychiatrists.

For example, the California corrections system has increasingly relied on psychologists to perform the job usually held by psychiatrists, who train for an additional 4–5 years. Michael Golding MD, the California Department of Corrections and Rehabilitation's chief psychiatrist, filed a whistleblower report in U.S. District Court in October of 2018, alleging that the department was providing substandard psychiatric care by routinely replacing psychiatrists with psychologists.[227] In his report, Golding outlines how psychologists at the department were granted independent medical privileges including admitting and discharging patients to in-patient units, as well as ordering physical restraints on mentally ill patients—privileges denied to psychologists by California law outside of the correctional system. The report also alleges that psychologists failed to seek consultation with psychiatrists, and even overrode psychiatrist's medical orders. Golding notes that substituting psychiatrists with psychologists caused inmate harm, including suicide attempts and psychotic episodes that occurred when psychologists failed to take appropriate medical action.

One of the arguments that William Robiner lists in criticizing psychology prescribing is that it will create a slippery slope: If psychologists are permitted to prescribe, why not allow the same rights to other mental health professionals like clinically trained social workers, licensed professional counselors, and marriage and family therapists? Indeed, the Golding Report cites examples of the California Department of Corrections doing this very thing—allowing unlicensed psychologists, interns, and even social workers to treat inmates medically.

This dumbing down of mental healthcare is affecting not only prisoners, but all members of society. After discovering that her alma mater, Tulane University in Louisiana, had replaced the student health psychiatrist with a "medical" psychologist who was prescribing psychotropic medication to medical students, Torie Sepah, MD, was outraged. Sepah wrote to the provost of the university, "I will point out the inherent conflict of providing care that is well below the community standard, is not evidence-based, and is opposed by both the AMA and the American Psychiatric Association to one of the most vulnerable patients, medical students, who have 15–30% higher rates of depression disorders than the general population." Sepah, a practicing psychiatrist herself, considers the practice of replacing psychiatrists as one of social injustice. "Why is it that those with psychiatric disorders are considered acceptable test cases for a lower standard of care delivery? Are the mentally ill more disposable? Does society feel comfortable lowering the standard for them because they happen to have a disease involving a brain?"[228]

PHARMACISTS—FROM FILLING PRESCRIPTIONS TO WRITING THEM

Pharmacists are advocating for the right to not only dispense medications, but also make medical diagnoses, order lab tests, and prescribe medications without physician involvement.[229] While only two states, New Mexico and California, currently allow significant expansion in pharmacist authority, other states are following suit. In March 2020, Florida passed a law allowing pharmacists to perform, order, and evaluate clinical and laboratory tests, such as strep and flu tests. The law also permits pharmacists to "initiate, modify, or discontinue drug therapy for a chronic condition." Some chronic conditions that Florida pharmacists are now permitted to treat include asthma, emphysema, diabetes, and HIV/AIDS. They are also permitted to treat head lice and "minor, uncomplicated skin infections."[230]

The federal government has encouraged states to expand the scope of practice for pharmacists. A 2017 bulletin by the Center for Medicaid and CHIP Services advised that allowing pharmacists to independently prescribe and dispense medications could "facilitate easier access to medically necessary and time-sensitive drugs for Medicaid beneficiaries."[231]

Advocates for expanded practice rights for pharmacists have closely followed the path laid out by nurse practitioners. In fact, an article published in the American Journal of Health System Pharmacy in 2003 begins: "The evolution of nurse practitioners and their subsequent recognition as primary health providers is an excellent example of a health profession's effort to reengineer practice and achieve change."[232] The article notes several essential strategies that nurse practitioners used that pharmacists should follow, including:

- Demonstrating to legislators and the public that the profession can play a larger role
- Developing and presenting research to show how the profession can provide value
- Creating educational and credentialing standards

- Working through powerful professional organizations
- Patience, or "Having a passionate, persistent commitment to the cause and being willing to accept small, incremental gains over time."

Physician professional organizations have opposed an increased scope of practice for pharmacists, arguing that the professions are trained differently and should work collaboratively for optimal patient safety. Moreover, pharmacists and consumer advocates point to concerns over an increased workload for already strained pharmacists. A February 2020 article from the Advisory Board, a healthcare industry think tank, notes that pharmacists are already feeling overwhelmed and say that they are "spread too thin."[233] While pharmacists complain that an increasing workload may cause them to make mistakes and compromise patient safety, pharmacy chains like CVS and Walgreens can only stand to benefit from an increased role for pharmacists.

If pharmacists are overburdened, corporations are prepared to follow the slippery slope, delegating increased responsibility to the next level down—pharmacy technicians. While pharmacists study for at least 6 years to receive a doctorate in pharmacy (PharmD), followed by at least another 1–2 years of residency training, pharmacy technicians only require one year of training after high school.[234] However, the American Society of Health-System Pharmacists and its Research and Education Foundation have sponsored the "Pharmacy Practice Model Initiative," which includes recommendations to "advance the role of technicians" to allow pharmacists more time to provide direct patient care, or, to practice "at the top of their license."[235]

This sounds remarkably similar to the origin of nurse practitioners and physician assistants. Originally created to free up physicians to provide care to more complex and seriously ill patients, the professions have demanded an increasingly larger role, culminating in the right to practice independently. How long will it be before pharmacy technicians demand the right to fill prescriptions independently without pharmacist supervision?

OPTOMETRISTS—FROM EYEGLASSES TO EYE SURGERY

Optometrists are aggressively lobbying to expand their scope of practice to include surgical procedures. Historically, only ophthalmologists, who train for four years more, have been entitled to these privileges.[236] Now, four states—Louisiana, Kentucky, Oklahoma, and Arkansas—have granted optometrists the right to operate on the eyes, including providing laser surgery and retinal procedures. Other states have introduced legislation to allow optometrists to perform eye surgery and to prescribe pharmaceutical medications.

In a 2019 report by Ocular Surgery News, Richard Lindstrom MD, an ophthalmologist, notes that any physician with a medical license could theoretically offer eye surgery as part of their "legal scope of practice," but that no physician would have the hubris to operate on the eyes without performing a specialized residency training in ophthalmology. "We don't let our fellow ophthalmologist do every type of surgical procedure ... even though I'm an MD, even though I've completed 4 years of medical school, an internship, 3 years of ophthalmology residency and another 2 years of ophthalmology fellowship, there are a lot of surgical eye procedures I don't do and shouldn't do. If I walked into my own [surgical center] where I'm the practice founder and a partner, and wanted to do a retinal detachment surgery, it wouldn't be allowed. We police ourselves."[237] Lindstrom and other ophthalmologists point out that optometrists do not have the same degree of education and training, and that a small mistake could cost a patient their vision—or even their life.

CHIROPRACTORS—MORE THAN JUST THE SPINE

Chiropractors typically complete a four-year undergraduate degree followed by a four-year chiropractic program. While most chiropractors limit their practice to treatments of the musculoskeletal system, some are providing more extensive medical care. For example, chiropractors are allowed to complete sports physicals for children in 36 states, exams that are intended to ensure that children do not have life-threatening cardiac conditions that would exclude participation. Many physicians question the ability of chiropractors to be able to hear cardiac murmurs in children, a skill that requires extensive practice to master. In every state except Michigan, New York, and Washington, chiropractors are also permitted to perform Department of Transportation physicals, exams meant to ensure that operators of heavy vehicles are safe to be on the roads.

In some states, chiropractors have won the right to practice certain medical procedures. In Oregon, chiropractors are permitted to perform minor surgery, practice proctology (examination and treatment of the rectum) and perform obstetrical procedures. They may also draw blood, give nutritional advice, and dispense nutritional supplements.[238] Other states allow chiropractors to perform pelvic examinations, conduct electrocardiograms, and perform nerve studies.[239]

While chiropractors are permitted to call themselves "Doctors of Chiropractic," some have also incorporated terms traditionally associated with medical doctors. For example, Zach Walker, DC, calls himself a "chiropractic neurologist," and advertises the use of traditional chiropractic treatments combined with "functional neurology," what he describes as, "brain-based therapy to address a wide range of neurological disorders such as migraines, brain fog, balance issues, and even anxiety."[240]

What can go wrong when practitioners step outside of their traditional scope of practice? A lot.

Gary Giles, a 55-year old Utah man, died from the first fatal case of rabies in the state in over 80 years. Giles had a history of handling bats and even allowing them to lick him. When he developed pain in his neck and back, followed by numbness and tingling in his arms, he sought treatment from a chiropractor, which helped at first, but then the symptoms worsened. By the time he finally sought medical attention, it was too late.[241] In May 2014, Kate Tietje took her toddler to a chiropractor because her child would not use one of his arms. The chiropractor was unable to diagnose the reason, which was discovered days later after a trip to the emergency room—a broken arm.[242]

While one may argue the admonishment "let the buyer beware," it is important to note that many consumers are led to believe that chiropractic care is as good—or better—than care by physicians. Noting that some chiropractors were advertising cures and treatments to medical conditions from autism to Alzheimer's disease, the College of Chiropractors of British Colombia announced an ultimatum in 2018: remove all scientifically unsupported claims from websites, social media sites, and printed advertising, or face potential discipline.[243]

NATUROPATHS AS PRIMARY CARE PHYSICIANS

Naturopathic medicine is a field of study that promotes 'the healing power of nature.' Many physicians and medical experts note that the study of naturopathy includes "pseudoscientific, ineffective, unethical, and potentially dangerous practices" such as enemas, fasting, hydrogen peroxide baths, detoxification regimens, and desiccated animal parts.[244] Although naturopaths, who call themselves "naturopathic doctors," only receive a fraction of the training of medical doctors, they have succeeded in gaining the right to function as primary care physicians in 13 states.[245]

Naturopaths now receive payment from insurance and Medicaid in Washington, Oregon, and Vermont.[246] Advocates for naturopathic practice are seeking payment for care provided to Medicare patients, with two naturopaths appointed to the US Medicare Coverage Advisory Committee in 2003.[247] In response to criticisms that the use of the term "family medicine" by naturopaths may confuse patients, advocates argue that "there can be more than one source of primary care in healthcare." For example, Nicole Basque, a naturopathic physician, says that she practices family medicine. Basque states that the term indicates "the fact that I treat all ages, from a newborn to an elderly person, not that I am a general practitioner or an MD."[248]

What's the harm in allowing patients to receive so-called natural care? A website dedicated to treatments that may cause harm includes a list of over 200 cases of patients who were killed or seriously harmed by naturopathic treatments.[249]

In 2008, 79-year old Roger Matern died after naturopath Mitra Javanmardi injected him with a magnesium solution. When he began to complain that he felt hot and had nausea after the injection, she told him to drink a smoothie. Despite this recommendation, Matern worsened and died. Investigators later found the medical vial to have been contaminated with bacteria.[250]

In 2017, 30-year old Jade Erick died after receiving an intravenous injection of the spice turmeric by naturopath Kim Kelly. According to news reports, this naturopath was treating him for eczema.[251]

In 2012, 19-month old Ezekiel Stephan died of bacterial meningitis after his parents sought care from a naturopath rather than a physician. Ezekiel's mother first treated him with natural remedies and homemade smoothies containing "hot pepper, ginger root, horseradish, and onion" before requesting a tincture of echinacea from a local naturopath. According to news reports, the child's father told police that he and his wife had planned to seek medical attention if the natural remedy for meningitis didn't work. Unfortunately, Ezekiel died shortly after he was taken to the naturopath's office.[252]

INCREASING ACCESS—IS LOW-QUALITY CARE BETTER THAN NO CARE?

Calls for expanded scope of practice for various medical professionals generally stems from a well-intentioned ideal—increasing access to healthcare to patients. However, many advocates fail to realize that expanding access to lesser trained practitioners may be more harmful than providing no care at all.

Good intentions and well wishes are just not enough when it comes to providing medical care. Consider the example of American missionary Renee Bach. Bach operated the nonprofit "Serving His Children" in Uganda, which focused on malnutrition but also offered preventive care programs. Although she had no formal medical training, Bach worked alongside Ugandan nurses and other medical professionals, aiding them as they cared for patients. According to her attorney, she felt that this experience had given her the skills to help provide medical assistance when necessary.[253]

According to witnesses, Bach dressed in a white coat and wore a stethoscope. The missionary's blog posts describe her starting IVs, running blood tests, administering medication, and even providing blood transfusions. Following the deaths of two children, Bach and her nonprofit were sued for operating a medical facility without a license. While it is still uncertain if Bach committed any wrongdoing, ethical questions about the care that Bach provided abound. Did Bach misrepresent herself as a trained medical professional by wearing a white coat and stethoscope?

Did Bach's attempts at treatment ultimately cause more harm than good? Perhaps. Studies show that poor-quality care is more dangerous than no care at all. A study published in the Lancet in 2018 estimated that 5 million people die every year worldwide due to poor-quality healthcare—significantly more than the 3.6 million estimated to die from a lack of access to care.[254]

Examples of poor care cited in the study included short visit times, incorrect diagnoses, and delays in care. For example, researchers noted that more than half of healthcare providers in sub-Saharan Africa did not know how to accurately diagnose the common conditions of diabetes or pneumonia. These medical clinicians simply did not have the foundational training to properly care for patients. The study authors noted that commonly used strategies to improve quality of care amongst these providers (checklists, refresher trainings and supervision) were not as helpful as anticipated. Researchers instead recommended that the system "move further back to a much more foundational strategy," which includes a focus on quality care and problem-solving skills for healthcare practitioners.

Based on the findings of the study, the authors suggest that policymakers consider a fundamental change in the way we think about access to healthcare. Current strategies to increase patient access have emphasized bringing clinics into underserved areas, "a lot of small clinics spread out over a large territory." Researchers found, however, that patients may be better served by focusing on several large, centralized sites that patients can be brought to for care.

Dr. Margaret Kruk, the co-commissioner of the study and professor at the Harvard T.H. Chan School of Public health says that the key to providing care to the underserved is not only just access to care, but rather, access to quality care. Kruk emphasizes that healthcare leaders must focus on producing high-quality medical care and "stop flooding countries with quick fixes and shiny solutions."[255] The same recommendation should apply to public health strategy in the U.S.

CHAPTER 4

THE DEATH OF MEDICAL EXPERTISE

Despite receiving multiple doses of medication to slow her rapid heart rate, Alexus Ochoa remained acutely ill. Nurse practitioner Antoinette Thompson seemed unsure of what to do next. Alexus's heart rate continued to increase, her oxygen levels remained dangerously low, and now, the young woman's blood pressure began to drop, signaling impending cardiovascular collapse. It was at this point—if not long before—that the nurse practitioner should have contacted her supervising physician for assistance.

State law in Oklahoma at the time required that all nurse practitioners work under the medical license of a supervising physician. Dr. Brent Wilson was the medical director of the Mercy-El Reno emergency department and the supervising physician—at least in name—for Antoinette Thompson, as well as another advanced practice nurse.

Despite his position of authority as medical director and supervising physician for two nurse practitioners, Wilson was rarely on-site at Mercy-El Reno, averaging shifts less than once a month in the emergency department during 2015. Wilson admitted under oath that he could not keep track of the nurse practitioners he was supposed to be supervising. When asked if he could remember who he supervised during 2015, Wilson could not answer, stating, "people come and go in my life. And the nurse practitioners and mid-levels/PAs come and go." The cavalier attitude toward physician supervision of non-physicians appears to have been pervasive throughout the Mercy Oklahoma system.

For example, Sheri Cullers was Mercy Hospital-Oklahoma's operations manager. Tasked with various aspects of personnel management, Cullers worked directly with Dr. Jeffrey Reames, the Mercy Health System regional emergency medicine director. Email chains show Cullers and Reames strategizing on ways to circumvent Oklahoma's nurse practitioner supervision requirements for newly hired nurse practitioner

Antoinette Thompson. In one email, Cullers points out that with the addition of another nurse practitioner, the hospital did not have enough staff physicians available to comply with the Oklahoma Board of Medicine's maximum ratio of two nurse practitioners per physician.

The two noted that staff physicians were reluctant to sign on to supervise newly graduated nurse practitioners. Doctors were worried about potential liability risks, especially considering the loose requirements for supervision in the Oklahoma statutes. "I understand there is some apprehension in [physicians] signing for providers [they] have never met," Cullers wrote. To respond to physician reticence, Mercy executives instituted a policy of having new nurse practitioners shadow their supervising physician on a few shifts, hoping physicians would grow more comfortable with the idea of signing off on the new hire caring for patients underneath the physicians' medical license.

When this didn't work, Reames and Cullers decided to ask the Oklahoma Board of Medicine for an exemption from state law to allow Mercy physicians to supervise more than two nurse practitioners at a time. They asked Dr. Brent Wilson for help. Cullers sent an email to Wilson writing, "We desperately need your help in getting our new nurse practitioners licensed … The PA licensing board, we have workarounds, but for advanced practice RNs, the requirements are very strict … We are pulling the regulations for your reference, but from what we know, we can only have two NPs on each physician's license." Dr. Wilson appeared before the Oklahoma Board of Medicine and sought permission to supervise more than two nurse practitioners, which was the maximum permitted by state law. The board denied his request.

A second obstacle that Cullers and Reames faced was the nurse practitioner supervision requirements written into the hospital bylaws, a set of hospital rules written and approved by the medical staff. Mercy Hospital bylaws required physician supervisors to have privileges at the same individual Mercy facility where the nurse practitioners they supervised were working. This rule was intended to ensure the staff physicians were physically present on-site to supervise nurse practitioners directly. Cullers acknowledged understanding the hospital bylaws, writing, "I understand Mercy's bylaws state the supervising physician must have privileges at the same facility as the advanced provider they are supervising." Despite this, hospital executives developed a workaround by having physicians working at other hospitals in the area apply for staff privileges in-name-only at whichever hospital was short-staffed.

This was not an unusual practice. Through deposition testimony, Reames confirmed that Mercy Health doctors would commonly apply for privileges at specific hospitals in-name-only so a non-physician could work there under the physician's license. Reames indicated that he believed allowing nurse practitioners to work without direct physician oversight was safe practice: "After [nurse practitioners] come out of nursing school, we view their training as it qualifies them to [work in emergency departments]." Reames further argued that the practice of hiring unsupervised nurse practitioners was "common ... across the state of Oklahoma ... for small, rural emergency departments." Although at 10 miles outside of Oklahoma City limits, Mercy El-Reno could scarcely be qualified as a rural hospital.

To facilitate nurse practitioner Thompson's hiring, Reames reached out again to Dr. Brent Wilson, who was not yet on staff there and asked him to apply for privileges at Mercy-El Reno. Wilson applied for and was granted privileges at Mercy-El Reno Hospital. Hospital administrators utilized his privileges to assign the new nurse practitioner to work at the facility, though Wilson's actual supervision was quite minimal.

Wilson testified as to the limited nature of his supervision. He considered retrospective chart review to be a sufficient level of supervision, "when I see [nurse practitioner] charts, I review their charts, see if there are any issues that I thought might have been handled in a better [way.]" In fact, we now know that Wilson's supervision was so negligible that nurse practitioner Thompson was not even aware that he was her supervising physician at all. According to testimony, when she was asked if Dr. Brent Wilson was her supervising physician at Mercy-El Reno, she answered, "not to my knowledge, no."

It is certainly possible that because Thompson was unaware Wilson was her supervising physician, that it never occurred to her to ask Wilson for help when she ran into trouble treating patient Alexus Ochoa. However, other factors that can influence why a nurse practitioner would not think to consult a physician for help with a difficult situation, importantly, something called Dunning-Kruger effect.

DUNNING-KRUGER EFFECT

In 1995, McArthur Wheeler, a middle-aged, stocky man standing at five foot six and weighing 270 pounds, robbed two Pittsburgh banks in broad daylight. Wheeler wore no mask and did not attempt to disguise himself.

When exiting both banks, he looked directly at the surveillance cameras and smiled.

Later that evening, police arrested Wheeler and showed him the surveillance footage. As he viewed himself on video, Wheeler appeared shocked, muttering, "but I wore the juice." Wheeler later confessed that he had rubbed lemon juice on his skin. He had read that invisible ink was made from lemon juice and believed that applying the juice to his face would render him invisible.

The tale captured the interest of Cornell University psychologist David Dunning and his graduate student, Justin Kruger. The two theorized that some people were at risk for a faulty thinking pattern—the false assumption that their capabilities were far better than they really were. In their landmark study, *Unskilled and Unaware of It: How Difficulties in Recognizing One's Own Incompetence Lead to Inflated Self-Assessments* (1999), Dunning and Kruger developed the idea of illusory superiority, a false and over inflated sense of self-confidence. They classified the condition as a form of cognitive bias or faulty thought process.[256]

McArthur Wheeler was not stupid—just outrageously inept. His faulty thinking, or cognitive bias, was that he genuinely believed that lemon juice would make him invisible to surveillance cameras. Wheeler's misunderstanding of the chemical properties of lemon juice allowed for his identification and capture. This concept of illusory superiority, now known as the "Dunning-Kruger effect," describes a phenomenon in which people of lower ability overestimate their cognitive capability. Without adequate knowledge, some people are unable to recognize their own ineptitude, and without accurate self-awareness, those who are less capable cannot objectively evaluate their incompetence.

Dunning and Kruger performed studies to confirm their theory. They followed college students over a semester and learned that students who performed highly on tests were able to predict their future exam scores more accurately. This indicated that students who scored well had better insight into their own knowledge base. On the other hand, the lowest performers showed no aptitude to recognize they were performing poorly. These students with the least amount of knowledge had unrealistically high expectations about how they would score on future tests.

Dunning and Kruger found that high-performing students underestimated their competence, while low-performing students overestimated their own skills. Also, when high-performing students were given feedback to help them understand their performance, they were able to accurately adjust their self-assessment. Poorly performing students could not do this. Even when given clear and specific feedback about their performance, these students were unable to recognize and adjust their own self-assessment. These poorly performing students remained fiercely and unrealistically overconfident of their knowledge, despite all evidence to the contrary.

Dunning and Kruger learned that the phenomenon of overconfidence extends beyond the classroom, spilling into everyday life. For example, in one follow-up study, Dunning and Kruger went to a gun range to evaluate the expertise of gun hobbyists. They found that the people who answered the least number of questions correctly were most likely to overestimate their knowledge of firearms.

The Dunning-Kruger effect can be described in a simple graph form. The "y" axis is level of confidence and the "x" axis is actual knowledge of a subject, starting at novice and moving towards an expert level of understanding. The level of confidence of the complete beginner often starts extremely high. Self-confidence then decreases as the learner begins to acquire knowledge about a subject—and realizes how little they truly know. As the learner gains more understanding, self-confidence slowly rises in a curve until the learner achieves expert status. Interestingly, even top experts in a field may never achieve the self-confidence level of those with minimal knowledge on a subject (see diagram).

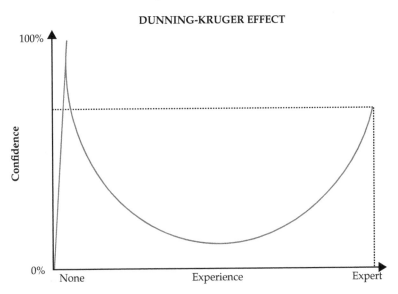

DUNNING-KRUGER EFFECT

The Dunning-Kruger effect explains why people with the least amount of knowledge may insist that they are correct, instead of being confused, perplexed, or reflective about their erroneous ways. They genuinely believe the illusion of superiority. The effect is seen in the hubris of medical practitioners who have only trained for a fraction of the time as physicians, and yet insist that they are just as good, or that those extra years of training are unnecessary. This false self-confidence is dangerous, and the illusion of competence can lead to failed medical judgment with life-threatening consequences.

The flip side of Dunning-Kruger is true mastery of a subject and includes the humility found in those who are top experts in a field. However, even those who are masters in a field must be wary of the Dunning-Kruger effect, particularly in the sciences. Physicians are vulnerable to becoming stuck in outdated beliefs and practices that are no longer supported by the latest research. To avoid becoming "confident idiots," as David Dunning terms it, we must constantly challenge our own knowledge and look for gaps in our understanding. Dunning recommends applying a sort-of Socratic Method to challenge our thinking, and that we seek advice by questioning and dialoguing with experts.[257] Recognizing the concept of illusory superiority is vital to avoid ending up like the foolish bank robber. Without insight into our own self-assessment skills, we may act in an irrational, inept, or even stupid manner—like using lemon juice to make ourselves invisible. The key is to continually re-evaluate our competence to avoid being fooled by illusions of our superiority.

EXAMPLES OF DUNNING-KRUGER

On Sunday, November 5, 2017, 10-year old Mya-Louise Perrin began vomiting. Two days later, she vomited again and had trouble standing up, so her parents brought her to Cromwell Primary Care Centre on the coast of England where nurse practitioner Ruth Loveday evaluated her. When she arrived at the clinic, the previously healthy child could barely walk down the hall. Despite the severity of her symptoms, this nurse practitioner diagnosed a urinary tract infection and sent the child home. That same night, Mya-Louise died of appendicitis.[258]

At an inquest into Mya-Louise's death, Loveday noted that at the time she was evaluating the child, she was quite sure that nothing was seriously wrong: "I felt confident my diagnosis was correct." This is the fundamental element of Dunning-Kruger; nurse practitioner Loveday was overconfident in her knowledge. She truly didn't know what she didn't know. It never occurred to her to consider a more serious diagnosis. She didn't have the experience to realize that simple urine infections don't cause healthy children to struggle to walk.

Although there was no physician onsite when Loveday examined Mya-Louise, she acknowledged that she always had the opportunity to contact a doctor if she had any questions or concerns. However, she did not have the clinical acumen to realize that she needed to seek consultation with a physician. "With hindsight, I would seek GP advice," she told the inquest.

Without extensive training, clinicians may experience gaps in their knowledge. Without experience, clinicians may not even realize that they need to ask for help—they don't know what they don't know. This lack of insight is particularly dangerous because it may impair a clinician's ability to recognize a life-threatening problem.

For example, pediatric emergency room physician Chelsea Majerus, MD describes the case of a 6-year old child she recently treated.[259] The child was initially brought to a family medical clinic for problems with urinary frequency and urgency. According to the child's family, the nurse practitioner at the clinic ordered a urinalysis, which was abnormal, including evidence of sugar in the urine. The nurse practitioner told the family that she suspected a urinary tract infection and recommended that the child be given more fluids to drink, including cranberry juice. After about six weeks, the child's symptoms worsened, and her family brought her back to the clinic, where she saw a different nurse practitioner. This time, the child was noted to have an elevated blood sugar of 325 mg/dL (normal 70–100) as well as a large amount of sugar and ketones in the urine. These results should have indicated the life-threatening diagnosis of diabetic ketoacidosis, but instead of immediately referring the child to the emergency room, the nurse practitioner instructed the family to give the child more water and to schedule an appointment with a pediatric endocrinologist, a diabetes specialist. When the child's family called the specialist for an appointment, the office triage nurse told them to immediately bring the child to the emergency department, where Majerus admitted her for emergent medical care, including an insulin drip to control her blood sugar. According to Majerus, without urgent treatment with insulin, this child would have died due to a lack of knowledge from her treating nurse practitioners.

The biggest pitfall for medical practitioners, as described by Dunning and Kruger, is having overconfidence in the incorrect diagnosis, while at the same time, failing to consider alternative, more serious causes of a patient's complaint.

HOW IS EXPERTISE ACQUIRED? THE TEN-YEAR RULE

In *Toward a General Theory of Expertise* (1991), psychologist K. Anders Ericsson explains that expert performance can only be acquired through years of dedicated effort. He further explains that expert performance is not dependent on innate ability or talent. Instead, all expertise is acquired slowly and deliberately as a result of thoughtful practice over time, and the highest levels of performance and achievement require at least ten years of intense preparation, a concept called the 10-year rule.[260]

The 10-year rule is a well-accepted theory of achieving expert performance across multiple domains. While studying expertise in the game of chess, researchers Simon and Chase found that obtaining the level of grandmaster required "a decade's intense preparation."[261] Ten years of experience is required to master the fields of mathematics, tennis, and even long-distance running. The same ten-year requirement has been shown throughout scientific disciplines. For example, when research published by 120 of the most important scientists of the 19th century was analyzed, it was discovered that scientists published their first work at around 25 years old. However, their greatest work was not published until they were 35 years old, fully ten years between their first and their best work.[262]

Research shows that the level of expertise, rather than intellectual capability, is strongly predictive of diagnostic accuracy. For physicians, it takes at least a decade of experience to gain the top level of expertise in their area of practice. For example, it has been shown to take ten years to develop mastery in radiology, the science of interpreting x-rays and other radiologic tests.[263] Experts in the fields of cardiology, endocrinology and internal medicine with at least ten years of experience are statistically more likely to make the correct medical diagnosis when compared to those medical practitioners with fewer years of training.[264]

There are several important factors that make a ten-year time period efficacious in developing expertise. First, learners must be motivated to acquire knowledge. They must exert maximal effort toward improving their performance. Learning must be active, and not merely repeating an activity without a thorough understanding of why it is being done. For physicians, this process occurs throughout medical school and residency training. Dara Grieger, MD, who was a nurse practitioner before becoming a physician, explains physician training in this way, "It's like learning a musical instrument. You must practice scales over and over. While you may not see it as relevant at the time, it builds the foundation." She notes that her nurse practitioner training was not as foundational. "It's like the difference between playing music for fun, versus playing it seriously. The time involved is completely different."[265]

A second essential component of acquiring expertise is the need for immediate and informative feedback about the learner's performance. This feedback must be accompanied by an explanation of the outcomes of the learner's decisions—learning from mistakes—as part of the performance improvement process. In the absence of such feedback, only minimal improvement will occur. For physicians, this happens during residency, when physicians practice medical care under the supervision of a fully trained attending physician. It is during this time that new doctors are instructed and mentored to improve their performance.

Residency is one of the most intense times in the lives of many physicians, as the senior doctors drive home the importance of accountability, precision, and critical thinking. New doctors must present every patient case to their attending physicians, where they are interrogated about their plan for the patient. Mistakes that result in the harm or potential harm of a patient are dissected in auditoriums for 'M&M'—morbidity and mortality—rounds. In the past, physicians who experienced a negative outcome would stand before an audience of their peers to account for their errors and analyze how to prevent making a mistake in the future. According to current residents, today's M&M rounds are not quite as personal, removing the identification of the physicians involved. Nonetheless, the acknowledgment and identification of errors remain an important part of medical education.

While difficult and sometimes painful, learning from mistakes is an essential part of developing expertise. Studies show that successful learners actively attempt to refine their methods when confronted with errors. This effort and growth in the face of mistakes is an essential part of physician residency training.

Another aspect of residency training is the development of milestones to help trainees and their supervising physicians to assess a resident physician's readiness for independent practice. These milestones include areas of strength and areas that require improvement and are formally evaluated at least twice per year. As physicians-in-training prove increased competency, they gain responsibility. The increase in responsibility occurs in graduated increments rather than all at once.

Unfortunately, this kind of directly supervised training is not required for non-physicians, who are more likely to learn on-the-job. This on-the-job training is not standardized and can be incredibly variable. Sometimes the only way that a practitioner learns is when they discover that a fatal outcome has already occurred, as in the case of the nurse practitioner who missed 10-year old Mya-Louise Perrin's appendicitis.

HOW DO DOCTORS LEARN TO THINK?

Physicians are trained to think in a specific way. Psychology research has examined the development of reasoning between the novice thinker (medical students, residents, or non-physicians) and the expert (experienced physicians). The difference is that when problem-solving, the novice thinker is more likely to use a strategy of reasoning backward while the expert uses the strategy of working forward. The ability to reason in the forward direction is the specific skill best correlated with diagnostic precision.

Reasoning backward begins with a hypothesis and ends with a search for facts to support the thinker's initial premise. When considering a patient's symptoms, the novice will speculate about the diagnosis based on probability, contemplating only the most common causes for the symptom. They will then look for clues to support their assumptions. For many novices, analysis stops at the first sign of a potential answer, even when it seems almost illogical.

In the example of the 6-year old child with a new diagnosis of type 1 diabetes, the nurse practitioner who treated the child initially was using backward reasoning to diagnose the child. Hearing the child's symptoms were urinary frequency and urgency, the nurse practitioner immediately thought of one of the most common diagnoses for these symptoms—a urinary tract infection. While she ordered the appropriate test to evaluate the possibility (a urinalysis), she proceeded to disregard result findings that did not support the diagnosis, such as sugar in the child's urine.

Henry Travers, MD, a clinical professor of pathology at the University of South Dakota, Sanford School of Medicine, describes this type of thinking as "foreclosure of the diagnosis." He notes that the novice thinker often limits diagnosis possibilities very quickly, latching on to the first diagnosis that occurs to them and failing to consider other potential causes. Furthermore, novice thinkers fail to incorporate additional evidence to support or reject their preliminary reasoning. "An expert begins with an expanded set of possibilities, modifying the probabilities as new information becomes available."[266] Travers says that not only do practitioners need to think this way from the onset of the diagnostic process, but they also need time to process information, something he calls "thoughtfulness time." Taking the time to consider all the possibilities can be tough to do when practitioners are busy, and Travers notes that "those who are less well trained actually require more thoughtfulness time because of the narrowed breadth of their training and experience." The perils of working backward or of "foreclosing the diagnosis" include the chance of jumping to conclusions about which diagnosis "seems right" while overlooking rarer, life-threatening conditions with the deadliest consequences.

Physicians do not diagnose this way. Instead, through the process of forward reasoning, physicians learn to pick out salient clinical details to determine which conditions should be included on the extensive list of diagnostic possibilities. Only by reasoning in the forward direction can an extremely broad list of diagnoses be compiled that may explain what is happening with a patient. In medical terminology, this list is known as a differential diagnosis, and it is a hallmark of medical training.

However, this kind of deliberate strategy cannot be implemented without first becoming a venerable subject matter expert. Only through the development of a broad fund of knowledge can a physician begin to organize the medical facts of a case and then sort through the details to develop an organized plan to rigorously evaluate, diagnose and treat patients. This skill is not about being smart or good; rather, it is about internalizing a methodology that requires at least 10,000 clinical hours to master.

Everything starts with a medical history, which is the story a patient tells the doctor when they meet. While a medical history is a critical component of making an accurate diagnosis, the patient's story often includes a litany of erroneous details that are irrelevant to the situation at hand. Patients do not always know which facts are critical and which are not. They may be confused about the specific details of their symptoms, leading them to provide inaccurate information to the physician. In the worst-case scenario, an occasional patient may provide deliberately misleading information, an obstacle that may sometimes derail the entire process. A physician must be a translator of sorts, not only putting puzzle pieces together for each patient but also setting aside unnecessary pieces that do not contribute to making the correct diagnosis.

Learning to ignore irrelevant information without missing critical aspects of a medical history is one of the most challenging parts of becoming an expert diagnostician. The skill is even more important when the patient is not a perfect historian, provides excessive details, or skips around in the story. This endeavor can be especially challenging when working in a fast-paced, disordered setting such as a busy emergency department or when working with a poorly designed electronic medical record. The ability to focus on the critical components of a medical history while simultaneously ignoring immaterial or incorrect details is the hallmark of high-quality care.

Sir William Osler, the father of modern medicine and a master at diagnosis, said, "If you listen to the patient, they will tell you their diagnosis."[267] While this is indeed a true statement, gleaning a patient's diagnosis from the information patients share with physicians (even when some are omitted) can be much harder than it seems. Physicians are constantly required to sift through information, one of the most challenging skills to develop, and one that can only be refined through a minimum of 10,000 hours of trial and error. This kind of experience can only be developed through the rigorous and demanding hands-on residency training process.

Another problem with backwards thinking occurs when practitioners use test results to try to explain a patient's symptoms. For example, many inexperienced practitioners begin a patient evaluation by ordering a "shotgun" panel of bloodwork and then searching for a way to make the results match up with the patient's symptoms. This type of practice can lead to serious errors when the practitioner is misled by a false result or a red herring—a meaningless test result that can lead the diagnostician astray. A master clinician never starts a patient evaluation with laboratory or imaging tests. Instead, the first step in evaluating a patient is the creating of an extensive differential diagnosis, based on the patient's symptoms and other relevant clinical facts. Only after this list has been formulated will the clinician begin to order specific tests to rule in or rule out each possibility.

In the case of a patient with symptoms of shortness of breath, low oxygen level, and low blood pressure, a pulmonary embolus would almost certainly be on the list of differential diagnoses. An experienced clinician would then order laboratory and imaging tests to rule out this life-threatening diagnosis, and would not be distracted by unrelated test results, like a positive drug test. After all, could a patient not have both a pulmonary embolus and use illicit drugs? But without the proper training, practitioners rely on backward thinking techniques. In the case of Alexus Ochoa, when the nurse practitioner learned that Alexus's urine had tested 'presumptively positive' for methamphetamine, she simply accepted that as fact, stating under deposition, "I just went by what the test said." Her acceptance of this incorrect fact, or "foreclosure of the diagnosis" colored the remainder of her treatment of the patient—with catastrophic results.

THE MAKING OF A PHYSICIAN

The pathway to becoming a licensed physician in the United States requires nine to eleven years of formal education: an undergraduate college degree, which is typically completed in 4 years, another 4 years of medical school, and several years of post-graduate residency training. Each state has different requirements for licensure, with some states requiring a minimum of 1 year, and others requiring 2 or 3 years for U.S. trained medical students, and all states requiring at least 3 years for those graduating from schools outside of the United States.

Entry to medical school is incredibly competitive, with an acceptance rate of 39.6% of applicants.[268] Admission requires top grades in advanced science classes as well as a high score on the MCAT, a standardized medical school entrance exam. Being a good student isn't enough; most medical schools also consider extracurricular activities when determining entry, and a round of personal interviews can make or break an otherwise academically worthy applicant.

All medical schools in the U.S. must be accredited by one of two organizations. There are 154 allopathic medical schools that grant a 'medical doctor' (MD) degree, and 38 osteopathic medical schools that award a 'doctor of osteopathic medicine' (DO) degree. Medical school typically takes four years to complete. While the first 2 years of medical school focus on the core sciences, most medical schools also incorporate longitudinal clinical experience immediately in the curriculum.

After the second year of medical school, students take the first of 3 high-stakes standardized examinations, in this case, Step 1 of the United States Medical Licensing Examination (USMLE). Following this exam, students move into the clerkship phase of medical school, in which they rotate through hospital wards and clinics to gain exposure to the core medical fields of internal medicine, pediatrics, obstetrics and gynecology, surgery, psychiatry, and other subspecialty areas. A second exam, USMLE Step 2 is taken at the end of the third year, which measures the students' clinical knowledge and assesses clinical skills which are evaluated by simulated patient encounters.

After graduation from medical school, new physicians must continue into a formal post-graduate program, called a residency, for a minimum of 1–3 years to receive a medical license to practice medicine independently. While most U.S. trained medical students will be accepted to a residency program, only the top students from schools outside the U.S. are accepted. During the first year residency training, physicians take their third and final exam, the USMLE Step 3, which must be passed before receiving medical licensure. The first-time pass rates for U.S. trained physicians in 2015 were 91% for DOs and 98% for MDs, while the pass rate for physicians trained outside the U.S. and Canada was 89%.[269]

From 2008–2014, the National Board of Medical Examiners conducted an interesting experiment. Nurse practitioners seeking a doctorate degree were given the opportunity to take the USMLE Step 3, the same exam that physicians must pass before becoming licensed to practice medicine. The results showed a low pass rate, and the exam was discontinued in 2014 due to "limited utilization."[270]

	Number Tested	Pass Rate
2008	45	49%
2009	19	57%
2010	31	45%
2011	22	70%
2012	18	33%

According to the United States Medical Licensing Exam website, the pass rate for the step 3 exam is 97% for U.S. graduates from allopathic medical schools (MD programs) and 94% for U.S. osteopathic graduates (DO).

Keep in mind that the version of the exam that nurse practitioners took was a less comprehensive version of the exam that physicians take. The National Board of Examiners published a white paper clarifying that "the DNP [doctorate of nurse practice] certifying examination is not designed to replicate the USMLE assessment for medical licensure. It does not include the in-depth assessments of fundamental science, clinical diagnosis, and clinical skills that are provided through USMLE [for physicians].[271]

While the years of medical school are long and onerous, residency, particularly the first year, or intern year, is known to be even more demanding. Most medical specialties like family medicine, internal medicine, and pediatrics require at least 3 years, but other fields require even more years of training, such as the 7 years necessary to become a neurosurgeon.

Standardization of residency programs began in the 1940s, and the term residency developed because physicians would live or reside at the hospital where they performed their duty. Even today, residents spend a significant amount of their lives at the hospital. Before the Accreditation Council for Graduate Medical Education (ACGME) rule changed in 2003, medical residents routinely worked 100–120 hours per week. New regulations limit work hours to 80 per week, averaged over four weeks, and in 2011 the ACGME added limits on overnight shifts, including no more than 28 consecutive hours for senior residents.[272] Despite these rules, most residents report exceeding the work hour restrictions.[273]

While residents are gaining essential knowledge and skills, hospitals also benefit from the cheap, skilled labor pool, paying new physicians only slightly more than they pay hospital maintenance workers.[274] Because residents make such a low salary, many cannot start paying off medical school debt until after they complete their training program. This debt can be considerable, with the average medical student graduating with nearly $200,000 in student loans.[275]

Residency training is considered the bottleneck for increasing the number of practicing physicians. Federal funding for residency programs was frozen in 1997, and no additional funds have been allocated to increase the number of physicians being trained. At the same time, some residency programs have closed due to financial insolvency. After Hahnemann University Hospital in Philadelphia filed for bankruptcy, 550 physicians-in-training were forced to scramble for positions at other centers.[276] Since residency positions must be standardized, accredited, and demonstrate the financial stability to support an academic training environment for residents, they lack flexibility in growth. While federal funding for additional positions has not increased in over two decades, hospital organizations can choose to expand their programs by demonstrating the ability to financially support these positions. Because this financial support goes beyond mere salary and benefit expenses and extends to support for additional program leadership, attending physicians, and other learning resources, some hospitals have been hesitant to expand physician residency training.

MEDICAL EDUCATION AND THE FLEXNER REPORT

At the turn of the 20th century, medical education looked quite different than it does today. Many medical schools were essentially small
trade schools owned by one or more doctors. These schools were rarely
affiliated with a college or university and were often for-profit. Admission standards were low, and laboratory work and dissection were not
always required. Students typically earned their medical degrees after
2 years of study.[277] In 1904, the American Medical Association formed
a council to reform medical education, intended to raise admission
standards and develop a standardized curriculum. They contracted
with the Carnegie Foundation, which tasked Abraham Flexner with
the job of evaluating medical schools and providing recommendations
for reform.

Flexner, a non-physician, was the son of German immigrants. He
respected the European model of medical education and emphasized
a Germanic approach to teaching.[278] Flexner crossed the United States
and Canada, visiting medical schools along the way. His report was published in 1910, and included the following recommendations:

- Increase medical school admission requirements to include a mini-
  mum of 2 years of college study, primarily devoted to science.
- Increase the length of medical education to 4 years
- Incorporate all medical schools into colleges or universities
- Focus on standardized scientific training and research
- Appoint full-time clinical professors at medical schools

Critics of the Flexner report note that his recommendations resulted
in the closure or consolidation of nearly half of all medical schools,
which disproportionately affected Black medical schools and negatively
impacted the opportunity for women to become physicians. Others
point out that by taking medical education out of the community, physicians ran the risk of becoming isolated in ivory towers, losing touch
with the needs of patients. They also note that the Germanic emphasis
on science neglected the importance of the humanities in medical education. Preventive health and population health also took a backseat to the
study of disease processes. While these criticisms were valid and would
be addressed through ongoing reforms in the decades to come, the
report was immediately successful in standardizing medical education
very quickly, as well as increasing the quality and amount of education

that physicians were required to receive. 100 years later, medical schools across the country continue to follow much of the doctrine laid out in the Flexner Report.

With the rapid increase in nurse practitioner and physician assistant training programs, is it time for a new Flexner report? Concerns about these programs hearken to the days before medical education reform: a large number of for-profit programs, often unassociated with a true college or university, low admission standards, variable curriculum and clinical experience. Changes to medical education were called for by the medical profession itself. Will the nursing profession and physician assistant profession do the same?

STATE OF THE UNION

Americans enjoy a better quality of life than ever before, and until recently, mortality rates have steadily declined over the last thirty years.[279] Despite this good news, studies show that the U.S. lags behind many other industrialized nations in certain health quality measures, including mortality. Why does the U.S. fare worse than similar nations?

One possibility is that Americans have less access to expert physician care. There are far fewer physicians per capita in our country compared to other industrialized nations. Here are the facts: In 2013, the U.S. ranked 24th of 28 countries in the number of practicing physicians, with only 2.56 physicians for every 1000 people.[280] The only countries ranking worse than the U.S. were Canada (2.46 physicians per 1000), Poland (2.24), Mexico (2.17), and Korea (2.16). For contrast, the top physician ratios occur in Austria (4.99 doctors per 1000), Norway (4.31), Sweden (4.13), Germany (4.04), Switzerland (4.04), Italy (3.81), and Spain (3.69).

This is important because continuity of care with a regular doctor is associated with lower rates of death.[281] Increasing the number of specialists by 10 physicians per 100,000 people led to a 19.2-day increase in life expectancy over ten years. Even more benefit occurs by increasing the number of primary care physicians by the same proportion, increasing life expectancy by 51.5 days over ten years.[282] Increasing the number of primary care doctors was associated with a:

- 0.9% reduction in cardiovascular death
- 1% reduction in cancer death, and a
- 1.4% reduction in death due to lung disease.

Unfortunately, Americans have one of the lowest rates of primary care physicians, resulting in longer wait times for patients than similar nations, with only 48% of patients being able to obtain a same or next-day appointment and 26% waiting six days or more. In a comparison of eight similar nations, including Germany, the Netherlands, Australia, Sweden, and France, only Canadians wait longer for care than Americans.[283] Not surprisingly, these patients resort to using the emergency department (ED), with 15% of Canadians and 13% of Americans being treated in the ED for conditions that could have been treated by a regular doctor or place of care. In countries with a higher ratio of physicians, much less unnecessary care was provided in the ED setting (3% of Germans, and 6% of French, for example).

Not only do we not have as many physicians in the U.S. compared to other similar nations, but we also are not keeping up with the production of new doctors. While the U.S. has increased the number of medical schools and therefore enrollment by 28% since 2003,[284] it is still behind most other industrialized nations, ranking 30th out of 35 countries in producing medical school graduates. In 2013, the U.S. graduated only 7.26 new doctors per 100,000 population, compared with countries like Ireland, (20.13/100,000), Denmark (18.38), Australia (15.44), and Austria (14.85).[285] Can the difference be made up by replacing physicians with nurse practitioners?

Probably not. First of all, the number of nurse practitioners entering primary care has declined by 40% since 2004, probably for the same reasons that many physicians hesitate to enter primary care.[286] Efforts to encourage nurse practitioners to enter into rural care have not been effective. A 2012 pilot project providing over $179 million in funding to train nurse practitioners in rural and underserved areas did not see the hoped-for increase in nurse practitioners. After five years, only 9% of nurse practitioner graduates went to rural areas, 25% went to underserved areas, and just 12% elected to work in primary care, with 66% entering into hospital work.[287]

Another limitation is that nurse practitioners spend 33% of their careers on average in primary care, compared to 90% of family physicians. Using workforce studies, Robert C. Bowman, professor of family medicine at the A.T. Still School of Osteopathic Medicine in Mesa, Arizona, has calculated that it would take 10 nurse practitioners to equal the contribution of one family medicine resident.[288] The bottom line: the U.S. needs to produce more qualified primary care physicians.

MEDICAL EDUCATION OUTSIDE THE U.S.

In European countries, top high-school students forgo the traditional 4-year undergraduate degree and instead enter directly into a 6-year medical school curriculum which integrates both undergraduate and graduate level course work. Medical education at public universities is generally free or very low-cost to residents. Medical school in Germany, for example, is divided into a 2-year preclinical segment of core sciences, and then a 4-year clinical segment which includes clinical rotations in the final year. Students must pass 3 national exams; at which time they receive a license to practice medicine.[289]

In France, medical school is also 6 years, a 2-year pre-clinical phase and 4 years of clinicals. After this, graduates can choose a general medicine pathway of 2 years or a specialist pathway of 4–5 years.[290] Medical school in Sweden is a 5 ½ year undergraduate program followed by an 18-month clinical internship (3–6 months each of surgery, internal medicine, psychiatry, and family medicine), which then grants medical licensure.[291]

Many countries around the world, including those in Africa, Asia, and South America follow a European model of medical education—5 or 6 year generally government-subsidized undergraduate program followed by a 1–2-year residency period. While medical education both in the U.S. and abroad emphasizes core science (preclinical years) and clinical training, the major difference is that the European model eliminates two college years and allows med students to graduate a few years younger (potentially) and debt-free.

NON-PHYSICIAN PRACTITIONERS AROUND THE WORLD

The U.S. has the highest rate of non-physician practitioners in the world. The nurse practitioner profession originated in the U.S., and currently, there are 40.5 nurse practitioners per 100,000 population in the U.S. After the U.S., the use of nurse practitioners is most common in the Netherlands, which has 12.6 nurse practitioners per 100,000, an annual increase of 27.8%. Nurse practitioners are becoming increasingly common in Canada at 9.8, Australia at 4.4, Ireland at 3.1, and New Zealand with 3.1.[292] While nurse practitioners are also utilized in England, Scotland, Northern Ireland, Wales, and Finland, there is no data registry to calculate the total number of nurse practitioners practicing in those areas.

As the nurse practitioner profession, the physician assistant program began in the U.S., and there are currently 40 physician assistants per 100,000 population.[293] Other countries are only now beginning to utilize physician assistants. Total numbers are small, with the highest number in Canada, where physician assistants have been utilized in the military for about forty years, but only recently began to work in the civilian setting. In 2014, there were about 500 physician assistants currently in practice in Canada, mostly in Ontario.[294]

Other countries are expressing interest in the physician assistant model, with England, Scotland, and the Netherlands establishing pilot physician assistant programs in 2007.[295] Taiwan also created a physician assistant-type program to train nurses to become physician assistants in 2002.[296]

IS THERE TRULY A PHYSICIAN SHORTAGE?

We know that the U.S. produces fewer physicians than most developed nations, and the American Association of Medical Colleges (AAMC) says that we aren't graduating enough physicians to meet our needs, predicting that the U.S. will face a shortage of up to 120,000 physicians by the year 2030.[297]

But not everyone agrees that there is a physician shortage. Some argue that we don't have a doctor shortage, but rather a distribution problem. These critics point out that like many other professionals, doctors tend not to accumulate in rural and poorer areas of the country, particularly where patients have lower rates of health insurance coverage.[298] Indeed, there is a great variation of the doctor-to-patient ratio between states in our country, with states with the most physicians per capita tending to be healthier in general, with longer life expectancies, lower smoking rates, and lower rates of obesity.

If the problem is simply distribution, how to get physicians to these needy areas? The AAMC contests that the answer is increasing residency slots, those 1–3 years that doctors are required to train before they can receive a medical license. They point out that medical schools have increased enrollment by about 30% since 2002, but residency slots have remained flat due to a cap in payment support from the government, which has been frozen into place since 1997.[299] Lifting this cap would produce nearly 4,000 more physicians per year. Increasing residencies can also increase physicians within a geographical area, with studies showing that more than half of family medicine physicians practice within 100 miles of where they completed residency.[300]

States with very few residents-in-training tend to produce lower numbers of practicing physicians for that state. While the national average is 35.8 doctors-in-training per 100,000 people, states like Idaho (the 4th lowest state in terms of total physicians per capita) trains only 3.9 residents per 100,000. Wyoming, (9th lowest physicians per capita) trains 7.1 medical residents per 100,000, and Nevada (7th lowest physicians per capita) trains 10.5 residents per 100,000.[301]

Other proposals to improve the physician supply include shortening medical education to a more European-like model,[302] creating provisional licenses for graduate medical students who haven't yet matched into a residency program[303] and creating incentives to lure physicians to less desirable areas of the country through scholarships and grants.[304]

Although it makes sense to increase physician supply—states with a higher physician ratio per capita have improved health outcomes, after all—some critics argue that the answer isn't in creating more physicians. Instead, they argue that we just need to make better use of teams, telemedicine, and electronic communication.[305] Ezekiel Emanuel, MD, chairman of the Department of Medical Ethics and Health Policy at the University of Pennsylvania, has strongly opined that the physician shortage is a myth. Instead, he suggests that physicians just need to get more efficient by improving their scheduling and using "video chats and text messaging."[306]

Of course, many organizations have used the physician shortage argument as an opportunity to promote an agenda of increasing non-physician healthcare providers. These groups propose that the best way to ease the physician shortage is to replace those physician spots with alternate care providers. For example, the Institute of Medicine (IOM) published a report in 2004 arguing that there was no need to increase funding to physician residency programs and suggested the use of non-physician providers like nurse practitioners and physician assistants as an alternative to creating more physicians.[307] But will independent nurse practitioners and physician assistants work in the underserved areas that are in such desperate need of medical care?

The answer seems to be, no. Workforce data shows that non-physician practitioners do not work in rural areas in greater numbers than physicians. Analysis of data from states that have passed independent practice laws for nurse practitioners shows that these states have not seen the promised increase of healthcare providers to underserved areas.[308]

A DEARTH OF BEDSIDE NURSES

An additional downside of increasing the production of nurse practitioners is the toll that it has created on bedside nurses. Health policy experts already note that there is a shortage of registered nurses across the nation and that 11 million nurses are needed to avoid a future shortage.[309] A lack of nurses puts patients at risk, with a 2002 report by the Joint Commission on Accreditation of Healthcare Organizations noting that "inadequate nurse staffing has been a factor in 24 percent of the 1,609 cases involving patient death, injury or permanent loss of function reported since 1997."[310]

The nursing shortage has been attributed to a variety of reasons. The most common explanation is an aging population which requires an increase in the number of available nurses. Other explanations include an aging nurse workforce and high burnout rates in nurses. One reason that is rarely cited, however, is the growth of the nurse practitioner model. It is estimated that the transition of nurses to nurse practitioners has reduced the number of practicing registered nurses by 80,000 nationwide, without a clear plan to replace those positions.[311] While organizations such as the Institute of Medicine have called for nurses to expand their education to become advanced practice nurses, little emphasis has been placed on how these bedside nurses who go on to become nurse practitioners will be replaced.

In fact, the Institute of Medicine's Future of Nursing report discouraged nurses from pursuing an associate degree, the faster and less expensive track to becoming a registered nurse, in favor of a longer bachelor's degree program.[312] According to the American Association of College of Nurses, bachelor programs include the same course work that associate degree students take in actual nursing, but add more "in-depth training in social sciences, management, research, public and community health, and leadership."[313]

Critics of the call for increased bachelor's degrees note that sixty percent of all registered nurses enter into practice with an associate degree, in part because programs usually offer more options for students who need to work while attending school.[314] They also point to a State of Nursing 2016 study which reported that 2-year associate nurse graduates were often better prepared to care for patients with more real-life experience obtained during training. In the study, bachelor's degree graduates reported feeling less-equipped to care for patients with practical bedside skills than their associate-trained peers.[315]

The big advantage that bachelor's degree grads found was to use the degree "as a stepping stone to larger roles, including graduate school or positions in management."[316]

Another factor impacting the production of bedside nurses is a shortage of qualified nursing instructors. The American Association of Colleges of Nursing reported that in 2018, U.S. nursing schools turned away over 75,000 qualified applicants partly due to a lack of faculty. The report notes that potential instructors are being lured away from teaching by the higher amounts of compensation that can be earned in the private sector as a nurse practitioner.[317]

Advocates for the expansion of nurse practitioners in the U.S. often point to a shortage of physicians. Meanwhile, little is being done to address the very real problem of a nursing shortage which is only growing as nurses move from a bedside RN role to a provider NP role.

THE SLIPPERY SLOPE CYCLE CONTINUES

Just as a shortage of physicians led to a call to expand the scope of practice for nurses, a shortage of registered nurses is resulting in a call to allow less qualified nurses to take on the roles previously restricted to only registered nurses. Over 105,000 licensed practical nurses signed a petition asking the Board of Nursing to allow them to challenge the registered nurse exam. "With this country's nursing shortage," the petition reads, "experienced LPNs should be able to challenge the [RN exam] and if able to pass, should be granted an RN license."[318]

The Alberta Health Services released recommendations in February 2020 that included reducing the number of registered nurses in favor of "licensed practical nurses or health care aids." This request was met with sharp criticism from higher-level nurses, who warned that replacing "higher-educated nurses with cheaper staff could backfire."[319]

Nurses cited some of the same concerns that physicians have expressed with being replaced by nurse practitioners and physician assistants. Nursing professor Cathy Carter-Snell said, "while RNs are more expensive, they have two years more education than LPNs, which helps with the complex multi-system problems many patients have." She notes that the different professions "work wonderfully together" but have different skill sets— "it's the critical thinking, the complex problem-solving, and the deeper path of physiology and pharmacology that they're applying to these acute patients."[320] Sound familiar?

CHAPTER 5

BAIT AND SWITCH

According to the Mercy Health Systems website, emergency department page:

> The Mercy emergency department—El Reno is here to serve you in any medical emergency, at any time of the day or night. We proudly serve El Reno and Canadian County. Our ED is staffed round the clock with a team of highly trained emergency physicians and nurses. And as part of the Mercy health network, we offer quick access to physicians practicing orthopedics, neurosurgery, internal medicine, and other specialty areas. Regardless of your emergency, Mercy Hospital El Reno stands ready to assist you by providing the high-quality care you deserve.[321]

At the time of Alexis Ochoa's treatment, Mercy Health systems advertised that emergency room physicians were available at Mercy-El Reno 24 hours per day. Although the organization has since taken down the El Reno/Canadian County emergency page, as of the publication of this book, all their remaining county-specific emergency pages still include this boilerplate statement above. Yet when Alexus Ochoa arrived, the nurse practitioner who treated her was on duty alone.

Nurse practitioner Antoinette Thompson was hired by a staffing agency, Mercy Health Ministries Support Services, which was contracted by Mercy Hospital, Inc. to recruit, credential, and hire medical professionals. A completely separate second corporation, Mercy Health Oklahoma Communities, was utilized in the finalization of her credentialing. The hospital's recruiting and credentialing agencies decided to hire a family nurse practitioner without certification in the care of acutely ill patients to work in the emergency department. In doing this, the supposed hiring experts made a serious error, violating the Oklahoma Nurse Practice Act and putting patients at risk.

The Mercy Health System hospital bylaws clearly listed the requirements for practitioners to be granted acute care privileges to work in an emergency room setting. Practitioners must be trained to: "manage acute respiratory failure patients, manage life-endangering traumatic injuries, perform procedures concerning emergency medical management of surgical patients who have had a cardiac arrest or respiratory arrest, etc., and manage any acute life-threatening situation that is presented to the emergency room to include: cardiac arrest, acute respiratory arrest, life-endangering traumatic injuries, hypertensive crisis, diabetic coma, and accidental or deliberate ingestion of poisonous/dangerous substances."[322] Antoinette Thompson had no experience in any of these areas.

Thompson had graduated from a family nurse practitioner program focused on providing primary care services in an outpatient or other clinic setting, just a month before she was hired. Her 500 clinical hours of practice experience consisted of the routine follow-up care of healthy, pregnant women in a local health department. She had no experience as a nurse practitioner in an acute care setting, nor did she have any training or credentials that should have permitted her to fill this role.

Not surprisingly, it wasn't long before things began to go wrong. At first, the complaints against Thompson were relatively minor: She brought her dog to work with her and made personal phone calls while working. Concerns progressed when she amassed an assortment of patient complaints, some involving misdiagnoses. Her supervising physician, Dr. Brent Wilson testified that he specifically counseled her not to "get tunnel vision when an abnormality is identified." Within that first eight months of practice, the nurse practitioner made a more serious error, by failing to advise a patient that his intestinal infection required surgery. At this point, Mercy Hospital decided to terminate Antoinette Thompson. However, executive leaders did not terminate her immediately. Instead, they decided to allow her to work another thirty days to complete her previously scheduled shifts. It was during those thirty days when she was already terminated from employment, that the nurse practitioner would treat 19-year old Alexus Ochoa.

CORPORATE DECEPTION

Most experts agree that granting acute care privileges to an advanced practice nurse with training in primary care is inappropriate. Jan Sinclair, an investigator for the Oklahoma Board of Nursing who had been a nurse for more than 4 decades, signed an affidavit stating that Mercy-El Reno violated the Oklahoma Nursing Practice Act and the Rules of the Oklahoma Nursing Board by hiring a family nurse practitioner to work in an acute care setting.[323] Sinclair noted that a certified nurse practitioner is a "limited license," in that healthcare delivery must be consistent with his or her advanced education preparation in a particular area of specialty. In particular, Ms. Sinclair called attention to the fact that prior work as a nurse or paramedic has no bearing on the scope of practice for a nurse practitioner.[324]

Sinclair emphasized the fact that the nurse practitioner license issued by the Oklahoma Board of Nursing was "statutorily limited to the specialty area of Family Medicine." In addition, the affidavit states, "An Oklahoma Family CNP [certified nurse practitioner] is licensed to provide healthcare across the lifespan to *medically stable* patients but it NOT licensed to provide healthcare to acutely or critically ill patients, nor is an Oklahoma Family CNP licensed to manage the healthcare of acutely or critically ill patients." The treatments Thompson was credentialed to provide were not within the scope of a Family CNP license.[325]

In essence, neither the nurse practitioner, the chief nursing officer, the hiring and credentialing agency, nor the Mercy Health System followed the Oklahoma Nursing Practice Act. Sinclair summarized her findings: "Based on my education and experience, it is my opinion the Nursing Board would have taken action against Ms. Thompson's license had it been aware of these violations." She went on to state that the Board would have also taken action against Mercy's Chief Nursing Officer, both for credentialing Thompson as well as for not reporting her to the Oklahoma Board of Nursing after Mercy concluded that Thompson was guilty of 'an act that jeopardized a patient's life, health, or safety according to the rules of the Board.'[326]

While the hiring and credentialing agency either did not understand or chose not to follow the training requirements for nurse practitioners established in law by the Nurse Practice Act, the hospital parent company, Mercy Health, Inc., also claimed to lack the knowledge of the qualifications of medical staff. Douglas Danker, Mercy-El Reno's CEO, denied accountability for improperly hiring Thompson, arguing that the in-depth analysis of hiring practices was outside of his duties. Alleging that the recruitment and hiring of medical staff were handled by a contracted organization that was separate from the Mercy Health, Inc., Danker said that he did not need to know the background training and education of his employees. Although Danker was a former registered nurse who went on to become a hospital administrator, when he was asked about what the training of a family nurse practitioner entailed, he stated, "That's beyond my scope. I have no knowledge of what their training is, what their qualifications are." Danker appears to have washed his hands of all culpability, stating, "I have processes and people in place to make those decisions."

Another hospital leader who claimed ignorance of nurse practitioner credentials was Brent Wilson, an emergency medicine physician and medical director of the Mercy-El Reno emergency department. According to legal records, Wilson stated that nurse practitioners "had a license to practice family medicine," just like emergency physicians. Wilson also said that he believed a nurse practitioner with primary care training could safely care for patients in an acute care setting, irrespective of educational background and training. Jeffrey Reames, Wilson's boss, Mercy-Oklahoma director of emergency services, was equally dismissive of the laws regulating nurse practitioner scope of practice. Wilson and Reames both admitted under oath they had never read the Oklahoma Nurse Practice Act or even those sections related to the scope of practice for a nurse practitioner.

THE DEMISE OF PHYSICIAN-LED CARE

Fifty years ago, most Americans reported having great confidence in their physicians. By 2019, only 57% reported trusting physicians.[327] Why have physicians lost the trust of the American people? What changed?

A key factor in the development of trust, fidelity—the belief that a caregiver has the patient's best interest at heart and will not take advantage of his or her vulnerability—has all but disappeared. The practice of medicine was once grounded in intimacy, a sacred relationship between two people. The boundaries were clear: doctors were accountable to their patients directly, with few outside factors influencing their medical decision-making. This powerful dyad created a bond between doctors and patients. Patients trusted their physicians, and doctors felt valued for the care they provided.

Medicine is no longer about two people. Instead, the healthcare system has devolved into an impersonal maze of bureaucracy that has distanced patients and physicians from each other. The sacred trust between patient and physician has been eroded. Patients no longer believe that doctors want the best for them. Instead, they see physicians as interested in them simply as a source of revenue. Patients also fear that doctors will take advantage of them in times of illness for financial gain. Sensing this distrust, physicians feel hurt and undervalued. They often respond by becoming guarded, defensive, and even hostile with patients. This adversarial attitude is the natural consequence of a dysfunctional health-care system—one that physicians have helped to create.

Healthcare as a business and commodity took off during World War II, when employer-sponsored health insurance became a popular benefit to compete for workers during a tight labor market. This was the first time that physicians truly began to accept payments for their services from someone other than the patient directly. A third participant was now introduced into the examination room, the insurance payer.

In 1965, Medicare and Medicaid were created, adding the government as an additional physician payer and third-party in medical decision-making. With the onset of this medical ménage-a-trois, physicians could no longer give patients their undivided attention. Doctors were forced into a new and unsettling dilemma: weighing the values and interests of the insurance company or government payer against that of the patient. As payers demanded more and more loyalty and oversight, patients began to question the fidelity of their doctors, and trust in physicians began to wane.

The 1980s ushered in the HMO era. Capitation—a payment arrangement that perversely incentivized physicians to provide less care to patients—was touted by Medicare and other insurance payers as the solution to controlling escalating medical expenditures. Primary care physicians, once trusted family doctors, were relegated to a gatekeeping role, paid to restrict patient access to care. Rather than rejecting this morally compromising situation, some doctors chose the side of the insurance payer over that of the patient. And with that, patient trust in their physicians began to disappear.

Fast-forward to the last twenty years. The colossal failure of capitation has given way to the rise of the medical-industrial complex, massive healthcare systems with million-dollar C-suites that promise value-based care by improving the patient "experience." Control has been further wrestled from the hands of physicians, as small practices are overshadowed by hospital conglomerates. The electronic medical record has become the next Holy Grail. Doctors who used to write office notes on 4x6 index cards must now click from screen to screen, producing pages of clinically meaningless information to meet unachievable "quality measure" mandates, simply to be paid for their labor.

In this environment, the solo doctor has struggled to survive. Many saw no other choice than to sell themselves into corporate indentured servitude. Physicians no longer served the patient—they now served new masters. Patients have felt the sting of this betrayal. Rather than being true patient allies, doctors have become cogs in a complicated machine that they helped to build.

Physicians no longer look patients in the eye because computer screens and corporate protocols demand their full attention. With a rising demand for increased productivity, visits pass in the blink of an eye, with no time to build the committed relationships which are the foundation of quality care. Rather than spending time with one trusted physician, patients are ping-ponged from one specialist to another in a system that mandates institutional loyalty through in-network referrals.

There is much money to be made from keeping patients within a health system. With every doctor visit, medical test, and procedure, corporate profits balloon, earning companies $2.4 million annually per employed physician, an unthinkable sum to the solo practitioner.[328]

The greatest tragedy is that while patients no longer believe that physicians have their best interests at heart, when faced with illness or disease they have no choice but to seek help. Instead of looking to a trusted family physician for guidance, patients are turning towards the big-name hospital systems dripping with prestige; the very institutions which created this disconnect in the first place. The medical-industrial complex is eager to fulfill this role.

Companies spend billions on marketing and public relations campaigns to gain public trust. They award themselves "Best Hospital" prizes by measuring outcomes like "patient experience"—as if a visit to the hospital were a trip to Disney World instead of a life or death endeavor. These organizations have found great profit in hiring non-physician practitioners to take the place of physicians. Companies can pay nurse practitioners and physician assistants less than doctors, and they can also count on the increased test ordering and referrals by these non-physicians to keep profits growing.

For example, after acquiring insurance giant Aetna in 2019, the drugstore chain CVS began piloting a new "HealthHub" project, with a goal to turn nearly 10,000 CVS stores into a "healthcare destination." CVS hopes to build on its 1,100 walk-in MinuteClinics, which are designed for simple problems, by adding care for patients with chronic conditions, staffed by, you guessed it, nurse practitioners. Naturally, patients will fill the many prescriptions written by these prescribers right at the store, possibly using their Aetna insurance card.[329]

Efforts to drive patients into these walk-in clinics and retail stores are succeeding. A 2016 analysis found an 18% decrease in office visits to primary care physicians over the preceding 4 years. At the same time, there was a 14% increase in office visits to "other providers," and visits to nurse practitioners and physician assistants increased 129%. The study noted that the average cost of an office visit to a primary care physician was $106 in 2012, compared to $103 for a nurse practitioner or physician assistant visit.[330]

To ensure that patients accept this replacement of physicians, companies have made great efforts to equalize physicians and non-physicians. Physicians are no longer identified separately from nurse practitioners and physician assistants—all are mere "providers." The doctors' lounge is now the provider lounge. Doctor-reserved parking is provider-parking. "Doctors' Day" is no longer celebrated—only "Provider's Day," although there is a special day for nurse practitioners and another for physician assistants.

The long white coat, once reserved for physicians only, is now worn by nearly everyone, sometimes even orderlies and housekeeping staff. While all staff members are required to wear identification badges, physician badges sometimes include their first name only and fail to identify them as a physician, confusing patients. Even prestigious teaching centers like the University of Wisconsin Madison fail to list physicians by their credentials on their website. The Department of Obstetrics and Gynecology Faculty page shows a photograph of the faculty members with their name and no title such as MD, DO, NP, etc. Instead, the faculty are identified by titles like Associate Professor, Clinical Instructor, and Professor. Even the gynecology oncology department chair, an MD, PhD, is titled simply by her first and last name, and "Department Chair," with credentials only being visible by clicking her name.[331]

Prestigious institutions are quick to tell patients that nurse practitioners are 'just as good' as doctors. For example, Cedars-Sinai Medical Center in Los Angeles, CA posted an informative blog for prospective patients in January 2019 titled, "Can I see a nurse practitioner instead of a doctor?" The answer: yes, indeed. The article includes a quote from Sylvia Estrada, a breast cancer nurse practitioner, who says, "We can pretty much do anything that a doctor can do with the exception of performing surgical procedures independently."[332]

Meanwhile, as the role of doctors is being downplayed, the roles of nurse practitioners and physician assistants are being played up. Nurse anesthetists are demanding a change in terminology to nurse anesthesiologists, despite the possible confusion to patients. Nurses with a DNP (Doctor of Nursing Practice) are referred to as "doctor," and even nurses without a doctorate or physician assistants are sometimes referred to as doctors on organization websites. Many doctor review sites persist in calling nurse practitioner and physician assistant school "medical school." This misrepresentation of credentials is meant to confuse patients and create a sense of equality between physicians and non-physicians.

While corporations replace physicians with non-physicians, they simultaneously and effectively capitalize on physician branding when advertising. For example, Dallas, Texas medical group MD Medical owns and operates MD Kids Pediatrics, Clinicas Mi Doctor, and MD Family. Despite the extensive use of the moniker "MD" and "Doctor" in its branding, the group fired 27 pediatricians in May 2018, replacing them with nurse practitioners.[333] The CEO of MD Medical, Alvaro Saenz, told a reporter that the new medical clinics would put a "greater emphasis on nurse practitioners and physician assistants, while staffing one to two pediatricians per location."[334]

Mercy Health System, Inc., also used the lure of "24/7" physician access when marketing to patients, but by 2015, Mercy-El Reno Hospital had nearly completely phased out physicians, instead hiring nurse practitioners to run the emergency department and manage hospitalized patients. In fact, 90 percent of the time, the Mercy-El Reno emergency department was staffed by a nurse practitioner working completely alone.[335] Moreover, many of these nurse practitioners were improperly trained for the role of caring for acutely ill patients.

This is not an uncommon phenomenon. Physicians are increasingly being replaced in hospitals across the country. In 1997, only 5.5% of emergency room patients were treated by non-physicians, but by 2006, that number increased to 12.7%, or 15.2 million patients, an annual growth of 13%. That same year, 77% of all emergency rooms were utilizing non-physician practitioners, and not only for lower acuity patients. While many facilities do triage less severely ill patients to non-physicians, studies show that 11% of the patients treated by non-physicians were in the highest risk category, with 8% requiring hospital admission. Many of these non-physicians are not being supervised by a physician. Of those patients treated by non-physicians in an emergency department setting, 45% had no documentation showing that a supervising physician ever saw them.[336]

The same trend is occurring on hospital floors and in outpatient settings, coinciding with the massive increase in hospital and healthcare organization mergers across the country. Following legislative changes in 2010, hospital consolidations have increased by 70 percent.[337] Large hospitals engulfed small medical clinics during a buying spree of physician offices and small rural hospitals. Bringing numerous facilities under one umbrella organization was a smart business move, ensuring steady access to patients and a guaranteed revenue stream for hospital executives.

Private equity firms have also wanted in on the financial action. Just like every other business sector across the country, medicine is on sale to the highest bidder. Venture capital firms and private investors have moved into the healthcare sector, buying up physician practices and hospital physician groups, and often replacing physicians with non-physicians to increase profits. Profits are generally the bottom line in these private equity transactions. CEO Alvaro Saenz of MD Medical, which replaced pediatricians with nurse practitioners, noted that 2016 revenue for the organization was $55 million, with $8 million in earnings.[338]

Profits were also a factor in the Chicago-area health system Edward-Elmhurst firing of fifteen physicians in April 2020. These doctors were replaced by nurse practitioners and physician assistants as a form of cost savings. An internal memo sent by Edward-Elmhurst Health CEO and Nurse Mary Lou Mastro blamed the decision on patient desire to save money. "Patients have made it very clear that they want less costly care and convenient access for lower-acuity issues (sore throats, rashes, earaches), which are the vast majority of cases we treat in our Immediate Cares."[339]

The dermatology field has been particularly lucrative in the private equity market, valued at about $14 billion nationally. About 1,000 dermatology practices are presumed to be associated with private-equity groups, employing 1,100 dermatologists and 750 nurse practitioners and physician assistants. These practices are expected to make a tidy profit for their shareholders, and patients may have no choice but to be treated by a non-physician, with the associated risk of unnecessary procedures. One dermatologist at a private equity company said that non-physician practitioner schedules were filled preferentially to her own schedule "because they were more profitable," even when patients requested a physician.[340] When doctors push back or refuse to comply with unethical procedures, they face punishment. Douglas Robins, a dermatologist, resigned when the company insisted that he supervise a physician assistant at another office. Although Robins joined another practice, the private equity organization placed an ad in the paper saying that he had retired.[341]

Government policies have aided and abetted corporations in these activities. In 2010, physicians were banned from owning hospitals, forcing specialists who rely on hospital services to cooperate with corporately owned facilities.[342] The 2010 legislation prioritized funding for the education and training of non-physicians by increasing funding for the training of nurse practitioners and physician assistants, whereas, as stated above, funding for physician residency programs has remained frozen since 1997.[343]

Corporations are profiting from America's waning trust in physicians, but the pendulum can swing the other way. Physicians must both regain autonomy as well as the public's trust through upholding the tenets of our profession, namely, serving patients first and always. Additionally, patients must learn how to protect themselves from an increasingly corporate healthcare system that sees them as no more than an entry on the accounting ledger.

IS THERE A SUPERVISING DOCTOR IN THE HOUSE?

Supervise: to be in charge of; see also superintend or oversee
Collaborate: to work jointly with others or together especially in an intellectual endeavor, to cooperate with or willingly assist
— Merriam Webster Dictionary, 2020

Physicians created both the nurse practitioner and physician assistant professions. Historically, nurse practitioners and physician assistants worked side-by-side with a physician, often functioning as the doctor's extender, providing counseling and education of routine patients while allowing the physician to see the more complex patients. Often, physicians delegate responsibilities to these staff members, asking them to see follow-up patients or treat simple medical problems.

This delegation of responsibilities generally includes the use of protocols or clinical pathways. These policies and procedures are often written in the form of a checklist or algorithm. The physician also educates staff members on situations in which referral back to the physician is indicated and develops emergency protocols in case the supervising physician is unavailable. In this type of truly supervisory relationship, the physician is ultimately responsible for the care provided by a non-physician practitioner.

As mentioned, over time, nurse practitioner organizations began to demand more autonomy in caring for patients. In 1994, they took an important step in separating themselves from physicians, insisting that the term for the relationship between the two groups no longer be called "supervision" but instead, "collaboration."[344] The American Nurses Association (ANA) defined collaboration as physicians and nurses working "together as colleagues, working interdependently within the boundaries of their scope of practice,"[345] with the change in semantics implying a collegial relationship and inferring equivalence to doctors.

Many states followed the ANA's recommendation, changing the requirement for nurse practitioner physician supervision to that of collaboration, with each state defining the term differently. For example, Alabama state law defines collaboration as "physician direction and oversight" and requires that the collaborating physician be available to the nurse practitioner for consultation. The collaborating physician must be present at least 10% of the nurse practitioner's scheduled hours and must visit each collaborative practice site at least quarterly. The state requires written standard protocols for medical treatments implemented by a nurse practitioner, including a pre-determined plan for emergency services. Physicians must also monitor nurse practitioner quality, including reviewing at least 10% of medical records and all adverse outcomes. Wisconsin, on the other hand, has a looser definition of collaboration, simply indicating that "the collaborative relationship is a process in which an APRN is working with a physician, in each other's presence when necessary, to deliver healthcare services within the scope of the practitioner's professional expertise. The APRN and the physician must document this relationship."[346]

While the American Medical Association has no formal definition for collaboration, in a truly collaborative relationship, a physician and non-physician practitioner would be personally responsible to each other. Having worked closely together, the physician would have a strong familiarity with the non-physician's skill and fund of knowledge and would trust them to come forward with any question or doubt. The non-physician would trust the physician to be immediately available to answer clinical concerns and to act as a mentor and guide. But like the waning trust between patients and physicians, the bond between physicians and non-physician practitioners has been breached. Some doctors have misused practitioners, treating them as their own personal cash cow. Others have neglected to nurture the clinical skills of practitioners, instead using them to manage an increasing burden of paperwork and administrative responsibilities.

For example, consider the case nurse practitioner Kevin Morgan who was found to be responsible for the deaths of several patients due to the improper prescribing of testosterone. Morgan was supposedly being supervised by three different physicians while he was prescribing these high-risk medications. One of the supervising physicians was a general surgeon who worked 150 miles away from the nurse practitioner's location. When a physician colleague threatened to report her to the Board of Medicine for improper supervision of the nurse practitioner's work, she withdrew her supervision of him rather than address the issue of improperly supervising him. Unfortunately, within days, Morgan was back in business, having established a supervisory relationship with a new physician, a local obstetrician. It was only after the deaths of patients that any disciplinary action by the Board of Medicine was taken against all three supervising physicians.[347]

As has been established via testimony, although Oklahoma required physician supervision of nurse practitioners, the requirement was so loosely followed at Mercy Hospital that nurse practitioner Antoinette Thompson did not even know who was supposed to be supervising her. Brent Wilson, the physician assigned to her, was seldom on-site, and it never occurred to Thompson to call him for help when she got into trouble caring for a patient.

PHYSICIANS FORCED TO COLLABORATE

Although some physicians have neglected their responsibilities, many practitioners have also turned away from physician mentorship, chafing at being called an 'assistant,' or denying that a physician's education has anything to offer them. This strained relationship becomes more difficult when collaboration is a term of employment, an increasing requirement for many physicians who have turned to corporate jobs. For the first time in history, corporations employ more physicians than physicians own their own practices. Through cleverly written contracts, these employed doctors are being forced to supervise non-physicians while having little to no input on who is being placed under their medical license. From a revenue standpoint, this makes perfect sense. Administrators can pay nurse practitioners and physician assistants significantly less than physicians. To keep costs under control, corporations hire fewer physicians and instead, hire non-physicians who will technically be under physician supervision, or collaboration. Doctors often have no choice but to supervise or collaborate.

Jou Jou Hanna, MD, a Texas pediatrician faced this exact situation. Hanna took a job at a pediatric urgent care right out of residency in 2011. When she began, there were thirteen physicians and one nurse practitioner. Gradually that ratio began to change. Hanna noted that every time a physician would leave the group, a nurse practitioner or physician assistant would be hired—and worse, Hanna and her physician colleagues were expected to take on the supervision of these new non-physicians. "We were told by our administration that supervision was not an option. Do it or quit. This is how it is." Hanna noted that physicians were not given any compensation for supervising non-physicians. They were given no administrative time to review charts, much less to do actual supervision. "I was in a state of high anxiety," Hanna recalled. "I couldn't physically see every patient that I was supposedly supervising, and I worried about patients being harmed." Ultimately Hanna left the organization because of the supervision conflict, but she has found that most jobs in her field in Texas require her to supervise non-physicians. "I really don't have any option—every job offer I have had requires supervision."[348]

Shannon Mitchel, MD, a wound care specialist, also lost her job providing care to patients at skilled nursing facilities because she refused to sign off on non-physician charts without adequate supervision. "My contract required me to supervise a physician assistant and two NPs," she explained. "These were all new graduates who were given a two-day course on wound care and then sent off to work independently at different facilities, but I was given no time to supervise or train them." Ultimately, Dr. Mitchel found herself at an impasse. She left the wound care company but is still struggling to find a job that doesn't come with similar strings. "Every physician contract I see has a supervision clause built into it."[349]

This is a major problem for doctors who depend on hospitals for their line of work, like emergency physicians. Edwin Leap, MD, an emergency physician, wrote about the tangible impact that supervision requirements are causing physicians. "When [the physician shortage] is coupled with corporatization, the increasing complexity of medical care, unrelenting electronic charting requirements and the explosion of administrative tasks, physicians barely keep up each day." Doctors are ultimately responsible for the care of patients they supervise, yet they have no time to properly take on this role. Leap explains, "Sure, I try to be constantly aware of what's going on all around me and give guidance as much as I can. But to sit down and do a thorough evaluation of a chart? Next to impossible."[350]

Despite their best effort, a supervising physician may not be able to catch every potential error made by a non-physician working under their license. Leap wrote, "I'm frightened that I may one day sign off on a dangerous mistake just because I didn't have time to provide proper supervision. And that possibility should make physicians, PAs, NPs and especially administrators very nervous indeed."[351]

Without proper supervision, patients should also be concerned. Brent Wilson, the doctor assigned to supervise Antoinette Thompson, said that he supervised nurse practitioners by reviewing their charts. He described it this way: "When I see their charts, I review their charts; see if there are any issues that I thought might have been handled in a better [way]." When asked if he had reviewed the chart for Alexus Ochoa, whose life-threatening blood clot was missed by nurse practitioner Antoinette Thompson-Ducasse, Wilson replied, "Yes, sir. After she had left the ER." After the patient had been transferred to another hospital for more intensive care.

MEDICAL ALGORITHMS, ARTIFICIAL INTELLIGENCE, AND SOCIAL JUSTICE

Because the training period for nurse practitioners and physician assistants is completed in a much shorter time than that of physicians, an alternate approach to education is emphasized. Although these professionals do indeed learn to think critically and develop some forward reasoning skills, they simply do not have the time to develop an adequately extensive knowledge base in five years that physicians acquire in twelve. Therefore, non-physicians must rely upon the use of protocols, medical algorithms, and even drop-down menus in electronic medical record systems to make medical decisions about patient care.

Early in the development of the nurse practitioner and physician assistant model, these professionals generally provided care by following physician-developed protocols. For example, Silver's child-care specialists in the late 1960s followed written guidelines for performing well-child examinations and administered recommended vaccinations and tests by a protocol. Likewise, in 1980, a family planning clinic in Missouri that utilized nurse practitioners to provide contraception successfully defended itself against the medical board's accusation of practicing medicine without a license by providing evidence to the court that nurse practitioners were following specific protocols and standing orders developed by supervising physicians.[352] For straightforward problems like contraceptive management, minor infections, and treating chronic diseases like well-controlled hypertension or diabetes, protocols allow non-physicians to provide care with minimal physician supervision. When a more nuanced evaluation is necessary though, algorithms are insufficient to provide high-quality care. While algorithms may be able to suggest treatments for established medical conditions and help track preventive services, they cannot diagnose patients.

Advocates for the use of protocol-based care point out that algorithm technology is rapidly improving due to the use of artificial intelligence and deep learning models. These artificial intelligence systems utilize complex algorithm software to compete with human cognition in analyzing complex medical data and allows computer algorithms to draw conclusions without direct human input. What distinguishes artificial intelligence from more traditional technology in healthcare is the ability to process information and give a well-defined answer to the end-user. Artificial intelligence does this through machine learning algorithms, which recognize patterns in behavior and create a logical pathway based on experience. Of course, to reduce errors, artificial intelligence algorithms need to be tested repeatedly.

However, it is worth noting that artificial intelligence algorithms behave differently in two ways when compared to human counterparts: (1) algorithms are literal: they only understand exactly what they have been told. Therefore, if you set a goal, the algorithm cannot adjust itself accordingly and (2) algorithms can make precise predictions but cannot determine causal relationships well. Information technology enthusiasts argue that as deep learning techniques continue to improve, perhaps one day physicians may no longer be required at all, but while algorithms may provide an answer using predictive reasoning, they are missing the most common question asked of physicians by their patients: artificial intelligence will never understand the "why." This becomes a particular problem when a deep-learning model comes up against an unusual data point, like a new disease or a unique case. Even the best artificial intelligence systems still require human intervention, as deep learning experts point out that sometimes these learning systems "can make baffling predictions that could prove harmful if [clinicians] unquestioningly follow them."[353]

For example, Rich Caruana, a researcher on artificial intelligence, worked on a system that was designed to predict which patients with pneumonia were at higher risk and required more intensive hospital admission. Evaluating the data, his team discovered that the machine was incorrectly labeling asthma patients as low risk. Why? The computer saw that asthma patients had higher survival rates—but it didn't understand why. These patients were surviving not because they were low risk, but because doctors recognized the increased risk in these patients and intervened more aggressively.[354]

Once a computer is stuck in a mistaken prediction, only human intervention can resolve the problem. For example, flawed computer software in Boeing Max airplanes activated anti-stall measures that forced the plane's nose down on takeoff. Several pilots reported experiencing this dysfunction before the fateful crashes of Ethiopian Airlines and Lion Air. One pilot noted that immediately after engaging the plane's autopilot, the plane began to descend. "I immediately disconnected [Autopilot] and resumed climb," he wrote in a report.[355] Fortunately, the pilot was able to take over the flight manually, avoiding a crash. While pilots of Ethiopian Airlines Flight 302 seemed to consider autopilot error as the cause of systems problems upon takeoff, they were unable to deactivate it in time.[356]

Yet another problem with algorithms is that they must make certain assumptions to do their work. These assumptions may be racially, ethnically, and socioeconomically biased, leading to unsafe treatment for patients. In 2019, a study found that one of the most commonly used algorithms in healthcare was racially biased against patients of color, resulting in Black patients receiving less healthcare than white patients.[357] Bias has been shown in artificial intelligence use in the non-medical sector. For example, Amazon, the internet retail giant, built a hiring software tool that was found to discriminate against women. Facial recognition technology used by the U.S. government has been found to misidentify Black people more often than white people.[358] Before we can relegate the care of patients to computers, these dangerous biases must be eradicated.

That is not to say that human reasoning does not have its own constraints. There are nearly always hidden assumptions behind reasoning through any problem. The difference between artificial intelligence—as we know it today—and humans is that humans can understand there may be such assumptions and can actively accommodate and work with them. While artificial intelligence may offer some benefits to patient care, it comes at a price. The big picture question is this: Which human beings will receive algorithm-driven care by a non-physician practitioner—the poor, people of color, children, the elderly, veterans—and which will receive care from a fully-trained physician? Rationing healthcare by restricting access to physicians and substituting lesser trained practitioners is very much a question of social justice.

If the nation has learned nothing else throughout 2020, there is no lesson more timely or important than understanding how race, economics, and social circumstances lead to disparate health outcomes. As the Covid-19 pandemic spread across the United States, it quickly became clear that the burden of disease and fatality fell most heavily on patients and communities of color, with mortality rates among Black individuals substantially higher compared with white populations across the nation.[359] While the reasons for health disparity are likely a combination of social and structural determinants of health, economic disadvantages, and healthcare access, there is no doubt racism and discrimination play a larger role than previously understood.

Healthcare access, specifically to physician-led care, is becoming increasingly difficult for patients of color like Alexus Ochoa. Like many other Black patients, Alexus's symptoms were incorrectly attributed to drug intoxication rather than a medical condition. In a February 4, 2020, Facebook post, Lakesha Benson described a similar occurrence, noting that the death of her son, Javaris Daques Benson, whose cardiac symptoms were initially disregarded by a nurse practitioner as possibly due to drug use, was a "perfect example of systemic racism."[360]

Assuming young Black patients with chest pain are using illicit drugs, like in the cases of Javaris Benson and Alexus Ochoa-Dockins, anecdotally demonstrate how disparate treatment results in fatal outcomes for these patients. Black Americans are no more likely than whites to use illicit drugs. Yet, studies show Black patients are systematically undertreated for pain relative to white patients, likely due to implicit bias of individual healthcare practitioners.[361] It is bad enough the systems themselves have implicit racial bias built into their protocols. Effectively addressing disparities in the quality of care will require better data systems, increased regulatory oversight, and training medical professionals appropriately to think beyond negative stereotypes ingrained in all of us.

CHAPTER 6

LIES, DAMN LIES, AND STATISTICS

19-year old Alexus Ochoa lay on a hospital gurney in the Mercy-El Reno emergency room. Her heart was racing, and her blood pressure was dropping, signaling impending cardiovascular collapse. Nurse practitioner Antoinette Thompson had already tried all of the treatments she could think of and seemed unsure of what to do next. She finally decided to contact a physician for help, but rather than calling emergency physician Brent Wilson, her supervising physician, the nurse practitioner made a phone call to Dr. Jonathan Valuck, a cardiologist at Oklahoma Heart Hospital.

Thompson told Valuck that she was treating a 19-year-old girl with an elevated heart rate who had tested positive for methamphetamines in her urine. She did not mention Alexus's low oxygen level and blood pressure, nor did she report Alexus's symptoms of fainting, chest pain, and shortness of breath. She also failed to tell Valuck that Alexus was taking birth control pills, a significant risk factor for pulmonary embolism. Based on the few details that nurse practitioner Thompson provided, the cardiology consultant recommended admitting Alexus to Mercy-El Reno overnight for observation for methamphetamine toxicity.

Nurse practitioner Susan Abrahamsen corroborated Thompson's failure to tell Valuck the complete medical story. Abrahamsen was also on-duty at Mercy-El Reno, working on the in-patient unit managing patients once they were formally admitted from the emergency room into the hospital. After emergency room nurse practitioner Thompson called cardiology consultant Valuck, she then contacted Nurse Abrahamsen to admit Alexus Ochoa to the hospital with a working diagnosis of methamphetamine intoxication. In her note, nurse practitioner Abrahamsen documented the same history that was provided by Thompson to Dr. Valuck, also failing to note any discussion of abnormal vital signs. Based on a history that indicated that Alexus was stable and simply needed observation and supportive care, Abrahamsen accepted Alexus for admission to the in-patient unit.

Alexus Ochoa was transferred from the emergency room to a hospital bed. However, upon arrival to the hospital floor, the patient's blood pressure dropped precipitously, likely a response to the medication labetalol, which had been administered in the emergency department before she was transferred. Realizing that Alexus was acutely ill and required more aggressive medical intervention, hospital nurse practitioner Abrahamsen called Thompson to advise that the patient was too unstable and must return to the emergency room for more intensive treatment. Acutely ill with unstable vital signs, 19-year old Alexus Ochoa was shuttled from the hospital floor back into the care of Antoinette Thompson.

Thompson once again contacted cardiologist Valuck to solicit advice about the patient. Hearing that the patient was unstable, Valuck recommended ordering a D-Dimer level, a blood test that may indicate the risk of a blood clot, as well as a CT scan to rule out a pulmonary embolus. Nurse Thompson took Valuck's advice and ordered the recommended chest CT. However, she did not choose to order the CT scan as "stat," meaning it would have been done as an urgent or emergent request. The only possible explanation for this oversight would have been that Thompson did not believe that Alexus had a blood clot in her lung. Indeed, later testimony from Paul Turley, a nurse on the hospital floor, supported this notion, "When I talked to her [Nurse Thompson] at some point ... she said ... she didn't think the patient had a pulmonary embolism."

It was not until 1:30 am on the morning of September 28, 2015, ten hours after Thompson began treating Alexus Ochoa that the nurse practitioner finally obtained the critical CT scan. Despite a lack of formal radiology training, the nurse practitioner reviewed the CT scan herself as she awaited the official radiology physician's reading, which was performed off-site. Thompson looked at the films and thought that she saw an unusual finding. She diagnosed Alexus with a crushed sternum.

The sternum is also known as the breastbone. Only a major traumatic injury can fracture the breastbone, much less "crushing" this structure. Alexus had not experienced any type of mechanism that should have caused such a finding. Later, a board-certified radiologist would provide an alternate interpretation of the CT scan findings—including a normal breastbone.

While Thompson's diagnosis was incorrect, it at least motivated her to call to request Alexus's transfer to a larger hospital system with physician specialists. At 2:30 AM, physicians at the University of Oklahoma

Medical Center accepted the nurse practitioner's transfer for a crushed sternum, and Alexus was loaded into an ambulance.

THE ORIGINS OF EVIDENCE-BASED MEDICINE

Before the 1960s, the practice of medicine was more of an art than a science. The use of scientific methods such as research, statistics, and epidemiology were not yet considered the standard of care. Instead, expert opinion and experience formed the foundation for medical decision making. While scientists and physicians had begun to perform controlled trials and document the role of the scientific method in the 1940s and 1950s, evidence-based medicine took a huge leap forward with the creation of the first Department of Clinical Epidemiology and Biostatistics at McMasters University Medical School in 1967.

Epidemiology is the study of the frequency and distribution of disease, intended to use this knowledge to understand novel infections and control their spread to save lives. For example, John Snow, a British physician, traced the outbreak of an 1854 London cholera epidemic to a tainted water pump. By carefully tracking and recording infected patients, Snow successfully stopped the epidemic by intervening at the source of the infection. Snow's methodology formed the foundation of modern epidemiology, and his work led to fundamental changes in waste and water systems, improving public health throughout the world. The vital role that epidemiologists play in the health system cannot be underestimated. Epidemiologists are critically important in understanding the behavior of pathogens and helping to control the spread of infection. The emergence and worldwide spread of the novel coronavirus, SARS-CoV-2, in late 2019 demonstrates the ongoing need to advance the field.

This first university epidemiology department was chaired by a young physician, Dr. David Sackett, who had completed his education at Harvard School of Public Health. Sackett was joined at the Clinical Epidemiology Department by Walter O. Spitzer, who had spent a year at Yale studying with Alvan Feinstein, a mathematician-turned-physician. Together, Sackett and Spitzer shared a vision: that physicians practicing medicine could apply the knowledge acquired through epidemiological research to patient care decisions. First, a fund of medical research knowledge would need to be established for physicians to draw upon.

This medical research rapidly evolved throughout the 1970s and 1980s. As more data became available to help doctors treat patients more effectively, by 1990 the medical community began to embrace the concept of evidence-based medicine—the application of scientific evidence gleaned from research studies directly to the treatment of patients at the bedside. Doctors were urged to provide only the treatments shown to be helpful by careful research and to avoid treatments shown to be unhelpful or harmful.

The introduction of evidence-based medicine would forever change the medical profession. Henry Travers, MD, points out the importance of this new standard of treatment. "Evidence-based medicine was and remains the most effective means to counter medical practice motivated solely by financial gain."[362] Ironically, it is this very concept of using evidence that has become a stumbling block for the healthcare system today. With government and corporations becoming more powerful in the physician-patient relationship, financial gain has become a central component of the healthcare business rather than evidence-based strategies that promote the health of patients first.

Applying research is challenging. First, to be considered valid, research must be performed meticulously and then interpreted cautiously to avoid drawing conclusions that cannot be substantiated later. Peer-reviewed medical journals play an important role in ensuring that inaccurate or biased articles are not published. However, Henry Travers, MD, notes that "the rise of for-profit, online medical journals has obfuscated the landscape of evidence."[363]

Scientific research must be reproducible. In other words, to confirm that a result is accurate, findings should be able to be demonstrated again and again by other researchers. It can be challenging to prove something is true through repetition and easier to prove something is false with a single observation. Consider the ancient belief that all swans were white, and that black swans did not exist. While repeated observations of white swans could not prove all swans were white, the observation of a single black swan proved the hypothesis false. That being said, repeated observations giving the same answer increases the probability of something being true. If scientific principles are not meticulously followed, then research results cannot be considered valid. Instituting change based on invalid research findings can mislead the public, patients, and the entire healthcare system. Furthermore, it can unintentionally cause harm.

A BRIEF STATISTICAL PRIMER

Nurse practitioner and physician assistant advocates state that five decades of research prove the safety and efficacy of these professions.[364,365]

They are correct that both physician assistants and nurse practitioners can provide safe and effective care in the right circumstances. However, none of this research has been designed to demonstrate that the professions can provide the same level of care as a physician, and no credible study has evaluated the work of nurse practitioners and physician assistants working independently without physician supervision and oversight.

To properly analyze the research available on this subject, it is important to understand some basic principles of medical research and statistical analysis. In the scientific process, the first step is always the generation of a hypothesis or educated guess about the relationship between two variables. The hypothesis is then subjected to critical tests through observation and experimentation. The goal of a research study is to design an experiment to provide evidence of sufficient power to allow the researcher to support or reject their hypothesis.

The goal of a study must be clearly stated at the beginning. This goal, or hypothesis, is the *only* question that the study is designed to answer, and therefore, the only results that matter. Sometimes frustrated researchers who do not get the results they had hoped for will sift through data points, adding in additional hypotheses after-the-fact to yield something significant from their pool of data. While these incidental findings uncovered by researchers may be interesting and lead to additional research, these results are not considered definitive unless the study was originally designed to provide that data.

Statistical analysis includes the evaluation of something called the "null hypothesis," which holds that there will be no significant difference between two defined populations. The goal of a given study is to either reject the null hypothesis (finding a difference) or to confirm that there is indeed no difference. In rejecting the null hypothesis, one would accept the "alternative hypothesis," that there is indeed a difference between two groups not caused by random chance.

Null hypothesis = there will be no difference in outcomes between groups
Alternate hypothesis = there is a measurable difference between groups not caused by chance

An important term in research is "statistical significance," which refers to the probability that an outcome is due to a specific cause, and not simply due to random chance. Statistical significance can be strong or weak depending on a study's design. For example, studying larger populations for a longer time increases the chance that results will be true and not simply due to chance.

Statistical significance is measured using a calculation of the "probability value," commonly called a *p*-value. A study result has traditionally been considered statistically significant if the *p*-value falls below 0.05. Conversely, if the *p*-value is higher than 0.05, the finding is not considered significant. For example, consider a study in which the clinical outcomes for patients of physicians and non-physicians are found to be the same. However, the calculated *p*-value of the comparison is 0.1, higher than the required cutoff of 0.05. The *p*-value of 0.1 indicates that there is a 10% chance that the conclusion is not true, and instead, due to random chance. Thus, although researchers might claim that their study showed that physicians and non-physicians had the same outcomes, the result would not be statistically significant, and potentially invalid.

It is also important to understand that statistical significance does not always equate practical importance. If the result cannot be applied to a real-world situation, then it may be meaningless. For example, one study reported that patients of nurse practitioners had a diastolic blood pressure that was 3-points lower than that of physicians in the group. Researchers used this result to conclude that nurse practitioners may be "better" than physicians at controlling blood pressure. But what are the real-world consequences of a 3-point reduction in diastolic blood pressure? The diastolic blood pressure is the lower reading of a blood pressure measurement and has long been considered far less important in determining a patient's risk for cardiovascular disease than the systolic blood pressure, or top number reading. While this result may make headlines—"nurse practitioners better at controlling blood pressure than physicians"—the reality is that a minimal improvement of a relatively unimportant variable is unlikely to translate into any real-world improvement in patient outcomes.

TYPES OF RESEARCH STUDIES

The most rigorous and reliable type of scientific study is a prospective randomized, controlled trial. In this type of study, a research question is posited, with tests designed to try to specifically answer the question. "Randomized" means that participants are divided by chance and then randomly assigned to separate interventions. Researchers determine ahead of time what endpoints they will measure. After a period of time, data is collected on the outcomes of each group and then statistically analyzed.

Imagine an experiment in which researchers wanted to determine whether nurse practitioners could provide the same quality of care as physicians. Researchers would need to consider the following variables:

What type and how many patients do we need to include in this study to show a difference in outcomes?

The more patients in a sample, the greater the ability to determine a difference in outcomes, especially if researchers are trying to determine differences in more serious and rarer endpoints, like death, heart attack, or stroke rates. Researchers must also consider the diversity of the patients being studied. The more diverse the patient population, the larger the sample size needed to show differences in outcomes. In many cases, studies comparing nurse practitioners or physician assistants to physicians utilize small data sets (a few hundred patients) or evaluate patients with isolated problems in specific settings (middle-aged women with diabetes, for example). Even if the study determines similar outcomes, it is not possible to generalize these results to a larger population including more diverse and less healthy populations.

What endpoints should be measured?

Researchers need to determine ahead of time what endpoints to use to compare care between physicians and nurse practitioners. The best type of study would evaluate the most meaningful outcomes, like death rates, heart attacks, or strokes. However, because these serious conditions are relatively rare, accurately measuring differences would require an enormous sample size and a long period of time. Most researchers instead choose substitute markers like blood pressure or blood sugar levels, easier information to gather. In some cases, researchers choose measures that are harder to quantify, like "general health," or outcomes that may not translate into better health, like "patient satisfaction."

Randomized, controlled studies tend to be expensive and time-consuming. A less reliable but simpler type of study is an observational study, in which researchers analyze data points without actually designing an experiment to change any of the variables. One type of observational study is a retrospective analysis. Rather than designing an experiment and then following it through to see the outcome, a retrospective study examines data that have already been recorded for other reasons and applies statistical measures to try to find differences. For example, many retrospective studies examine patient charts or billing records to try to discover differences or similarities in care between physicians and non-physicians. This type of study is known to have a high risk of bias and confounding variables. For example, while billing records may reflect that a non-physician treated a patient, they cannot say whether the non-physician sought consultation with a physician during that patient's encounter.

Keeping these statistical variables in mind helps to evaluate the strength of the evidence provided by "five decades" of research on non-physician care.

THE FIRST INKLINGS OF A PROBLEM

As nurse practitioners and physician assistants gained popularity during the early 1970s, the question of whether or not they could provide care equal to that provided by physicians became important. One of the first studies to examine the issue was published in the American Journal of Public Health in June 1974.[366] The study developed out of the needs of a Midwestern county hospital medical clinic in 1970. The program had trained four registered nurses for an extended role in internal medicine, with didactic education and precepting with physicians, the goal of which was to assess the quality of care provided by these advanced nurses.

Sixty patients were studied. Two-thirds of patients were assigned to the nurse group (experimental) and one-third to their physician (control group). The patient populations were equivalent for economic status, age, race, gender, and education across both groups. The study collected data on health status, patient knowledge of their disease, the effect of illness on activities of daily living, and patient's understanding of dietary needs, medication compliance, and use of outside medical facilities.

Investigators hypothesized there would be no difference between the health status of either group of patients. While they assumed the experimental group would spend more time with the nurse than did controls with their physician, researchers hypothesized that patients cared for by the nurses would spend less time in the clinic overall.

Two important outcomes were found. The first was that nurse clinicians spent far more time educating patients about exercise and diet than physicians. Second, patients cared for by nurse clinicians had significantly increased utilization of healthcare resources. Nurses referred patients more frequently to community agencies, such as specialty clinics, private eye doctors, and hospitals. In fact, 73% of their patients used outside care facilities, compared with fewer than 50% of those patients cared for by physicians.

In addition to increased healthcare utilization, nurses saw patients three times more often than physicians and nurses visited more patients at home. Nurses saw almost 70% of their patients 5 to 10 times over the study period, whereas physicians saw close to the same proportion merely once or twice during the study period. Study authors surmised that nurse clinicians were insecure in their new role and that frequent patient contact reassured them they were providing appropriate care. They also considered the possibility that the nurse clinicians had more time to see patients than the physicians and therefore scheduled more frequent follow-up visits.

In addition to seeing patients more frequently, the nurse group also ordered far more diagnostic tests, ordering more than 3 times as many electrocardiograms, almost 7 times more blood tests, 3 times as many urinalyses, and five times as many X-rays. The authors speculated the reasons for this fact was insecurity on behalf of the nurses, so they depended more on laboratory studies to assist decision-making with patients. These results were consistent with those reported by Lewis et al (1967), which found nurse clinicians ordered tests 3 times more often than physicians. When it came to medication, nurse clinicians also ordered more medications than physicians except in two categories. Nurse patients were more likely to take more medications per day than physician patients.

The study was designed to prove there was no difference in health status between patient cared for by nurse clinicians and physicians—and it did prove this point, but equal outcomes required a far greater quantity of health services when the patients were cared for by nurses. Theoretically, utilizing nurse clinicians in place of physicians should have been less expensive, but the exact opposite was true. Due to more frequent clinic visits, more testing, and more home visitations, costs were higher to achieve the same health outcomes for the patients cared for by nurse clinicians. Today, U.S. healthcare expenditures have increased exponentially, with researchers noting that up to one-third of medical care is unnecessary. If care by nurse practitioners is more costly than that of physicians, as these early studies showed, is it possible that allowing non-physicians independent practice has contributed to this increase in healthcare spending?

Sometimes when we get answers we aren't looking for, rather than accepting that result, researchers change the question and try again. From this very early study, it became clear that nurse clinicians could not deliver the same healthcare as physicians in the same amount of time or for the same cost. Yet, instead of focusing on improving efficiency and reducing quantity without sacrificing quality, researchers keep trying to show "no difference" in health outcomes for those cared for by non-physicians.

THE BURLINGTON RANDOMIZED TRIAL

Remember Drs. Sackett and Spitzer, the physician-scientists who started the first epidemiology department at McMasters University? In 1972, these forefathers of evidence-based medicine published one of the most important randomized controlled studies comparing physicians and nurses in practice.

Drs. Ian Hay and Pat Sweeney were two overwhelmed family physicians in a large urban medical practice in Ontario, Canada. Due to a shortage of primary care physicians, in 1970, half of the physicians in the province of Ontario were too busy to accept new patients. However, highly experienced and well-educated nurses were abundant. Hay and Sweeney employed two such nurses, Georgi Lefroy and Isabel Vandervlist. The physicians thought so highly of their nurses that they wondered if the two could assume some of the primary care responsibilities traditionally carried out by physicians. Hay and Sweeney approached Sackett and Spitzer about studying whether or not nurses could be safely "substituted" for primary care physicians to alleviate their workload. This important research, known as the Burlington Randomized Trial, would forever change the future of the medical profession.[367]

In 1971, Sackett and Spitzer designed the first randomized controlled study ever conducted at McMaster University and the fourth ever done in history. The question they asked was this: Could the capacity to deliver primary care be increased by having nurse practitioners work in collaboration with family practice physicians? The answer was a resounding yes.

Working together as a team, the four highly motivated clinicians—two physicians and two nurse practitioners—provided exceptionally high-quality personalized medical care to their patients. Recognition of their care became legendary throughout the province. The collaboration was so successful and efficient that the practice's capacity to take on new families increased by 22%.

However, the study also showed very clearly that physician supervision was required to make such a model successful. Lefroy and Vandervlist were experienced nurses who received an additional year of advanced nurse training at McMasters School of Nursing to become nurse practitioners. Despite this experience, the nurses still needed input and assistance from their supervising physician about 33% of the time. The results also demonstrated that the nurse practitioners, under careful physician supervision, were as safe and effective as a physician 55–67% of the time.

This overall positive finding that nurse practitioners are "as good" as physicians 55–67% of the time has been quoted in literature reviews more than one hundred times. Usually, the results are cited this way: *Nurse practitioners working in primary care have outcomes equivalent to those of physicians.* But the citations rarely include the fact that the nurse practitioners in these studies were practicing under physician supervision, and they never point out an opposite way of looking at the findings, namely, that even under supervision, nurse practitioners were not as good as physicians up to 45% of the time. Patients are not receiving an accurate message. They are not being told that nurses are as safe and effective as a physician *most* of the time, *while under physician supervision*. Instead, they are being led to believe that unsupervised nurse practitioners are every bit as good as physicians—and maybe even better.

The American Academy of Nurse Practitioners states on their website that "five decades of research affirm that NPs provide safe, high-quality care." This statement is true, but incomplete. Over those 5 decades, the scientific literature provides solid evidence that non-physicians provide care approaching the same level of quality as physicians—when supervised by them.

A HOUSE OF RESEARCH BUILT UPON SAND

The question as to whether there is a difference or not between the care provided by physicians and independent non-physicians remains unanswered. While empirical research can provide a base of evidence, hypothesis testing has limitations. Research will never eliminate uncertainty, only quantify it.

One of the most thorough reviews of studies comparing physician and non-physician medical care was done by Robin Newhouse and colleagues in 2011, titled "Advanced Practice Nurse Outcomes: 1990–2008: A Systematic Review." Researchers reviewed 14 randomized controlled trials and 23 observational studies comparing patients cared for by nurse practitioners or physicians. Newhouse gave nurse practitioners high marks for delivering "safe, effective, quality care" but the authors concluded that "APRNs, in partnership with physicians and other providers … will need to move forward with evidence-based and more collaborative models of care delivery."[368]

Perhaps the best study example contained in the Newhouse review was that done by Mary Mundinger, DrPH in 2000. The central hypothesis was that there would be no difference between patients of non-physicians and physicians regarding selected clinical outcomes of general health status, diabetes control, asthma control, and blood pressure control.

While investigators determined there was no difference in patient health status after the 6-month endpoint, the *p*-value was 0.92, meaning there was a 92% chance this finding of no difference was by random chance or error. Test results for diabetes and asthma were also reported to be no different between those patients cared for by non-physicians and physicians, but again, these findings were not statistically significant. *P*-values show that there is an 82% and 77% chance respectively that these two findings were due to random error.

There were two statistically significant findings to emerge from this study by Mundinger. The first was that diastolic blood pressures were 3 points lower for the patients cared for by nurse practitioners. The second difference was that the patient satisfaction ratings were higher at the 6-month endpoint for physicians. Ultimately, the only statistically significant findings in this study, considered one of the best scientific studies comparing nurse practitioner to physician care, is that nurse practitioner patients had slightly lower diastolic blood pressures and patients of physicians were more satisfied with their care after six months.[369]

"NURSES AS SUBSTITUTES FOR DOCTORS IN PRIMARY CARE"—THE COCHRANE REPORT

Cochrane is a UK-based charitable organization that uses 13,000 volunteers throughout the world to organize medical research findings and make evidence-based treatment recommendations. Previously known as the Cochrane Collaboration, the group's mission is "to promote evidence-informed health decision-making." Cochrane formed in 1993, and within twenty-five years, the group has become so well-respected that it currently collaborates with the World Health Organization (WHO) and Wikipedia to provide medical information around the world. An editorial published in the Canadian Medical Association Journal called Cochrane Reviews "the best single resource for methodologic research and developing the science of meta-epidemiology" due to its standardization.[370]

In other words, when Cochrane publishes a review article, the medical world and policymakers take note. So, when Cochrane released a review—"Nurses as Substitutes for Doctors in Primary Care"—in 2018, everyone in the healthcare industry paid attention. The 2018 Cochrane report analyzed the 18 randomized, controlled studies published between 1967 and 2017 that met the group's criteria for inclusion. In summary, the Cochrane report noted these findings:

- The substitution of nurses for physicians is one alternative strategy that *may* improve access, efficiency, and quality of care.
- Cochrane authors found that the delivery of primary care by nurses instead of doctors *probably* leads to similar patient health and higher patient satisfaction.
- Using nurses instead of doctors makes a small amount of difference in the number of prescriptions written or tests ordered. This difference may not matter clinically.
- Nurses probably have longer consultations with patients.
- Regarding the impact of information provided to patients, the extent to which clinical guidelines were followed, and the costs of healthcare provided by nurses instead of doctors, the results were uncertain; conclusions about these issues could not be drawn.[371,372]

Most importantly, the Cochrane report does not address the work of independent nurse practitioners—*because the issue of working independently was not evaluated.* Every study that "substituted" nurses for doctors encompassed physician involvement because a physician supervisor could always be consulted whenever necessary by nurses caring for patients.

It's awfully hard to design a study that compares independent nurses to physicians, simply because of the ethical dilemma. Is it fair to randomly assign patients to an unsupervised nurse when unsupervised nurses have never been shown to safely provide care devoid of physician supervision? Despite the fact that scientific research has not determined whether substituting independent non-physicians in the place of physicians is safe, nearly half the states in the Union sanction this practice by law. This is one of the tallest tales being told by politicians and lobbyists in healthcare today.

COCHRANE'S 18 TALL TALES

It is astounding that despite more than 50 years of research, only 18 studies met the rigorous scientific criteria necessary to evaluate perhaps one of the single most important questions facing our healthcare system today: who should provide medical care to patients?

Moreover, of the 18 studies that Cochrane analyzed, only 3 were conducted in the United States: Lewis[373] Mundinger,[374] and Hemani.[375] 6 studies were carried out in the UK, where physicians supervised all nurse practitioners. 3 studies were conducted in the Netherlands, three in Canada, and one each in Sweden, Spain, and South Africa. Study lengths were short, averaging only 14 months for the 18 trials. The shortest study lasted just 2 weeks and the longest evaluated care over 4 years. The type of care provided by nurses in these studies consisted of first-contact, ongoing care for physical complaints, as well as the follow-up of chronic conditions.

All the studies had shortcomings. 2 out of 3 U.S. studies (Mundinger and Lewis) were judged to have a high risk of bias, meaning the study authors had a vested interest in the outcome of the research. Only one U.S. study (Hemani) was considered to be methodologically adequate to analyze whether doctors and nurse practitioners are "equal." Let's start there.

RANDOMIZED CONTROLLED TRIALS IN THE UNITED STATES

Study 1—Hemani (1999)

The single best scientific U.S. study in the Cochrane review was conducted at the Veterans Administration (VA) Medical Center in Baltimore, Maryland involving 450 patients. The conclusion: "In a primary care setting, nurse practitioners may utilize more healthcare resources than physicians."[376]

9 nurse practitioners, 35 medical residents, and 10 attending level physicians were evaluated on their first contact with patients in primary care. Nurse practitioners in the study had 5 years of education and an average of 13.3 years of practice experience. Medical residents had 8 years of education and 1 to 2 years of residency experience. The attending physician group had completed 11 years of education and had 7 years of practice experience.

In this study, attending physicians were required to review and sign all charts of nurse practitioners and medical residents, therefore this study qualifies as 100% supervision. In other words, if the attending physicians found a problem with the quality of work performed while reviewing charts, patients could be contacted, and mistakes corrected. Although they were being supervised, nurse practitioners and residents were permitted to make referrals, order tests, and develop treatment plans without explicit approval by their attending physician.

- The study found nurse practitioners utilized more healthcare resources than medical residents in 14 out of 17 outcomes.
- Nurse practitioners utilized resources more often than physicians in 10 out of 17 outcomes.
- Nurse practitioners ordered more lab tests, such as urinalyses or thyroid function tests.
- The finding that nurse practitioners ordered more imaging studies—ultrasounds, CT scans, and MRIs—was statistically significant.

Although nurse practitioners and attending physicians had the same number of years of experience in healthcare, the nurse practitioners ordered a strikingly higher number of specialty consultations, both medical and surgical. Study authors surmised that nurse practitioners may have felt more uncomfortable with diagnostic complexity and relied more on testing and specialty referrals to make up for the gaps in knowledge.

Hospitalization rates were higher for those patients in the nurse practitioner-patient group, even though patients in the nurse practitioner group were not considered higher risk—patients managed by the attending physicians had the highest rates of chronic disease. Patients managed by the nurse practitioners had a 41% higher risk of being hospitalized, translating into 13 more hospital admissions per 100 patients per year.

The only statistically significant conclusion drawn from this single best examination of U.S. nurse practitioner performance compared to physicians was that nurse practitioners utilize more healthcare resources in primary care. Interestingly, this is the same conclusion reached in one of the first studies on nurse practitioners in 1974.

Study 2—Mundinger (2000)

The second U.S. study analyzed by Cochrane was published in the Journal of the American Medical Association (JAMA) in 2000. This study, by authors Mundinger and Lenz, is the most commonly cited research in support of nurse practitioner equivalence, but Cochrane pointed out that the study showed the highest bias of all 18 trials included in their review.

The Mundinger study compared 17 physicians and 7 nurse practitioners in community out-patient primary care clinics. Study subjects totaled 1316 patients, predominantly low-income Hispanic women. One peculiarity about this study was that the patient population was highly transient, frequently relocating between New York City and the Dominican Republic.

Patients were assigned to either a nurse practitioner-run or physician-run primary care practice. While many believe this study compared independent nurse practitioners to physicians, it is noted in the fine print that at the time of the study, New York state law required nurse practitioners to practice with a collaborating physician—one who must be available upon request for nurse practitioner consultation.

After 6 months, the study reported no differences in health status or health service utilization among patients in this low-risk, generally healthy population. There was a statistically significant difference in patient satisfaction at the 6-month mark, with physicians rating higher than nurse practitioners.

The Cochrane report criticized this study in several ways, noting that study data was not only incomplete but also not completely accurate. Cochrane noted that researchers, including Mary Mundinger, who was a nurse, were heavily invested in the outcome of the study, which may have impacted the results.

Cochrane's critique included the fact that this study had the highest bias of all 18 studies reviewed:

- Subjects were not randomized (selection bias)
- Neither patients nor personnel were blinded to intervention (performance bias)

- Outcome assessments were not blinded (detection bias)
- Study authors reported only favorable data

Importantly, the patient population studied was very specific, therefore results cannot be scientifically generalizable to a high-risk or sicker population. The setting of the study, community health clinics, is also different from the setting in which most patients receive primary care in the U.S.

Nurse practitioner advocates often cite the Mundinger study, as demonstrating no differences in nurse practitioner care compared to physician care. It would be more accurate to say that the Mundinger study shows that "for Hispanic, low-income women receiving care in a community clinic, there are no differences when nurse practitioners are supervised by physicians compared to physician care in New York State after a 6-month time period."[377] An editorial that accompanied the article noted that "the short duration of the trial limits its ability to test a health professional's competence across the broad spectrum of primary healthcare."[378]

Study 3—Lewis (1967)

The third randomized controlled U.S. trial included in the Cochrane review was conducted at the University of Kansas Medical Center in 1967. The study was produced through a joint effort through the Departments of Preventative Medicine and Community Health and Nursing Education.

A total of 66 patients were examined, divided into two groups of 33. Most of these patients were women over 50 years of age with lower socioeconomic status. Patients in the study had 1 of 5 conditions: hypertensive disease, arteriosclerotic heart disease, obesity, gastrointestinal or musculoskeletal complaints, and arthritis. Nurse practitioners were 100% supervised throughout the study, protocols were written for all 5 conditions and all charts were reviewed daily by 1 or 2 of the physicians involved in the study. A total of 345 visits were made by 33 patients in the nurse group, and 153 visits were made by 33 patients in the physician group. No information was provided about the experience level of clinicians in either cohort.

The goal of this study was to determine whether or not patients would accept seeing an advanced clinical nurse in an expanded role.

The answer to that question was yes, patients were absolutely accepting of nurses as a primary source of care.

RANDOMIZED CONTROLLED TRIALS IN THE UK

Of the 18 studies included in the Cochrane review, 7 were performed in the United Kingdom. Nurse practitioners in these studies were practicing under physician supervision, based on the Royal College of Medicine's restrictive "scope of practice" statement. It may be worth noting that nurse practitioner education and training are different between the U.S. and the U.K., where there are no minimum educational requirements.[379]

The role of nurse practitioners in telephone triage

2 of 6 U.K. studies evaluated the efficacy of telephone triage performed by nurses for a general practice office. The first study was done in 1995 in Wiltshire, a landlocked county known for the tourist attraction Stonehenge. The study was designed to evaluate the safety and efficacy of after-hours telephone triage by nurses (Lattimer 1998). Telephone calls would be guided by decision support software, and nurses completed a 6-week training program before the study to improve telephone consultation skills.

Nurses could follow three management options:

1. Offer telephone advice directly to patients
2. Refer the patient for evaluation by a general physician
3. Refer the patient to the emergency department.

Nurses managed nearly half of all calls without referral to a physician. This reduced the need for physicians to take phone calls by 69%. The telephone triage system also reduced referrals to primary care clinics by 38%, and 23% fewer patients required a home visit by a physician.

Overall, nurse telephone triage produced substantial changes. The system reduced the workload of general practice physicians by 50% and provided efficient access to health information for callers. There was no increase in the number of adverse outcomes, such as death, hospital admission, or the volume of patients seen in the emergency department.

This study concluded experienced nurses could safely provide telephone triage advice after-hours independent of physicians using a software program guide.[380] However, this study provides no evidence as to the quality of independently practicing nurse practitioners not guided by protocol.

By the time the second telephone triage study commenced in 2013, many practices in the U.K had already implemented nurse telephone triage. Physician workload had grown 62% since the first telephone study was conducted in 1995. The average primary care practice managed 7,000 patients, with at least 20 patients requesting same-day consultation.

Researchers analyzed the effect of adding a nurse-run telephone triage call service on primary care workload (Campbell 2014). Outcomes were consistent with the previous trial. Telephone triage did indeed reduce the workload of face-to-face visits for primary care physicians with no increase in adverse outcomes. However, telephone triage increased the number of patient contacts by 33% for general practice physician-led calls and 48% for nurse practitioner-led calls, with no cost savings overall.[381]

Advanced Practice Nurses in Adult Primary Care

A third randomized controlled trial in the UK (Shum 2000) involved five practices in southeast London and Kent, in a semi-rural, suburban, and urban settings. This study evaluated practice nurses, not nurse practitioners, and narrowly focused on patients with only minor medical complaints. 5 nurses with an average of 8.4 years of clinical experience were recruited. They each completed a 3-month part-time educational course learning to manage minor medical complaints. 19 general practice physicians made up the comparison group.

The study evaluated only low-risk patients. High-risk patients were excluded: children under one-year, pregnant women, anyone with severe chest pain, abdominal pain, or difficulty breathing, anyone vomiting blood or fainting, and patients with psychiatric complaints.

Nurses acted semi-independently, taking histories, performing examinations, offering treatment, and issuing prescriptions, which required the signature of a physician. Nurses referred complicated cases to their supervising physician when necessary.

Out of 790 low-risk patients seen by nurses, 27% required evaluation by the physician. Nearly 20% required face-to-face contact with the physician, while 8% needed informal consultation with the supervising physician. In other words, almost one in three low-risk patients seen "independently" by clinical practice nurses required physician collaboration.

Researchers could not draw any conclusions about the safety of nurse-led care because the study group was not large enough to detect rare, adverse outcomes.[382]

Nurse practitioners in walk-in clinics

The fourth randomized controlled trial conducted in the U.K. (Venning 2000) evaluated the cost-effectiveness of using nurse practitioners to staff walk-in clinics. Patients were randomized into two groups: 651 saw a general practice physician and 641 saw a nurse practitioner. Again, nurse practitioners worked under the supervision of physicians. The study compared processes, outcomes, and costs of care between the groups.

Nurse practitioners spent more time with patients, averaging 12.9 minutes per visit, compared to 7.28 minutes for physicians. Nurse practitioners also performed more tests, ordering them 8.7% of the time, while general practice doctors ordered tests 5.6% of the time (p=0.01). Nurse practitioners also performed more follow-up visits than physicians.

Nurse practitioners were supervised by general practitioners as part of a primary care team. The nurse practitioners required direct assistance from their supervising physician 17% of the time. Ultimately, the study was inadequately powered to determine the cost-effectiveness of employing nurse practitioners in primary care.[383]

Nurse practitioners in disease prevention

The fifth study conducted in the U.K. evaluated the prevention of heart attacks and strokes (Moher 2001). This study compared how well doctors and nurses followed-up on 3 cardiovascular risk factors: blood pressure, cholesterol levels, and smoking status. Twenty-one Warwickshire practices were enrolled. Patients with known heart disease were randomized to care from either a doctor or a nurse. Both groups were trained on guidelines for prevention and protocols were established.

This study found that nursing care delivered by protocol was equally effective as the same care by doctors. However, this study found that following up on the 3 risk factors did not lead to fewer heart attacks and strokes in patients.[384] If an intervention does not save lives or cut costs, then protocol-driven assessments of cardiac risk may not have a practical application at the bedside.

Nurse practitioners in specialty care

The final 2 studies in the U.K. dealt with specialty care. The first, in 2014, assessed clinical outcomes and cost-effectiveness of nurse-led care for patients with rheumatoid arthritis (Larrson 2014). The study compared a clinical nurse specialist with 10 years of experience to a rheumatologist (a physician who specializes in diseases of the joints) with 9 years of experience. The nurse was directly supervised, with access to the rheumatologist for questions or concerns. The study showed that while nurse-led care in protocol-driven chronic disease was cost-effective, there was no effect on the quality of life scores for patients. The study also noted that "the clinical nurse specialist conferred more with the rheumatologist than vice-versa."[385]

The second study of U.K. nurses in a specialty setting assessed patients in a gastroenterology practice who suffered from dyspepsia, a condition of abdominal pain after meals (Chan 2009). The study excluded high-risk patients and anyone with symptoms considered to be high risk—vomiting, anemia, rapid weight loss, tumors, peptic ulcer disease, or any life-threatening condition.

All patients underwent endoscopy, a procedure of visually inspecting the stomach by placing a camera tube down the esophagus, to exclude a life-threatening condition, like cancer. After endoscopy, a standardized and structured protocol was performed by either a gastrointestinal nurse practitioner or a gastroenterologist, a physician who specializes in disease of the gastrointestinal tract.

The conclusion of the study: specialty-focused nurse practitioners could provide cost-effective follow up after endoscopy—assuming patients were low-risk without any concerning signs or symptoms.[386]

NETHERLANDS STUDIES

The Netherlands has not incorporated non-physicians into primary care to the same extent as the U.S. and the U.K. Nurse practitioners began to play a role in care in the Netherlands in 1997.

Three of the studies included in the Cochrane review were performed in the Netherlands.

First-contact primary care

The first randomized controlled trial in the Netherlands compared nurse practitioners to general physicians (Dierick-van Daele 2009). Nurses in this study completed a specialized 2-year clinical training program designed to teach them how to manage common medical complaints. Nurse practitioners were always working with physician supervision and required physicians to sign prescriptions and authorize referrals.

Nurse practitioners evaluated patients with a variety of primary care complaints, including respiratory problems, ear, nose and throat problems, musculoskeletal injuries, skin complaints, urinary problems, and gynecological problems. Nurses enrolled in this study had an average of 12 years of clinical experience and physicians had 16 years of experience.

The study did not enroll enough patients to determine whether using nurse practitioners was safe. That is not to say they are not, rather, that the study could not draw definitive conclusions about this. Considering its many methodological problems, it is unclear why this study was included in the Cochrane review at all. The only statistically significant finding was the patients cared for by nurse practitioners had more frequent follow-up appointments, a consistent finding in many of these comparison studies.[387]

Diabetes management

The second Dutch study investigated the safety of nurse practitioners managing type 2 diabetes mellitus in primary care (Houweling 2011). Patients with complicated diabetes who required an endocrinologist for care and those who were older or had other medical conditions were excluded from the study. The remaining low-risk diabetic patients were randomized to either the care of a nurse practitioner or physician.

Nurses at the practice received one week of training of a diabetes protocol intended to optimize blood sugar, blood pressure, cholesterol levels, and eye and foot care. For the study, nurses were permitted to prescribe only 14 different medications and adjust them accordingly. They were not permitted to prescribe insulin. In both groups, diabetic control and blood pressure improved. However, according to Cochrane, there were not enough patients enrolled to determine if there was a difference in care between the 2 groups.

Consistent with most comparison studies, nurse practitioners referred more patients for higher levels of care, in this case, initiation of insulin therapy (p-value=0.07.) Patients of nurse practitioners followed-up more frequently than physicians—6.1 times compared to 2.8 times (p-value=0.001). In essence, to achieve comparable outcomes, physicians spent 28 minutes per patient and nurse practitioners needed 128 minutes.[388]

Heart disease

The third Dutch study included in the Cochrane report was a prospective randomized trial conducted at 6 large centers involving 25 physicians, 6 practice nurses, and 30,000 patients (Voogdt-Pruis 2010). Eligible patients were 30–74 with at least a 10% 10-year risk SCORE (Systematic Coronary Risk Evaluation) for heart disease. This group of patients is at increased risk of heart disease progression. High-risk patients such as those with diabetes, known cardiac disease, and other chronic conditions were excluded from the study. Nurse practitioners chosen to participate were experienced, already managing patients with asthma, chronic obstructive pulmonary disease, and diabetes. They all practiced under physician supervision.

After one year of intensive cardiovascular management, the nurse group saw a greater reduction in risk factors compared to physicians, probably due to better adherence to chronic disease protocols. The study did provide strong evidence that experienced nurse practitioners can effectively modify cardiovascular risk factors in low-risk patients and in collaboration with physician supervision.[389]

CANADA

2 studies included in the Cochrane review were conducted in Canada. Both Canadian studies were done before 1980 and involved fully supervised nurse practice. The Burlington Randomized Trial of the Nurse Practitioner conducted by Walter Spitzer and David Sackett was the first study on nurse practitioners (Spitzer 1974). As previously discussed, the study demon-

strated that the nurse practitioners treating low-risk patients under careful physician supervision, were as safe and effective as a physician 55–67% of the time.[390] The second Canadian study was completed at St. John's Newfoundland and compared a doctor to a nurse in a family practice (Chambers 1978). Both clinicians were highly experienced; the physician had practiced in St John's for 15 years, while the nurse had twenty years of clinical experience overall, with 15 as a family practice nurse. Before the study, the nurse attended a 9-month training course to expand history, physical exam, and diagnostic skills. The physician managed 585 families and the nurse managed 292 families. There were no differences in patient outcomes when receiving first-contact care from a physician-supervised family practice nurse or care provided by a physician.[391]

SOUTH AFRICA

The Cochrane review included one study conducted in South Africa, where nurse practitioners cannot prescribe medicine. The study enrolled 812 HIV-positive patients who were then randomized into two groups: "doctor-initiated, nurse monitored" anti-retroviral treatment compared to "doctor-initiated, doctor monitored" anti-retroviral treatment, which was the standard of care (Sanne 2010).

This study followed protocols for the management of HIV-positive patients. Outcomes studied were death, viral load reduction, and drug toxicity events. This study was very well done and concluded that nurses are as capable of monitoring HIV therapy initiated by physicians as the physicians are themselves.[392] However, this study did not evaluate independent nurse practitioners managing various conditions without supervision.

SPAIN

Physicians in Spain are struggling with high demands for primary care services. Time constraints are increasing the proportion of patients referred for specialty care, which in turn is increasing healthcare expenditures. This study evaluated whether or not a proportion of physician workload could be safely assumed by nurses (Iglesias 2013).

Patients over 18 years of age with 6 specific complaints were included: burns, injuries, diarrhea, low back pain, cold symptoms, and pain with urination. Patients who were pregnant or breastfeeding, had a mental health condition, recent hospitalization, or those with a serious current or past health condition were excluded. After the patients were screened as having one of these low-risk conditions, 753 were assigned to the nursing group and 708 to the control physician group.

Nurse practitioners managed 72% of the low complexity conditions of burns, injuries, and diarrhea independently. However, they were only able to independently manage 17.5% of low back pain complaints, 16% of cold symptoms, and 15% of patients having urinary discomfort. This study shows that physician-supervised nurses trained in managing a few, specific, low-complex conditions provide care comparable to that of primary care physicians.[393]

SWEDEN

The final study in the Cochrane Review was conducted in Sweden. The study compared treatment outcomes in patients with low-disease activity in a nurse-led rheumatology clinic compared to care from a rheumatologist (Ndosi 2013).

The study recruited 5 registered nurses with clinical nursing experience ranging from 20 to 40 years and with 9 to 20 years of rheumatology-specific clinical experience. A group of 107 patients were randomized between nurses and rheumatology physicians. The years of experience of the rheumatology physicians were not reported.

The authors concluded that patients with stable chronic inflammatory arthritis on biological therapy can safely be monitored by a nurse-led rheumatology clinic with equivalent outcomes. Repeated contact through a nurse-led rheumatology clinic adds considerable value for patients with stable rheumatoid arthritis and it is probably safe to replace one of the two annual visits with a rheumatologist for monitoring biological therapy outcomes.[394]

SUMMARY

The Cochrane review summarizes the best available data on the use of non-physicians to supplement the care provided by physicians over the last 5 decades. Based on this data, it is unclear whether nurses can substitute for doctors in primary care or specialty settings. What is clear is that in patients with minor medical complaints or low-risk chronic conditions, non-physicians using protocols and being supervised by physicians can unequivocally provide safe, high quality, and cost-effective care. However, the data has not demonstrated that nurse practitioners or physician assistants can deliver safe care to patients independent of physician involvement.

ADDITIONAL RESEARCH

Other large-scale review studies have had similar results. The RAND Corporation produced a study sponsored by the Ohio Association of Advanced Practice Nurses in 2015.[395] The review sought to evaluate the impact of expanding scope of practice and nurse independence on patient care. Only 3 studies met their strict inclusion criteria, and only one of those studies was published in a peer-reviewed journal.

Based on these 3 studies, the report concluded that nurse practitioner practice would "likely" increase access and utilization, "possibly" improve quality and outcomes and that the effect on cost was "inconclusive." The only peer-reviewed study included in the analysis found a 2% increase in the number of office visits when a state allowed nurses to prescribe medications. This led to 3.5% higher visit charges and 4.3% more spending on office visits.[396]

The Veterans Association sought an answer to the following question: Do independent advanced practice nurses and physicians provide care of comparable quality? To answer this question, the group found 10 studies that met inclusion criteria: 4 in urgent care settings, 3 in primary care, and 3 that evaluated anesthesia care.[397] Of the 10 studies, 7 were evaluated by Cochrane. Only 3 focusing on anesthesia care have not been discussed previously.

Regarding anesthesia care, the report concluded: "no randomized trials compared outcomes of surgical patients managed by an independent CRNA with those managed by teams, anesthesiologists, or other physicians."[398] The report did note that one study (Silber 2000) showed that the 30-day mortality rate was higher when medical care was managed by a non-physician anesthesiologist, while the 2 other studies showed no difference.[399] Altogether, this data is not scientifically supportive of having unsupervised CRNA's manage anesthesia for surgical cases.

Although headlines summarizing the report conveniently concluded that there was no difference in health status, quality of life, mortality, or hospitalization between nurse practitioners and physicians, few mentioned the poor quality of available data. The report itself acknowledged that the strength of evidence for these conclusions was "insufficient to low." Additionally, all the studies were found to have a medium-to-high risk of bias.

The final summary from the VA report states that there is insufficient information on the quality of care by advanced practice nurses and no information on the quality of care of unsupervised nurse practitioners.

SLOW DEATH OF A GOOD IDEA

This chapter laying out the results of 5 decades of research would not be complete without returning to William O. Spitzer, the co-author of the famous Burlington Trial. In a 1984 editorial for the New England Journal of Medicine, titled, "The Nurse Practitioner Revisited—Slow Death of a Good Idea," he expressed concern about the lack of good quality research on nurse practitioners.[400] Spitzer warned about taking shortcuts in the randomized controlled trial phase of evaluation. Unfortunately, much of the research evaluating nurse practitioners have been rife with methodological flaws. The most common problems include a failure to randomly distribute patients and varied clinician experience favoring non-physicians. Another weak point is the use of self-reported, subjective information such as patient satisfaction, feelings about clinicians, and self-reported health status, outcomes that are notoriously unreliable and have very little to do with patient safety.

The nurse practitioner and physician assistant roles were created to provide complementary care with a physician carefully supervising and collaborating on complex patients. This model works well. Studies definitively show that when physicians and non-physicians collaborate, patients receive exceptional and cost-effective care.

Physician associations, like the American Medical Association (AMA) and the American Academy of Family Physicians (AAFP), acknowledge that physician-led teams incorporating nurse practitioners and physician assistants are successful. However, most physician groups oppose the independent practice of non-physicians, because there is no scientific evidence that the care provided is safe, let alone equivalent. Despite a lack of evidence, legislators have allowed nurse practitioners in 24 states and the Veteran's Administration to legally practice independently without any physician supervision or oversight.

PHYSICIAN ASSISTANT RESEARCH

The American Academy of PAs presents 30 references to support "optimal team practice," which downplays the requirement of physician supervision.[401] Most of the studies are retrospective, culling through data to try to determine outcomes. Every study cited involved some form of physician supervision or consultation.

Although the Cochrane database has not yet studied physician assistant practice, the meta-analysis "The Contribution of Physician Assistants in Primary Care: A Systematic Review" was published in 2013. The work analyzed 49 studies, most of which were performed in the United States, and concluded that "research evidence of the contribution of PAs to primary care was mixed and limited." The study noted, however, that physician assistants were judged to be "of value" by an increasing number of employers and suggested further specific studies to understand the contribution of physician assistants to the primary care workforce.[402]

Regarding in-patient care, a 2008 comprehensive review of the medical literature found no randomized, controlled studies that evaluated the performance of physician assistants in critical care settings.[403] The bottom line: there is simply not enough data to support the safety and efficacy of physician assistants when practicing independently of physician supervision.

CHAPTER 7

FAKE IT 'TIL YOU MAKE IT

At 2:30 am, after eleven hours under the care of nurse practitioner Antoinette Thompson in the Mercy-El Reno emergency room, Alexus Ochoa was loaded into an ambulance to be transferred to the Oklahoma University Medical Center. Nurse practitioner Thompson had arranged the transfer after interpreting from Alexus's chest CT scan incorrectly that the patient was suffering from a crushed sternum.

Shortly afterward, an off-site radiologist read the chest CT scan that Thompson had incorrectly interpreted. He called the emergency room immediately to report that the scan showed that Alexus had large blood clots in both lungs.

Alexus arrived at the University of Oklahoma Medical Center at 3:30 am, finally diagnosed correctly with a pulmonary embolus. Physicians there tried desperately to save her life by giving her the proper dose of blood-thinning medication—but it was too late. Alexus, who one day before had been an energetic, healthy 19-year old college athlete, died at 5:26 am.

WHAT IS THE DIFFERENCE BETWEEN THE PRACTICE OF MEDICINE AND THE PRACTICE OF NURSING?

Nurse practitioners say that they are capable of autonomously diagnosing and treating acute and chronic medical conditions. While this sounds like the practice of medicine, nurse practitioners insist that they do not practice medicine, but rather, they practice "advanced nursing." What is the difference, and why is the distinction important? Orla Weinhold, MD, a physician who was a family nurse practitioner for 8 years before attending medical school characterizes the differences. "Nurse practitioners are taught pattern-based thinking, and physicians are taught more critical thinking."[404] Another physician who was a nurse practitioner first, Dara Grieger, MD, agrees. "As a nurse practitioner, I was taught to recognize the patterns but not the 'why' behind them."[405] What Weinhold and Grieger describe as the difference in the way that nurses and doctors think is the difference between forward reasoning and backward reasoning.

Nursing education tends to emphasize a reverse reasoning methodology because it uses a framework built upon symptom identification from patterns rather than a diagnostically driven focus. There is nothing inferior about this method. It is a necessary technique when caring for patients at the bedside.

"Nursing is not medicine and medicine is not nursing. We care about different things," says Nixi Chesnavich, DO, a physician who worked as a nurse for ten years before attending medical school. "Nursing theory is what the patient would do for themselves if they understood or had the information or could physically perform themselves."[406] To provide this care, nurses learn to follow a multi-step framework called the "Nursing Process."

The Nursing Process involves the following:

1. **Nursing Assessment**
   The nurse collects and analyzes data about a patient's symptoms.
2. **Nursing Diagnosis**
   According to Characteristics of a Nursing Diagnosis (1985), a nursing diagnosis is a "statement of a patient's problem or state of health, based on a pattern or cluster of signs and symptoms."[407] A nursing diagnosis is based on the patient's symptoms and not a medical diagnosis—for example, "chest pain" or "headache." Once a nurse has determined a nursing diagnosis, a care plan is created to address the patient's needs from a nursing standpoint.
3. **Outcomes/Planning**
   Nurses are taught to set achievable goals for the patient, which are written into the patient's care plan. These goals may include improvement in the patient's activities of daily living, nutrition, or pain control.
4. **Implementation**
   The care plan is followed and documented in the patient's record.
5. **Evaluation**
   Patients are reassessed to determine the effectiveness of the care plan, with modifications made when needed.

In following this process, nurses become intimately acquainted with their patients, particularly when they are working at a patient's bedside. Joann D'Aprile, DO, worked as a nurse and taught nursing school before becoming a physician. "Nurses identify the biopsychosocial needs of patients, provide symptom relief and comfort, and assist patients in regaining optimal function." She compares the care that nurses give to that of a mother caring for an ill child. "Add in a fundamental understanding of the human body and condition, and what types of nursing interventions will help that person regain your health; that is nursing." D'Aprile also adds that the role of the nurse is to advocate for the patient. "If there is an error in an order, a nurse would bring the issue to the physician's attention."[408] Truly, there is nothing like a nurse.

Medicine follows a different model. Cheryl Ferguson, MD is a physician who worked as a nurse and even attended a semester of nurse practitioner school before she decided to pursue medical school. Ferguson notes that nursing is "knowing how to take care of patients' needs, whether they are physical, social, psychological. Medicine is much more scientific; diagnosing the disease, not just the symptoms, weighing risks and benefits of treatment, understanding lab results and what they really mean. Nursing is not medicine. Medicine is not nursing. They overlap but should be separate entities to be best for patient care."[409]

Rather than focusing on the moment-to-moment needs of the patient, physicians are trained to search for one unifying diagnosis for their symptoms and focus on the most effective way to manage their disease process. This does not mean that physicians do not deeply care about the patient's biopsychosocial needs. Henry Travers, MD, notes that just like nurses, physicians are also interested in becoming intimately acquainted with the patient and providing symptom relief and comfort. Travers says, "the point is that the total care of the patient is critically dependent on the correct diagnosis while being mindful of the difference between disease and illness."[410]

Physicians do not spend the same amount of one-on-one time with patients as nurses do. While nurses in the hospital may be assigned to 1, 2, or sometimes up to 6 patients at a time, physicians typically follow 10, 20, 30, or more patients. Physicians rely on the reports given by nurses at the bedside to understand how the patient is responding to a treatment plan, and this collaboration is essential for patient care. Patients do not always realize that even though they may see their physician for a shorter period, the doctor may still be working on their case throughout the day.

The difference in models may be one of the reasons that patients value nurses so highly. Indeed, the work done by nurses should be highly valued by everyone in healthcare. There is nothing that can replace the one-on-one personal attention and care that a good nurse provides. But patients also need a diagnostician—someone who can determine why they have a medical symptom—and ideally, help them to recover fully. This is where physician-training focuses. The training provided for a registered nurse as described in the nursing process does not provide the tools to independently diagnose and treat patients.

Can a nurse practitioner gain the necessary knowledge to take on this role in an additional 2 years of training? Physicians who were previously nurse practitioners say no. The biggest reason: nurse practitioner school did not adequately prepare them to be able to develop an adequate differential diagnosis, the essential list necessary to accurately diagnose disease.

THE DIFFERENTIAL DIAGNOSIS

A differential diagnosis is a comprehensive list of all possible explanations for a patient's physical signs and symptoms. The development of this list requires an exhaustive fund of knowledge; without knowing about a disease, one cannot consider it as a possible diagnosis. Fortunately, common problems are common, and most of the time, a patient will have one of the top three or four most-likely explanations for a medical problem. Take, for example, a child with a sore throat and fever. The most likely diagnoses, just based on prevalence, are:

- Viral pharyngitis
- Strep throat
- Mononucleosis

However, physicians are trained to think far beyond the top two or three potential diagnoses. A pediatrician encountering a child with sore throat and fever will entertain additional possibilities:

- Epiglottitis
- Retropharyngeal abscess
- Peritonsillar abscess
- Diphtheria

- Meningitis
- Lemierre syndrome
- Gonorrhea of the throat
- Trapped foreign body
- Herpetic stomatitis
- Kawasaki disease
- Stevens-Johnson syndrome
- Autoimmune diseases like Behçet's syndrome
- Periodic fever with aphthous stomatitis, pharyngitis, and adenitis (PFAPA syndrome)

Physicians are taught to prioritize the deadliest disease on the differential list over more innocent potential causes. While few patients will die from strep throat or mononucleosis, epiglottitis or tonsillar abscesses are often deadly, which is why a pediatrician must keep these potential causes in mind when examining a child with sore throat and fever. Physicians then work forward searching for reasons to exclude conditions from the list instead of building a case for only one diagnosis that seems probable.

Nurse practitioners do not have the time or in-depth training during a two-year program to learn how to develop a comprehensive differential diagnosis. Orla Weinhold, MD, notes that "When I was a nurse practitioner, I never knew how to form a differential diagnosis. This was one of the most challenging parts of my clinical rotations in medical school. I didn't know how much I didn't know."[411]

Ronald Epstein, MD writes in *Attending: Medicine, Mindfulness, and Humanity* (2017) that even a non-medical person can learn how to recognize the signs and symptoms of various medical ailments and be correct most of the time.[412] The need for physician training occurs during those rare times when a medical situation is unusual or more complicated—and potentially life-threatening. Epstein argues that this is the very reason for the long and arduous journey of medical training. Without additional training on how to perform a differential diagnosis and the fund of knowledge required to expand the potential diagnoses to include the most serious causes of a patient's symptoms, non-physician practitioners may put patients are at risk.

Fortunately, most of the time, patients do not present with a critical illness or life-threatening problems. The problem arises with the occasional patient who truly needs an expert diagnostician. As Dara Grieger, MD notes, "As a nurse practitioner, most of the time I was OK. The problem was that I couldn't recognize when things were not OK."[413] This seems to be what happened to nurse practitioner Antoinette Thompson when she was treating Alexus Ochoa.

LACKING A PROPER DIFFERENTIAL DIAGNOSIS LEADS TO FATAL CONSEQUENCES

When Thompson was asked whether or not she understood the concept of a differential diagnosis list, she testified "I do, "I do. What everything—what it could be—once you're presented with something, what everything could be, and then your actual diagnosis is what it is." When asked if she has ever formed one before, she stated, "Only in school. I have done differential diagnosis, yes, that's why I knew what it was."

However, her answers under deposition made it clear that she had difficulty creating an accurate differential diagnosis for Alexus Ochoa. For example, when plaintiff's attorney Travis Dunn asked Thompson if she was aware that shortness of breath and chest pain were common symptoms of pulmonary embolus, she replied, "Could be." She was asked if she knew that chest pain was the second most common symptom of pulmonary embolism. Her reply: "No … I wasn't aware of that, no." Dunn asked: "Are you aware that chest pain, rapid breathing, and rapid heart rate, taken together, are highly suggestive of pulmonary embolism?" "No," Thompson replied, adding that the symptoms of a pulmonary embolism were not taught to her during her online schooling.

Despite lacking an adequate differential diagnosis, Thompson began to order tests to search for the cause of Alexus's symptoms. She explained her methodology this way: "At first, I ordered a chest CT, [but] because she was a teenage girl … I worried about causing cancer or infertility. Then when they told me she was syncopal [had fainted], I ordered a head CT. Every time someone presented me with something, I went in and did something about it."

She stated, "When you interview a patient, you don't get everything, because they don't tell you everything, you just go by what you see and what they tell you." She explained why she did not consider a pulmonary embolus as part of her differential diagnosis: "those [symptoms] presented at different times for me. They didn't just present—ok this is what I've got. It wasn't on my differential because I didn't get all the information. I got spotty information at different times. So, I treated according to that."

Nurse practitioner Wendy Wright testified as an expert witness on behalf of Antoinette Thompson. Wright, considered a competent and experienced family nurse practitioner, runs a full-service family practice clinic employing five nurse practitioners that serves 4,000 patients in the state of New Jersey. She has made a second career out of testifying as an expert witness about the care standard for nurse practitioners, spending most of her time providing defense testimony. As a nurse practitioner, Wright is not an expert in the practice of medicine. She is an expert in the practice of nursing.

On the stand, nurse practitioner Wright laid out her method for generating a differential diagnosis list. "Is this patient tachycardic because there was a positive meth urine test? Is this patient having chest pain because of that test [methamphetamine]? Is she syncopal because she's got a head bleed? Does she have a tumor? Does she have a cardiac abnormality?"

As they explained their thought processes in evaluating Alexus's symptoms, nurse practitioners Thompson and Wright both appeared to evaluate her symptoms individually, rather than organizing them as parts of the whole condition. Compare this type of thinking to that of a physician. James Leo, a critical care medicine physician and expert witness for the Ochoa family, shared the differential diagnosis list that he would have created based on the Alexus Ochoa's history alone: "… pulmonary embolism, pleurisy, pneumonia, sepsis, arrhythmia … aortic dissection, pneumothorax, and less likely pericarditis, pericardial tamponade, viral syndrome."

Once provided with Alexus's physical exam findings, Leo refined the list further, adding on the possibility of an asthma attack or musculoskeletal chest pain as causes of Alexus' symptoms. Leo explained why these "loose ends" should not remain on the list of possibilities after considering two additional findings, Alexus's low oxygen level and fast heart rate.

While both nurse practitioners listed "bleeding in the brain" as a possible diagnosis, Leo did not mention a brain problem at all, because this diagnosis did not fit the patient's observations and clinical findings.

When asked to discuss Thompson's further evaluation of Alexus, Wright continued in the nurse practitioner's defense. "She was an athlete. She's tachycardic and short of breath. Could it have been a cardiac issue? You take what you are presented with and you work that up and then you respond to what you get back … you don't just order 9 million tests when someone walks in."

No one suggested that Thompson should have ordered millions of tests. In fact, in addition to the standard screening labs, physician expert witness James Leo recommended only two, a D-dimer and a CT scan of the chest. "If the D-Dimer is zero, the chance of a clot is zero, and so no further workup is necessary," he testified.

Unfortunately, it took nurse practitioner Thompson more than 8 hours to order a D-Dimer test on Alexus Ochoa, and only after cardiology consultant Valuck recommended it. Instead of flagging the test as urgent, she ordered it as a routine lab study, failing to understand the reason consulting cardiology physician Valuck had recommended the D-Dimer in the first place.

Brian Swirsky, MD, an emergency medicine physician who was an expert witness, summed the reasoning approach best, "If a 19-year old female on birth control pills presents to a hospital with chest pain, shortness of breath, tachypnea, tachycardia, and hypoxia, what is the number one diagnosis that needs to be ruled out or ruled in by the physician? The answer is simply and only pulmonary embolus."

He continues, "I am of the opinion that the diagnosis of a pulmonary embolus was as 'plain as the driven snow,' for any reasonable physician even before a CT angiogram or D-dimer. Asked about the decision-making of Nurse Thompson, Dr. Swirsky commented, "she either didn't have the skill set or she didn't use the skill set."

Nurse practitioner defense expert Wendy Wright disagreed with Swirsky's assertion that a pulmonary embolus was likely based on Alexus's risk factors, stating "I've seen patients with PE's who had no risk factors." Wright further testified that she doubted that the chest pain, shortness of breath and fast heart rate that Alexus Ochoa presented with were "highly suggestive" of a pulmonary embolus, the ultimate cause of death for the young woman. Instead, Wright suggested that Alexus Ochoa's fast heart rate could also have been due to fear of the emergency department, or from riding in the ambulance.

The Ochoa family attorney Glendell Nix asked Nurse Wright, "Do you agree that life-threatening conditions associated with fainting include cardiac [cause], blood loss, PE and [brain bleeding]?

Expert witness Wright answered, "that, and a million other things."

Nurse practitioner Wendy Wright's vague and ambiguous answers belie an inadequate understanding of the practice of medicine. Despite being asked about immediately life-threatening conditions, she seemed unable to separate serious causes from innocent ones.

In addition to defending Antoinette Thompson's handling of Alexus Ochoa, Wendy Wright also defended the hospital's hiring of the nurse practitioner to work in an acute setting. Although Thompson admitted in court that her nurse practitioner education had inadequately prepared her to function in an acute care setting, expert witness Wright disagreed. She told the court that the training Thompson received was enough to safely treat patients seeking care at Mercy-El Reno emergency department, testifying, "Her education and her experience allow her to evaluate and treat to the upper limits of her education and when she gets to the point where she does not feel—that she feels that this is exceeding my knowledge and experience, it's time to transfer, or consult or collaborate."

Thompson testified that her nurse practitioner training did not include the care of acutely or critically ill patients. Expert witness Wright again disagreed, stating, "every person who walks through your door with an acute illness is acutely ill, so I find it really hard to believe that she never saw a pneumonia and she never saw a chest pain." Wright went on to add that, "[Nurse Thompson] may not have known exactly what was going on with that patient … but she knew this patient was sick and this patient needed to be out of the ER."

Wright's testimony was contradictory. While she testified that Thompson's extensive education prepared her to work in an emergency department, she also testified that using adenosine—an advanced life support resuscitation medication that every emergency medicine physician in this country should be familiar with—is outside of her comfort level. The nurse practitioner expert witness said, "my scope of practice says I can perform that for which I am educated and experientially trained … when it gets to the point where it is beyond what I am comfortable with, it is time for me to consult, collaborate or transfer care."

Is this level of knowledge adequate for a medical professional to independently staff an emergency department? No. It is not enough for a medical practitioner to simply know that a patient is acutely ill. It is the responsibility of the clinician to recognize severe illness and then to promptly act medically to save lives, and therein lies the problem: It is simply impossible to exchange a profession with twelve years of education and 15,000 hours of clinical training for one with a year of education and less than 1,000 hours.

Patients presenting to an emergency room, especially if they are brought by ambulance due to a life-threatening condition, expect to be treated by a qualified healthcare professional. As hospitals and corporations replace physicians with nurse practitioners and physician assistants, patients no longer have a choice. One wonders if Alexus Ochoa or her family had recognized that she was not being treated by a physician and demanded further evaluation, whether she may have survived.

"WE CHOOSE NPS"—A HOLISTIC VIEW OF NURSING PRACTICE

Nurse practitioner organizations have aggressively marketed the nursing model to patients. For example, the campaign "We Choose NPs," was designed to show the benefit to nursing care. So, what is the difference between a nursing model and a medical model in the care and treatment of patients? According to nurse practitioner advocates, the advantage to the nursing model is that it is "more than identifying a problem and suggesting a solution; it is a quest to work collaboratively with patients, families, and others toward patient-centered goals."[414] The American Association of Nurse Practitioners puts it this way: "What sets NPs apart from other healthcare providers is their unique emphasis on the health and well-being of the whole person. With a focus on health promotion, disease prevention, and health education and counseling, NPs guide patients in making smarter health and lifestyle choices."[415]

It must be asked, how is this any different from what physicians do? According to the American Academy of Family Physicians: "Family physicians are personal doctors for all people of all ages and health conditions. They are a reliable first contact for health concerns and directly address most healthcare needs. Through enduring partnerships, family physicians help patients prevent, understand, and manage illness, navigate the health system, and set health goals. Family physicians and their staff adapt their care to the unique needs of their patients and communities. They use data to monitor and manage their patient population and use best science to prioritize services most likely to benefit health."[416] The American College of Physicians describes the role of the internal medicine physician as "focused on the care of adults emphasizing use of the best medical science available in caring for patients in the context of thoughtful, meaningful doctor-patient relationships."[417]

The commonality between nurse practitioners and physicians is the emphasis on patient care, and nurses don't have a monopoly on caring for the whole patient. The difference lies in the emphasis on science and rigorous, standardized training. A nurse studies nursing. A physician studies medicine. This basic fact more than any other leads to some of the differences in care between the professions.

RESOURCE UTILIZATION

Since nurse practitioners and physician assistants receive abbreviated training and education compared to physicians, they need additional tools to supplement limitations in their fund of knowledge. For this reason, non-physicians order more laboratory tests, x rays, and medications, and refer more often to specialists.[418] Often, these additional tests are not necessary to make a correct diagnosis but are more of a "shotgun approach" to discover the cause of a patient's symptoms.

This increased healthcare utilization leads to increased expenditures. While patients and society suffer from increased healthcare spending, corporations and health systems benefit, incentivizing them to hire more non-physicians. Increased testing and medications don't just increase the cost of care; these interventions can have adverse consequences, such as negative side effects from unnecessary treatments. Patients also face anxiety and fear as they wait for test results. They also lose valuable time as they bounce from one specialist to another.

Alternately, non-physicians have a higher rate of non-intervention—failing to act when medically necessary.[419] This failure to provide care when it is truly needed is where true harm can occur to patients. Diagnosing and treating patients with life-threatening conditions, where the stakes are perhaps the highest, is a scenario in which the level of expertise matters. Inappropriate medical intervention can be dangerous, but non-intervention, or failing to act in a situation where medical treatment is necessary, may cost patients their lives. Unfortunately, numerous studies consistently show that non-physician practitioners are less aggressive than physicians in managing medical conditions and intervening when medically necessary.

Take the case of James Neely (name changed), who was 24-years old when he developed the sudden onset of swelling of his eyes, fatigue, headache, and a diffuse rash. James called his pediatrician for an appointment, but since he was over 21, he was scheduled with a family nurse practitioner instead. The Sacramento, California college student was seen by the nurse practitioner, who referred him to an ophthalmologist because of his eye symptoms. When the ophthalmologist found no problems with his eyes, James returned to the nurse practitioner, visiting her three more times over the next month. Although he complained of progressively worsening symptoms, no blood tests or additional work-up were done.

When James's mother stopped by his apartment to check on him, she was alarmed. "His skin was covered with what looked like mosquito bites, and his eyes were yellow." She drove James to the emergency department at UC Davis, where he was promptly diagnosed with severe aplastic anemia—a profound lack of blood in the body. James is currently awaiting a bone marrow transplant, and his mother wants to raise awareness about his lack of care. "If she had just done a little bit more perhaps we would have discovered the situation sooner to improve his chances."[420]

James's experience is not an anomaly, but part of a larger pattern in which non-physicians are less likely to act when medically necessary. While non-physicians may be able to provide medical care safely in some instances, studies show that physicians are better at catching and treating conditions judged to be very serious or serious, and in arranging timely follow-up care than non-physicians.[421] Doctors are also more likely to intervene to initiate a change in treatment compared to non-physicians when necessary, and provide higher rates of medication intensification when appropriate.[422,423]

Failing to intervene when medically appropriate is not only dangerous but also adds to healthcare costs. Early treatments tend to be less expensive to manage. Waiting until disease processes are more advanced requires more aggressive treatment which tends to be more complicated and expensive. By failing to act when medically necessary, non-physician practitioners may increase healthcare spending and complications for patients.

Non-physicians also increase the cost of healthcare in other ways. One of the very first studies on nurse practitioners, published in 1974, revealed increased healthcare costs due to much higher utilization of care services compared to physicians.[424] Although well-established now, this finding stunned the study authors, who had theorized that the use of nurse practitioners would lower costs. The increased cost associated with the use of nurse practitioners was due to an increase in-office visits and testing. Patients of nurse practitioners were seen in the primary care clinic up to three times more frequently than patients assigned to physicians. They were also more likely to visit specialty clinics and community agencies. Also, nurse practitioner patients were subjected to far more diagnostic tests. In the 45 years since this work was published, test ordering by nurse practitioners has only increased. Between 2003 and 2015, the number of skeletal x-rays ordered by nurse practitioners and physician assistants increased by 441%. At the same time, the rate of x-rays ordered by primary care physicians decreased by 33.5%.[425]

Consider the case of 3-year-old Joshua. When Joshua fractured his arm, his pediatrician referred him to a local orthopedic physician for casting. Instead of seeing the physician at his first visit, a physician assistant saw Joshua. After looking at the x-ray films sent by the pediatrician as well as the radiologist's report noting a fracture, the physician assistant determined that additional x-rays were needed. Joshua's mother protested, stating that x-rays had already been taken and reviewed, but the physician assistant insisted the additional films were medically necessary. Over the next 5 weeks, Joshua received not one, not two, but fifteen unnecessary x-rays, all ordered by the same physician assistant at the orthopedic clinic.[426] Although x-rays use a small amount of radiation and are generally considered safe, radiation exposure is associated with an increased risk of cancer later in life—and this risk is higher in younger patients. Avoiding unnecessary x-rays, particularly in children, is an ethical obligation for all clinicians. Studies consistently show that non-physician practitioners order more radiology studies than physicians.[427]

A 1981 Air Force study of "routine cases of low or moderate complexity" revealed that nurse practitioners and physician assistants ordered x-ray films at three times the rate of physicians.[428] A 1999 study showed that primary care patients assigned to nurse practitioners underwent more ultrasounds, CT scans, and MRI scans than patients assigned to physicians.[429] These findings were replicated in studies published in 2015[430] and 2017.[431]

In addition to being potentially dangerous, ordering unnecessary tests can be expensive. For 3-year old Joshua, with each set of x-ray films costing approximately $300, the treatment of his simple fracture increased by $1500. Nurse practitioners and physician assistants have also been found to order more laboratory tests, including skin biopsies to rule out cancer. Compared with dermatologists, physician assistants both perform more biopsies on benign spots and miss more malignant cases compared to physicians.[432] In one study, physician assistants and nurse practitioners performed six biopsies for every one skin cancer found—twice the biopsy rate of physicians.[433] The costs of unnecessary tests and procedures are high—both in terms of dollars and patients' health and safety. In 2012, non-physician practitioners billed for 2.6 million dermatological procedures. With studies showing that non-physician providers lack physicians' accuracy when identifying benign from malignant lesions, many of these treatments have likely been unnecessary.[434]

69-year-old John Dalman experienced this type of unnecessary treatment. After enduring 10 skin lesion biopsies by a physician assistant during one visit, John was told that his other lesions would require radiation and surgery. Worried that a physician assistant would be performing the surgery, he fled from the waiting room of the dermatology office. A second opinion from a dermatologist proved his instinct correct: not only did he not need radiation or surgery, but the physician assistant had missed a malignant melanoma on his shoulder.[435]

Is ordering extra tests so wrong? Aren't nurse practitioners and physician assistants just being extra-thorough, and ensuring that nothing important is missed? Ordering tests that are not medically necessary can lead to unnecessary medical interventions, which can be time-consuming, painful, and even dangerous.

On December 19, 2018, 45-year old Emily Heigl (name changed at patient request) walked into an urgent care complaining of her heart "fluttering" for the last five days. The nurse practitioner on-duty ordered tests, including a chest x-ray. "The nurse practitioner came back and said she needed to give me some 'straight talk,'" recalls Heigl, who was told that she had "emphysema, a lung tumor, and a possible embolism." Heigl was referred to the emergency room, where repeat tests showed an innocent lung nodule and otherwise normal chest. "I thought I had cancer and was going to die. I shook for an hour," says Heigl, who remains traumatized by the experience. Heigl also noted that her insurance company denied payment for her emergency room visit since the referral was not a true "emergency."[436]

Ordering unnecessary tests is not harmless. False-positive tests can lead to painful or invasive interventions and can cause serious emotional angst for patients. Of course, these additional tests and procedures also add up. In 2013, the Institute of Medicine estimated that "unnecessary services" added $210 billion to healthcare spending in the U.S., making it the single biggest contributor to waste.[437] Unnecessary services include not only x-rays and lab tests, but also referrals to specialists. Studies show that physician assistants and nurse practitioners are more likely to refer patients to specialists than primary care physicians, increasing cost to both patients and the healthcare system.[438]

Rebecca McPherson, MD is a neonatologist who worked as a nurse and family nurse practitioner for 14 years before she decided to become a physician. She says that as a physician, she believes that she saves the system money. "It's the MD in me plus those years of medical training that allows me to establish a diagnosis and treatment plan without doing a gazillion tests." McPherson, who supervises neonatology nurse practitioners in her practice, notes that her additional training has led her to cancel or redirect unnecessary tests. "Because of my medical training, I have the confidence to home in on the most likely diagnosis."[439]

Besides ordering more tests, nurse practitioners and physician assistants also prescribe more medication than physicians,[440] including more high-risk medications like opioids and psychotropic drugs.[441,442] This includes a higher number of unnecessary antibiotics, a major concern due to the development of resistant bacteria.[443] Antibiotic overuse has caused the emergence of resistant bacteria, so-called "super-bugs" that can no longer be killed with routine medications. Antibiotic resistance is a big enough threat to society that national agencies like the Centers for Disease Control and Prevention have called for the issue to become a national priority. Yet studies from 2005, 2016, and 2018 have repeatedly shown that non-physicians are more likely to prescribe antibiotics than physicians.[444,445,446]

Suzanne Humphries (name changed), a 42-year-old mother of two, was one such patient.[447] Suzanne walked into an urgent care with a sore throat and cough, convinced it was her third case of strep throat in a year. She requested an antibiotic from the physician assistant who saw her and told him that she'd had strep so many times in the past that amoxicillin did not work for her anymore. Rather than explaining that the bacteria that cause strep throat—Group A streptococcal bacteria—have no documented resistance to penicillin-class drugs, the physician assistant offered Suzanne a choice between two other antibiotics. She could have azithromycin, which clears the infection 30% of the time, or clindamycin, which is highly effective but associated with rare side effects, including *Clostridium difficile*. A potentially deadly intestinal infection, *Clostridium difficile* affects about half a million people in the U.S. each year. The bacteria often reside in the intestinal system at low levels and are usually kept under control by healthy gut bacteria, but a new strain that is particularly severe and difficult to treat has emerged, most likely a result of overzealous antibiotic use. For some reason, most victims are young, healthy, and without risk factors such as recent hospitalization or nursing home care.

Suzanne, who had recently been prescribed azithromycin at a different urgent care clinic opted for the more effective antibiotic. Because she was young and in good health, she assumed she would be at a lower risk of harm. On her fifth day taking clindamycin, Suzanne developed diarrhea and abdominal pain, signaling the onset of *Clostridium difficile* infection. Less than a week later, she was dead from the bacterial infection, leaving a grieving family, community, and 2 young children.

PAY PARITY

Although nurse practitioners and physician assistants may increase healthcare costs in certain respects, do they save money overall due to shorter educational training and lower salaries? According to some studies, nurse practitioner care may be more expensive than physician care, despite lower salaries, because care from nurse practitioners takes longer, resulting in increased clinical staff time. In one UK study, employing nurse practitioners to provide first contact care was found to cost the same or more as the employment of a salaried general practitioner.[448] Another study showed that teams that included nurse practitioners resulted in higher healthcare costs than physician-only care.[449]

While nurse practitioner salaries in 1981 were one-third to one-half that of a physician, nurse practitioner organizations have been fighting for years to be paid the same as physicians. Pay parity is listed as part of the American Association of Nurse Practitioner's strategic plan.[450] This demand for increased pay was predicted by William Spitzer, MD, one of the first researchers on nurse practitioner use in a 1984 editorial in the New England Journal of Medicine. Spitzer noted that the nurse practitioner concept was designed to "improve access for disadvantaged patients, contain healthcare costs, and efficiently deploy health professionals throughout the country." He insisted that "unrealistic ambitions about income must be set aside," noting that pay equivalence would obviate predictions made about the cost-effectiveness of nurse practitioners.[451]

However, nurse practitioners continue to advocate for equal pay to physicians. So far, nurse practitioners have achieved pay parity in Oregon, which has required insurance to pay nurse practitioners and physician assistants at the same rate as physicians since 2013.[452] Advocates are seeking this pay parity in other states. In February 2019, dozens of nurse-midwives descended on the state capital in Hartford, CT to demand the same pay as obstetricians.[453]

On October 3, 2019, President Donald Trump called for nurse practitioners and physician assistants to be paid at the same rate as physicians. In Section 5 of his "Executive Order on Protecting and Improving Medicare for Our Nation's Seniors," titled "Enabling Providers to Spend

More Time with Patients," President Trump proposed regulation paying all healthcare providers at the same rate.

> 5 (c)—conducting a comprehensive review of regulatory policies that create disparities in reimbursement between physicians and non-physician practitioners and proposing a regulation that would, to the extent allowed by law, ensure that items and services provided by clinicians, including physicians, physician assistants, and nurse practitioners, are appropriately reimbursed in accordance with the work performed rather than the clinician's occupation.[454]

Currently, Medicare pays nurse practitioners and physician assistants 85% of the physician rate when billed under the non-physician's provider number. Advocates of Section 5 argue that paying non-physicians and physicians the same allows free market forces to 'let the market decide.' In theory, patients would have the freedom to select the healthcare provider that they prefer—whether a nurse practitioner, physician assistant, or physician. However, in today's profit-driven healthcare system, now overrun by private equity firms, the reality will likely be far different. If Medicare pays the same rate for physicians and non-physicians, corporations will be incentivized to hire more nurse practitioners and physician assistants, especially if supervision is no longer required. Patients visiting hospitals and large health centers will lose the choice of seeing a physician for their care.

This legislation would also blow a death-knell to primary care physician residency training programs, decreasing the ever-dwindling supply of primary care doctors. Why would a student select the rigors of 4 years of medical school and at least 3 years of residency training—a minimum of 15,000 hours—only to be paid the same as a nurse practitioner with fewer years of school and 500 hours of clinical training?

In addition, the President's executive order asks for legislation to remove the requirement that non-physicians be supervised. Such regulation would potentially override medical staff bylaws and company policies designed to provide proper oversight of clinicians with less training than a physician.

> 5 (a) ... eliminate burdensome regulatory billing requirements, conditions of participation, supervision requirements, benefit definitions, and all other licensure requirements of the Medicare program that are more stringent than applicable Federal or State laws require and that limit professionals from practicing at the top of their profession.

Several medical associations have spoken out against section 5 of the executive order. The Medical Society of the State of New York expressed concern that the proposal perpetuates "a false narrative that promotes equivalency of non-physicians despite the lack of similar education and training."[455]

California Medical Association President David H. Aizuss, MD wrote in a statement that "We must ensure that every American, regardless of age or economic status, has access to a trained physician who can provide the highest level of care. We agree that medical professionals should be able to practice at the top of their license, but care must be supervised by a physician who is highly trained and ultimately responsible."[456]

Texas Medical Association President David C. Fleeger, MD said that his group will notify the president, HHS Secretary Alex Azar, and members of Congress that, "Physicians, who shoulder the ultimate responsibility for patient health and safety, are the only ones who can or should lead and supervise the other members of our healthcare team. They do not know what we know. They can't do what we do."[457]

Nurse practitioners and physician assistants play a valuable role in healthcare. Studies have shown repeatedly that when physicians and non-physician practitioners work together, patients benefit. However, no credible study has shown safety, efficacy, or cost-savings by non-physicians working autonomously.

Criticisms of physician-led care

Although the differences in training and education between nurse practitioners, physician assistants, and physicians are vast, each profession has important strengths. Patients must be aware of both sides of the argument when seeking care from a physician or non-physician practitioner. Understanding the criticisms of physician-led care may assist patients in making the best decision for their medical care.

Patients should have the right to choose

Patients should have the right to make their choice of healthcare clinician. The right to choose requires the opportunity for patients to choose a physician, an option that is being taken away from many patients. To make the best choice, patients need transparency regarding the credentials of who is providing their medical care. In some cases, patients are being misled that their practitioner is a physician or being told that these practitioners are "the same" as a physician.

Doctors are engaged in a turf war

Advocates for physician-led care are often criticized with the argument that doctors are simply looking out for themselves. The reality is that there are plenty of patients to go around, and most physicians can find a job anywhere, anytime. The demand for primary care is so high that a 'turf war' in primary care cannot truly exist. For specialists, an increasing number of non-physicians will only increase their patient volume through referrals. It is possible that as more nurse practitioners graduate from online schools and work far outside their scope, like nurse practitioner Thompson did, the workload for physicians may increase as patients fail to improve or worsen when mismanaged. After all, the concern of multiple physician organizations is genuine and well-founded. There is absolutely no credible scientific evidence that non-physicians can provide equivalent care to physicians. Before implementing national policy to permit non-physicians to practice medicine without physician supervision, there should be quantifiable proof that this intervention is safe and efficacious for patients.

Some advocates of non-physician independence argue that there are plenty of patients to go around. But how will we decide which patients should have substandard care? Just the ones in rural areas? Those with lower incomes? Non-physicians are not flocking to underserved work in states where independent practice is permitted. The answer is to produce more trained physicians, rather than relying on the promises of non-physician advocates. Underserved patients deserve physician care, too. The truth is that as corporations replace physicians with non-physicians, a two-tier system is developing. Patients with financial means are seeking out fully trained physicians for their medical care, often paying out-of-pocket for private, concierge-level care. Patients without extra funds are relegated to whatever medical "provider" their insurance company or hospital allows them to see.

Doctors are looking out for their pocketbooks

One criticism of requiring physician supervision is that some doctors are collecting collaboration fees from nurse practitioners without actually performing true supervision. These fees can range from $400 to $2,000 per month, depending on the type of work that the nurse practitioner is performing, and the extent of supervision required.[458] Physicians who agree to supervise a nurse practitioner are agreeing to put in the work— to provide a service to review charts and to be available for questions or concerns. In essence, doctors who supervise are essentially accepting the responsibility for the work of the nurse practitioner, including potential liability in the case of a malpractice suit.

Some nurse practitioner legal experts insist that the risk to physicians that collaborate is low. Carolyn Buppert, MSN, JD, wrote in an article that if a collaborating physician "performs the required duties and collaborates when asked, then the physician should not be held liable for an NP's mistakes."[459] However, she cautions that supervising physicians must be prepared to defend themselves, and must be able to prove that they truly supervised by following collaborative requirements to the letter.

Consider the case of Morgan Vittengl, the supervising physician for nurse practitioner Diane Belanger. The nurse practitioner evaluated a patient for abdominal pain on two separate days, diagnosing him with gastritis. Several days later, the patient developed a ruptured appendix. The patient sued both the nurse practitioner and supervising physician Vittengl for negligence. Vittengl filed for a dismissal, arguing that he had never treated the patient and was always available for consultation, which the nurse practitioner failed to seek. While the court originally agreed with Vittengl, the dismissal was overturned by a higher court, which noted that Vittengl spent a certain number of weeks on vacation without coverage and reviewed fewer charts than required for proper supervision. An expert witness opined that while the nurse practitioner's act of malpractice may not have occurred if Vittengl was properly supervising.[460]

If independent practice by non-physicians is so bad, why don't more doctors speak out?

Many physicians fear repercussions from speaking out. Doctors have been fired from jobs and persecuted in other ways, such as cyberbullying and mass posting of negative reviews by those who disagree with their stance. Physicians who are dependent on hospitals are particularly susceptible to being fired or blackballed by their employers.

Certain specialties like emergency room doctors and hospital specialists cannot simply hang a shingle and provide care independently. They rely on the resources of hospitals and healthcare organizations. Speaking out can be a career-ender for these physicians.

There are bad doctors too

Despite the strenuous efforts of medical schools and residency programs, as well as multiple levels of required standardized testing, bad doctors do sometimes slip through the cracks. While some doctors are not competent to practice, state Boards of Medicine are far more aggressive in sanctioning physician licenses than Boards of Nursing. For example, it took the Texas Board of Nursing more than a year before they finally sanctioned nurse practitioner Kevin Morgan for the deaths of two patients due to excessive dosing of testosterone and thyroid medication. Despite clear evidence of patient harm, the Texas Board of Nursing delayed acting and Morgan continued to treat and harm patients. In contrast, rigorous standards have been established to weed out bad actors throughout the medical school and residency periods. Unlike nurse practitioners, physicians must all meet identical standards of education to receive a state license to practice medicine.

Another difference between physicians and nurse practitioners pertains to legal repercussions for malpractice. Physicians are held to higher standards in a court of law. Patients of nurse practitioners that experience malpractice may be less likely to receive justice.

Restricting nurse practitioners is sexist

Physicians who express concern about nurse practitioner education and training are sometimes accused of being sexist since the nursing profession is dominated by women. Florida Representative Cary Pigman, a physician with a longstanding agenda to expand nurse practitioner rights in the state, accused the medical profession of being "a predominantly male-dominated profession holding their boots against the neck of a predominantly female professional class."[461] Speaker of the House Representative Jose Oliva, who spent most of his tenure advocating for nurse practitioner expansion, brought a nurse practitioner to serve as "Doctor of the Day" for the first time on the opening day of Florida's legislative session in 2019. To the dismay of women physicians in Florida, many of whom had served as "Doctor of the Day" during previous sessions, Oliva and news media emphasized that this was the first time in its history that a woman held the honor.

While most nurse practitioners are women, increasingly men are entering into the field of nursing. In medicine, more than 50% of all current medical school graduates are women, and women play in increasing role in medical leadership. It is because many women physicians have had to work so hard to achieve a level playing field, they are often the loudest critics of short-cuts to becoming a medical professional. In fact, 6 out of 7 board members of the group Physicians for Patient Protection, an advocacy group dedicated to physician-led practice, are women physicians.

Why not just offer additional training for non-physicians, like a residency program?

There are some additional training programs available for both nurse practitioners and physician assistants. These programs are usually designed to help prepare practitioners to work in a particular setting, like a hospital, and are not standardized or required for practice. Unfortunately, without a well-established foundation on which to build knowledge, additional training still will not match the training of a physician. Instead, practitioners may wish to consider the option of attending medical school and then completing a true residency program, as many physicians who were once nurse practitioners or physician assistants have done. Ultimately, patients must consider all of these arguments when deciding which caregiver in which to place their trust.

CHAPTER 8

KNOWLEDGE IS POWER

Alexus Ochoa died at 5:26 am, having received 11 hours of inappropri-ate care from a family nurse practitioner who was incorrectly hired and credentialed by a multi-billion-dollar corporation. Alexus's family filed suit against the nurse practitioner, her supervising physician, and Mercy Health Systems.

During the trial, Travis Dunn, the attorney for the Ochoa family asked nurse practitioner Thompson: "Can we agree that your educa-tion and training in family medicine did not prepare you to deal with a patient like Alexus?"

Thompson answered, "It wasn't family medicine that prepared me, no."

Dunn: "Can we agree that her heart was beating fast because her body was desperately trying to get oxygen, and at that same time, you were giving her medicine to slow her heart rate down?"

Thompson became emotional. Her lawyer asked if she needed a short break, but the nurse practitioner refused. "I want to answer. Because I had this girl and I was trying to help her. I was never trying to harm her. I don't care about [audibly crying] methamphetamine or anything like that. I was not trying to harm this girl. I was trying to help her."

The statement by nurse practitioner Thompson was unequivocally true. Thompson was not a bad human being. She was not a bad para-medic. She was not a bad nurse. She was not even a bad nurse practi-tioner. She simply did not realize she was in over her head.

Thompson attended an online nursing school to obtain a master's degree in nursing, not a medical degree in medicine. She was certified as a family medicine nurse practitioner scarcely a month before being hired as a solo practitioner in a bustling emergency department just out-side Oklahoma City limits. She did not complete a master's degree in Acute Care Nursing, which may have properly prepared her to work in an emergency department with physician supervision. The nurse practitioner falsely believed her experience as a paramedic adequately supplemented her nursing education enough to fulfill this role. None of this changes the fact that she was not properly educated and trained for the responsibility for which she applied and had been granted. As she testified, "I knew something was wrong, but I just didn't know what it was." Nurse practitioner Thompson was functioning in the role of an emergency physician. However, she was not a medical doctor, and without the proper education and training, she was incapable of making the definitive clinical decisions required to run a hospital emergency department alone.

Nurse Thompson never correctly diagnosed Alexus despite managing Alexus Ochoa's care for nearly 11 hours. Medical expert Dr. Brian Swirsky testified that if Nurse Thompson had diagnosed Alexus properly before midnight, Alexus might have survived. Nurse Thompson simply did not have the education and training to manage a critically ill patient like Alexus Ochoa and should never have tried to do so.

Unfortunately, Thompson did not realize the dire risk she posed to patients. The hospital administration, including Director of Emergency Medicine for Mercy Oklahoma, granted her privileges to work in the emergency department without having acute care training. Dr. Brent Wilson believed Nurse Thompson was properly educated, trained, and certified to practice family medicine in the emergency department.

Rather than taking any responsibility, hospital leaders at Mercy placed full blame for Alexus's death on Antoinette Thompson, concluding after a medical review that, "Ms. Thompson was guilty of an act that jeopardized a patients' life, health or safety, as defined in the rules of the [hospital] board."

Supervising physician Brent Wilson took little responsibility as well, opining that the nurse practitioner was mistakenly distracted by the methamphetamine result. Wilson stated he hoped that "medical staff leadership recognize [that] it would have been more prudent to terminate her immediately rather than risk liability from subsequent quality safety issues." The hospital leadership concluded that "the termination process was already underway for this provider based upon quality, safety concerns. Thompson should have been paid out the 30 days rather than been allowed to continue working."

Alexus Ochoa had her entire life in front of her. She died for the most senseless of all reasons—a healthcare system corrupted by greed. It will happen again and again unless change is demanded.

What can be done to protect patients from this broken system? How do we prevent another Alexus Ochoa, or Brad Guilbeaux, or Mya-Louise Perrin from dying unnecessarily? Countering the 'dumbing down' of the healthcare system will not be easy. The promises of non-physician advocates to increase access are alluring, even when they are disproven. Corporations with financial interests in non-physician practitioner use are powerful. Training new physicians is not a quick or inexpensive process. To effect change, we must begin by empowering those who will be the most affected by the increase in non-physician practitioners—patients.

THE ROLE OF THE PATIENT

Back in 44 AD, Roman physician Scribonius Largus warned the community of the growth of practitioners calling themselves "doctors in name only." He complained of those who were practicing "medicine in whatever way he wishes," and disregarding "the ancient founders who shaped and perfected their professional abilities." Scribonius's advice to patients: "No man should entrust himself and his family to any doctor whom he has not carefully judged.[462]

In their lawsuit against Mercy Hospital, the family of Alexus Ochoa indicated that both Alexus and her family were under the impression that Antoinette Thompson was a physician rather than a nurse practitioner. They stated that the hospital falsely represented nurse practitioner Thompson as a doctor, and therefore the family relied upon her "to possess the skills, knowledge, learning and training of a 'doctor.'"

The lawyer for the family also argued that Mercy failed to provide adequate informed consent, stating that the hospital knew that patients who come to an emergency room have a reasonable expectation that an emergency room doctor will treat them. "[Nurse practitioner] Thompson and Mercy had a duty to disclose to Alexus that NP Thompson was not a doctor but was a nurse practitioner so Alexus could make an informed decision as to whether she wanted to accept or reject the treatment proposed by NP Thompson. Had Alexus known that NP Thompson was not a doctor but only a NP she would have chosen to go to another hospital where she could be seen by a doctor."

Patients deserve the opportunity to make an informed choice about their medical professional—but this information is not always granted. It therefore becomes the responsibility of the patient to become educated about the credentials of all treating practitioners and to understand how education and training differ between various medical professionals. The following steps will help patients to learn about who is providing their medical care.

It's ok to ask

Historically, patients have assumed that any person providing their medical care has had the proper training and education to provide them with safe and effective care.[463] Patients must now challenge this assumption and take the further step of confirming the qualifications of their medical clinician. When confronted with any medical professional, ascertain their credentials. Ideally, your clinician should be wearing an identification badge with his or her name and professional title (e.g., physician, nurse practitioner, physician assistant, pharmacist).

If you see a nondescript title like "Doctor" that does not specify the type (are they a Doctor of Medicine, Nursing, Psychology, or Pharmacy?), don't be afraid to ask for clarification. Without asking, you won't know.

This is particularly common in hospital settings, where patients may be visited by a multitude of medical professionals of all backgrounds— physicians, nurses, physical therapists, case managers, etc. In hospitals that train students, patients may also be seen by medical practitioners who are still in training.

Medical professionals don't always realize that their role may be unclear to the layperson, particularly if the patient is sick, in pain, or sleepy from medication. If your practitioner doesn't clearly identify themselves, ask them what their role is.

If you are having surgery, find out if your anesthesia will be provided or supervised by a physician anesthesiologist versus being provided by a nurse anesthetist alone. Robert Painter, a medical malpractice attorney in Houston, TX, believes that anesthesiologists should always supervise anesthesia. Painter says that all patients should ask questions about medical practitioners involved in their care, writing "Don't be shy—it's your life on the line!" Painter suggests that patients ask the following questions:

(1) Will a physician anesthesiologist be in the operating room the entire time?
(2) If not, will the anesthesiologist be in the operating room during the most important parts of anesthesia—induction (when anesthesia begins) and emergence (waking up)?

(3) How many other surgeries is the anesthesiologist supervising at the same time?

(4) If a nurse anesthetist is providing the anesthesia, how much experience do they have?[464]

Know the abbreviations—or ask

Understanding identification badges can be confusing, especially if instead of a clear title, a string of letters follows the practitioner's name.

Interestingly, sometimes the least number of letters signifies the highest level of training. Physicians are usually labeled simply as MD (Medical Doctor) or DO (Doctor of Osteopathic Medicine). These are the two types of equivalent physicians who must graduate medical school, complete residency training, and pass the same standardized examinations to be licensed.

PA means physician assistant, and NP means nurse practitioner. However, because there are different types of nurse practitioners, the letters may differ. (See the Appendix for a list of abbreviations used by medical professionals.) If you aren't sure, ask for an explanation of the letters and clarification of the practitioner's credentials.

Understand supervision

If your clinician is a nurse practitioner or physician assistant, ask if a physician is supervising them. Just ask outright: "Who is your supervising physician?" Or, "If I have a complicated problem, is there a doctor that you will check with?" It is also helpful to know if the supervising physician is available onsite or just by telephone.

If you are in an independent practice state (see Appendix), then your nurse practitioner may not be required to have a supervising physician. You can still ask if the nurse practitioner has a physician that he or she consults with if there are any concerns.

Most non-physician practitioners will not be offended by these questions and are as committed to honesty and transparency in healthcare. If the provider seems angry or offended, then you may want to consider rescheduling your appointment with someone else. If this isn't possible (for example, you are in a hospital setting), you can ask to speak with a patient advocate or ombudsman, as it will be difficult to establish a therapeutic relationship with any clinician who responds to questions in a hostile manner.

It can be intimidating for many patients to speak up about their care, especially if they are ill or under stress. One option is to create a directive that makes it clear that you desire your care to be provided by a physician and not a non-physician practitioner (see sample letter in Appendix).

Know when you should see a physician

New problems—If it is your first time being evaluated for a new problem, it is important to ask to see a physician for that initial visit. If your physician approves a follow-up visit with a non-physician—say, to discuss lab results or for education about a medical condition, then seeing a nurse practitioner or physician assistant may be reasonable. In fact, research has shown that care by nurse practitioners and physicians assistants is safe when effective for follow-up of specific conditions following protocols. However, your physician should still be seeing you periodically during your treatment and should always be available if you have questions or concerns.

Worsening problems—If your condition worsens or new problems arise outside of a standard protocol, research has shown a physician should re-evaluate you. Do not hesitate to ask for an appointment with your physician.

Demand a physician if necessary

It is not always easy to see a physician, even when you ask for one. Sometimes front-desk schedulers put up barriers to seeing the physician or encourage appointments with the non-physician provider. You may have to be quite insistent. Be prepared for comments like, "our physician assistant was trained by the doctor and will do the same thing," or "the nurse practitioner is just as good as the doctor." You may also be told that the wait time is much longer to see the physician, but the nurse practitioner or physician assistant can get you in "right away." Stand your ground and insist on a physician appointment, especially if you have a complicated medical problem.

Patients must watch out for a "bait-and-switch" when making an appointment at a medical office. If you ask for an appointment with a physician, then you should not find out on the day of the appointment that you are instead scheduled with a non-physician practitioner. Insist that you see the physician that you asked to be scheduled with. If you end up still seeing a non-physician despite your request, demand a refund of your copay or payment and file a complaint with your insurance company.

As you are researching healthcare clinics, check the website to see who is on staff. Most offices have a listing of clinicians, sometimes called "Our Team" or "Providers." How many physicians are listed compared to nurse practitioner and physician assistants? Is it easy to tell who is who? Are credentials (MD, DO, NP, PA) properly noted, or is everyone titled as "Dr.?"

If you find that it is difficult to see a physician at your practice, consider changing to a physician-only practice, or one with a lower physician to non-physician ratio. (See the Appendix for a listing of resources to find a physician practice).

Let the buyer beware

When Bill Clinton and Arnold Schwarzenegger had open-heart surgery, you can be sure that a physician anesthesiologist oversaw their care rather than a certified nurse anesthetist. These politicians signed legislation that allowed nurse anesthetists to provide anesthesia without physician supervision, but when their own lives were at stake, they wanted nothing but the best. Why should any other patient deserve less?

Patients must be engaged in the decision-making process of their own healthcare, and rule number one is *caveat emptor*—let the buyer beware. Americans are good at researching before we buy. We pore over Consumer Reports before we purchase a new car, read reviews on Amazon before we order a product, and check the ratings of hotels before we book. Applying these same principles of investigation to the purchase of healthcare services is critical for patients seeking high-quality healthcare. Research is more important than ever right now, with some unethical practitioners taking advantage of online marketing to lure in unsuspecting patients.

For example, a news report in February 2020 revealed that fake urgent care centers were "popping up" across Arizona. Using false addresses, the medical centers offer "doctor by phone." To investigate, a news reporter called one of these urgent cares for treatment. Communicating only by text, which asked questions about his medical symptoms, the reporter was prescribed 3 medications, including an antibiotic and a steroid. Upon investigating the billing charges ($196), the reporter was able to discover that the treating "doctor" was nurse practitioner Alice Minkoff, who had been previously sanctioned by the Colorado Board of Nursing.[465]

While you may not have a choice in an emergency, in most cases, we do make choices about our primary care doctor, what health system to use for specialty care, or whether we want to visit a retail clinic when we have the flu. Patients should consider whether seeing a non-physician practitioner will really save them money. The Journal of Law Medicine argued in 1992 that consumers will demand nurse practitioner care based on microeconomics. The report stated that if all other factors remain the same, patients will seek out and choose a less expensive service if it is available.[466] By now, it should be clear that not all factors are the same. Training, education, and level of care are not equivalent between physicians and non-physician practitioners. .

Regarding cost, do healthcare consumers actually pay less to see a non-physician practitioner than a physician? The answer is *not always*. Right now, patients with Medicare coverage will pay a little bit less to see a nurse practitioner or physician assistant. Currently, Medicare pays nurse practitioners 85% of the rate they pay a physician. Patients with Medicare have a co-pay of 20%, so if an office visit costs $100, Medicare would pay a physician $80, and you would pay $20. If you saw a nurse practitioner, Medicare would discount the $100 charge down to $85, and they would pay $68, making you responsible for 20%, or $17. You would, therefore, save $3 per visit by seeing a nurse practitioner instead of a physician. However, since patients of nurse practitioners often require more frequent visits, have more tests, and receive more medication prescriptions, that $3 savings may quickly disappear.

Know the risks in the event of malpractice

While working under physician supervision, nurse practitioners and physician assistants have traditionally had low rates of malpractice claims. However, with an increasing scope of practice, malpractice rates are rapidly rising. One of the largest malpractice insurance companies reported that nurse practitioner claims jumped 19% between 2009 and 2011.[467]

Importantly, patients have the right to know that non-physician practitioners who practice medicine "like a physician" are not held to the same legal standard in the event of a negative outcome. One of the earliest cases to show this was *Fein v. Permanente Medical Group* (1985), in which the court stated, "The jury should not be instructed that the standard of care for a nurse practitioner must not be measured by the standard of care for a physician or surgeon when the nurse is examining the patient and making a diagnosis."[468] This legal doctrine was supported by *Simonson v Keppard* (2007), in which the Texas Court of Appeals refused to allow an MD to testify regarding the standard of care for a nurse practitioner who failed to diagnose a cerebral hemorrhage[469] and *Lattimore v Dickey* (2015),[470] which stated that a "nurse's conduct must not be measured by the standard of care required of a physician and surgeon, but by that of other nurses in the same or similar locality and under similar circumstances."

One of the challenges in pursuing malpractice cases against nurse practitioners is the ability of attorneys to obtain an expert witness to testify against the care provided. Case law has not allowed physicians to testify against nurse practitioners as to the standard of care. Only another nurse practitioner can provide expert testimony regarding practice standards in a lawsuit against a nurse practitioner. As Nancy Brent, a nurse and attorney shared in a bulletin for nurse practitioners, "If, as a nurse practitioner, you are ever named as a defendant in a lawsuit … evaluate the expert report required when a lawsuit alleging negligence and/or wrongful death is filed. If the expert's report is not authored by a qualified professional [another nurse practitioner], the case is quite ripe for a dismissal against you."[471]

Consider a 2007 Texas malpractice case against a nurse practitioner who misdiagnosed a headache. Rather than being a simple migraine, the patient was suffering from a brain bleed and died. Lawyers for the family produced a physician as an expert witness, who testified that the nurse practitioner had "assumed the duties of a physician when he undertook to examine, diagnose and treat" the patient. After an analysis of Texas civil law, the court determined that a physician could not legally testify to the standard of care for a nurse practitioner.[472]

However, malpractice attorneys are starting to pay more attention and may begin to litigate these cases more seriously. According to its website:

MedicalMalpracticeLawyers.com has noticed a significant increase in inquiries from medical malpractice victims throughout the United

States regarding the medical care and treatment they received from NPs. Some of these potential victims have alleged that they were unaware at the time they received medical treatment (either in the hospital or in a medical office) that their medical providers were NPs. Many had no idea regarding the medical education and medical training that their NPs had received. Some even thought that their NPs were medical doctors (most NPs wore white lab coats with their names embroidered on them, just like medical doctors).[473]

Speak out

Patients must be ready and willing to walk away from facilities when they are denied access to a physician. Be aware that corporations are replacing physicians with non-physician practitioners to save money. If your doctor suddenly "disappears" from their practice and is replaced by a nurse practitioner or physician assistant, take your business elsewhere. Make sure that the company knows why you are leaving. If enough patients demand physician-led care and refuse non-physician care, then profits will suffer, forcing corporations to again hire physicians.

State medical boards have long encouraged patients to complain about being harmed by physicians. While we hope your experience never comes to this, if a non-physician's inadequate care has harmed you, file a report with the appropriate agency. The oversight board for nurse practitioners is their state Board of Nursing, while state Boards of Medicine govern physician assistants. For concerns about the care being provided by chiropractors, naturopaths, or other healthcare practitioner, contact your state department of health for reporting information.

In addition to reporting concerns to the appropriate regulatory board, tell others about your experience. Tell your friends and family, tell the management of the facility where it happened, tell the media, and tell your legislators. Speak out when you are told that non-physicians are the same as physicians. If a scheduler or clerk tells you that there is no difference, explain to them that you are aware of the differences in education and training. You can take it a step further by asking for the name of the individual and advising them that you will be reporting them for false advertising. If you ask for a physician but are forced to see a non-physician, make a complaint to your health insurance company. If you see an advertisement with false claims, like a nurse practitioner being misrepresented as a physician, report the advertisement to the

Federal Trade Commission.[474] The more we speak out about this issue, the more we can make a difference.

THE ROLE OF LEGISLATORS

Every year, legislation to expand the nursing scope of practice, as well as independent practice for physician assistants, pharmacists, psychologists, and others, is introduced. Most legislators propose these laws in an attempt to expand access to medical care in their state, but many are unaware of the potential harm that this expansion may cause for their constituents. A better alternative is for lawmakers to focus on increasing the physician supply in their state.

Increase the production of primary care physicians

Primary care physicians are associated with a decrease in mortality, yet little is being done to incentivize medical students to choose primary care as a specialty. Primary care physicians are paid significantly less than their specialist counterparts, and the cost of providing care has increased more than primary care wages. Medical schools and residencies must be incentivized to increase primary care, payment through Medicare and insurance companies should reflect the importance of primary care, and controls must be put in place to make it more affordable for doctors to provide care. Legislators should also support innovative models that decrease physician burden, like Direct Primary Care.

Expand physician residency slots

Public leaders can increase the physician supply by expanding residency training programs, especially in areas of high need like primary care in rural locations. In 1997, the government froze spending for physician training, limiting the number of slots for graduating medical students to complete their education. While medical schools have increased 30% since 2002, residency slots have not expanded proportionately due to the freeze in residency funding. This has created a backlog and placed severe pressure on physician graduates to find a residency position, which is required before doctors can begin to practice medicine.

Each year, hundreds of well-prepared U.S. medical school graduates fail to match to a residency program and must wait a year or more to find a program with space to accept them. In the interim, these doctors-to-be work in research, teach, or sometimes even wait tables to pay the bills.[475]

While almost a quarter of the physician workforce is made up of international medical school graduates, doctors trained abroad have great difficulty in becoming credentialed to practice in the U.S.[476] Qualified candidates who attended foreign medical schools are far less likely to find a residency spot. There were 2,300 unmatched U.S. citizens and 3,700 unmatched foreign medical graduates who applied for residency in 2015.[477] It has become so difficult for these new physicians to obtain a residency program that some have resorted to attending online programs to become a nurse practitioner, with special primary care pathway programs dedicated to assisting international medical graduates.[478]

Lawmakers must free up funding for physicians to complete their training. The Resident Physician Shortage Reduction Act of 2019 introduced by Senators Menendez (D-NJ), Boozman (R-AR), and Schumer (D-NY) is a step in the right direction. This bill increases the number of medical resident training positions by 15,000 over five years and requires a study on strategies to increase workforce diversity.[479]

Residency programs should be focused on areas of high need, rather than in urban centers or medical meccas because doctors tend to practice within a hundred miles of where they did their residency.[480] More funding should be dedicated to primary care physician training in areas that lack primary care physicians. We also need to increase residencies in states with low physician supply, like Idaho, Wyoming, and Nevada, which have some of the lowest numbers of physicians per capita. These states train fewer physicians: therefore, fewer doctors stay to practice.[481]

Expand the assistant/graduate physician role

Every year, hundreds of qualified physicians graduate from medical school but are unable to match into a residency program. Without residency training, these physicians are not legally allowed to practice medicine and must wait an entire year before they are eligible for new residency positions to open up.

Some states are allowing these graduate physicians to work in a new role called an "assistant physician" while they await entry into an approved residency program. The state of Missouri has created such a program,[482] and the idea is being explored in other states.[483] In Missouri, 99 assistant physicians were licensed in 2017, but only 25 began work with a supervising physician. 20 of those 25 worked in a health professional shortage area. Since they have not yet completed a residency program, assistant physicians would require careful and close supervision by a physician. The assistant physician role would not be a permanent position but could function as a stopgap on the way to completing a credentialed residency program.

Make it easier for doctors to work in physician shortage areas

Legislators should focus on encouraging physicians to work in underserved areas by providing loan repayment or financial assistance. Expand programs like the National Health Service Corps and incentivize programs to hire physicians over non-physician practitioners. Consider innovative strategies, like the bill introduced by Oklahoma's House Speaker Charles McCall in 2020. The bill provides tax credits to doctors who work in rural and underserved communities.[484]

In settings such as Federally Qualified Health Centers and the VA, lawmakers must make it easier for doctors to practice. Pay physicians who want to work in these challenging areas better and decrease their administrative burden. The VA, in particular, struggles to keep physicians because of low pay and poor management.[485] It would be far better to treat physicians well so that they want to care for our vulnerable patients than to replace them with lesser trained practitioners.

Make it easier for doctors to practice—period

The increasing regulatory burden on physicians has led to unprecedented levels of burnout, with 48% of all physicians making active plans to leave the practice of medicine.[486] Legislators should focus on plans that remove the administrative barriers that are driving doctors out of practice. One major hurdle is lifting the 2010 regulation that banned physician-owned hospitals. By allowing doctors to own hospitals again, hospital-based physicians will have the option of working for other doctors, rather than private equity corporations and hospital conglomerates.[487] Allow patients to choose which hospital they prefer to use—one owned by physicians, or one owned by administrators.

Create public safeguards for independent non-physician practitioners

If non-physicians are permitted to practice medicine, then legislators must establish safeguards to protect patients:

(1) *Require state medical boards to supervise independent non-physician practitioners*
State nursing boards, responsible for thousands of LPNs, RNs, and NPs, cannot provide adequate oversight for nurse practitioners with a scope of practice that expands into the realm of medicine. First, most nursing board members are registered nurses and not nurse practitioners, and therefore do not have the expertise to provide oversight for nurse practitioners. Secondly, nursing boards simply do not have the resources to ensure that nurse practitioners are practicing medicine safely. Carol Moreland, RN, the executive administrator for the Kansas State Board of Nursing opposed the independent practice of nurse practitioners in Kansas for this very reason. Providing testimony to the Kansas Health and Human Services Committee on February 11, 2019, Ms. Moreland explained that allowing unsupervised practice "will, quite frankly, overwhelm an already stretched agency."
Boards of nursing in some states simply cannot handle the volume of complaints against nurses in a safe time frame. It took over a year for the Texas Board of Nursing to revoke the license of Kevin Morgan, even after the deaths of several patients. Audits of the California Board of Nursing in 2016 found a significant backlog of complaints, and that the system allowed a nurse accused of causing the death of a child to practice for over three years. In 2020, the Board was further accused of falsifying documents to make it appear as if complaints against nurses were being investigated in a timely fashion.[488]
If non-physician practitioners wish to diagnose and treat medical conditions without physician supervision, then the Board of Medicine should regulate them. Using semantics by saying "we aren't practicing medicine, we are practicing nursing," which many nurse practitioners argue, defies logic.

(2) *Require mandatory reporting of complications by non-physician practitioners*
No published studies show the safety of unsupervised non-physician practitioners. States that permit unsupervised independent practice should require that non-physicians report complications to

determine whether independent practice is safe. Physicians who see complications caused by non-physician care should also be required to report this information to a database for monitoring. The authors of a JAMA report point out that a mandatory physician reporting program in Florida helped to reduce the rate of dangerous office surgeries and argues that similar tracking of non-physicians could help ensure patient safety.[489]

(3) *All advertising by medical practitioners must be truthful and transparent*
Patients often do not understand who is providing their care. In a study conducted by the American Medical Association in 2008, almost 40% percent of the public mistakenly believed a Doctor of Nursing was a medical doctor.[490] Therefore, medical transparency laws are needed to ensure that the training and degree of healthcare providers be prominently displayed. Patients should be informed of the credentials of the medical clinician providing their care, and medical practitioners should wear identification tags when rendering professional services which will clearly identify them by name and professional status.[491] In addition, corporations and medical offices that utilize non-physician practitioners should be required to provide informed consent to patients, especially when physicians are not directly supervising.

Non-physicians should not mislead patients by misconstruing their credentials in advertising and marketing campaigns. Representative Larry Bucshon (R) introduced HR 3928, the Truth in Healthcare Marketing Act of 2017 on October 3, 2017. The bill requires medical practitioners to accurately identify themselves and prohibits misleading or deceptive advertising or misrepresentation.[492] Unfortunately, no action has been taken since the bill was referred to committee in 2017.

(4) *Expand the Sunshine Act*
Independently-practicing non-physician practitioners should be subject to the same requirements as physicians, such as the Physician Payment Sunshine Act, a law that mandates that any payments made to physicians—cash, dinners, office lunches—are required to be reported and available to the public. The idea is that patients should know if doctors are receiving financial motivations to prescribe medications.

Currently, the law does not require nurse practitioners or physician assistants to report similar payment. In May 2018, Senators Grassley (R-IA), Brown (D-OH), and Blumenthal (D-CT) introduced the *Fighting the Opioid Epidemic with Sunshine Act,* a bill that would expand Physician Payment Sunshine Act reporting requirements to cover payments and other transfers of value made to advance practice nurses and physician assistants.[493]

(5) *Ensure that non-physicians are held to the same malpractice standards as physicians if they are practicing independently*
Currently, non-physician practitioners are not held to the same legal standard of care as a physician in the event of a negative outcome or malpractice case, even if the nurse practitioner in question is purporting to offer the same level of care. According to a legal review by Judge Janette A. Bertness, if non-physicians are legally allowed to practice medicine without physician supervision, then they should be held to the same standards as physicians.[494]

THE ROLE OF MALPRACTICE CARRIERS

Malpractice claims against nurse practitioners have traditionally been relatively uncommon, and therefore, malpractice insurance rates have also been much lower than those of physicians. However, with the increase in independent practice and changing demographics of nurse practitioners, malpractice claims against them are on the rise, increasing by 18% between 2007 and 2011. Claims against nurse practitioners resulting in severe indemnity payments have increased by 19% since 2009.[495] Interestingly, while claims for nurse practitioners are increasing, physician claims have decreased by 20% over the last decade.[496]

According to a review of closed claims by a large malpractice carrier, the majority of claims can be traced back to the failure of nurse practitioners to adhere to their scope of practice, inadequate physician supervision, absence of or deviation from written protocols, and failure or delay in seeking physician referral.[497] In 1993, Professor Edward P. Richards III, JD, MPH wrote in *Law and the Physician* that "medical malpractice insurance rates for [nurse anesthetists] are artificially low because the nurses do not bear primary responsibility for any negligent actions. Instead, either the supervising anesthesiologist or the operating surgeon is held legally responsible for the actions of the nurse anesthetist."[498]

Malpractice carriers should be aware of the increasing scope of practice of unsupervised non-physician practitioners, and rates must rise in accordance with their risk. Physicians must also be aware of the increased risk of collaborating informally with non-physician practitioners, as they may become entangled in a lawsuit.

THE ROLE OF THE MEDIA

While the current media climate rewards clickbait titles and sensational reporting, when physicians are portrayed as less than caring, this hurts patients too. A focus of negative reporting on the occasional bad actor can increase patient anxiety about receiving care from physicians, causing a delay in care. Studies also show that critical portrayals of doctors in the media take a toll on physicians and contribute to physician burnout, which may lead to more doctors leaving the profession.[499]

Nurse practitioners and physician assistants have effectively utilized the media to galvanize the public, an area historically neglected by physicians. For example, in 2018, the Robert Wood Johnson Foundation contributed $4 million to National Public Radio to "strengthen health coverage through new content and coverage areas," including reporting about nurse practitioners.[500] Physicians must also take the stage to remind patients of the importance of quality medical education and training, as well as demonstrating the care and compassion that most physicians offer to patients. When doctors see or hear inaccuracies in media reporting, they must take the time to provide feedback and clarity. Media organizations have shown a willingness to listen to physician feedback. When doctors complained about a biased report about midwives on NPR's Planet Money, the organization's ombudsman responded by acknowledging the need for more balanced reporting.[501]

THE ROLE OF THE EDUCATIONAL SYSTEM

Nursing organizations must standardize their education, training, and certification process to ensure the nurse practitioner profession is providing the best possible clinical care to patients.

Eliminate disreputable programs and the "direct-to-nurse practitioner" route

There are approximately 400 U.S. academic institutions with NP programs. Some of them are reputable and accredited programs, but others offer 100% online learning, direct-to-nurse practitioner programs that bypass a nursing background entirely, part-time programs, and accelerated programs. Some even boast 100% acceptance rates. It's not surprising that accreditation standards of nurse practitioner programs are slipping through the cracks.

For example, in March 2018, Joanne Beattie, a family nurse practitioner, received a letter from the American Nurses Credentialing Center (ANCC) informing her that the program she'd graduated from, Fresno State's Mental Health Nurse Practitioner program, was never accredited. Beattie was told that she would not be permitted to take her certification test to continue to care for patients, even though she had already been treating patients for some time. When nurse practitioners complained that this late notification was unfair, the ANCC agreed to allow them to continue to treat patients, as long as they completed an accredited program within the next five years.[502] Even though this program was considered inadequate to be accredited, the ANCC allowed graduates to continue to treat patients.

Require enhanced standardized clinical experience hours

Nurse practitioners are required to complete 500 clinical training hours with a physician or nurse practitioner instructor in the field, also known as a preceptor. Many students are now required to find their own preceptors without help from their training program. As the number of nurse practitioner programs has grown, students have become so desperate to find a preceptor that they resort to cold-calling doctors, posting on online forums, and even paying headhunters to help them find a preceptor.[503]

Preceptorship is also extremely varied, with some students receiving in-depth, hands-on clinical training, while others are relegated to merely shadowing a physician or nurse practitioner. Of course, a minimum of 500 required clinical hours with no standardization is simply inadequate to assure the adequate knowledge base to being caring for patients independently. PetSmart requires that its dog groomers have 800 hours of hands-on training. Barbers require 1,500 hours of training and cosmetologists require 1,600 hours. Nurse practitioners and physician assistants who wish to practice without supervision should be required to complete a similar number of standardized training hours to physicians.

MEDICAL EDUCATION

The medical education system has the responsibility to produce a high volume of quality primary care physicians or other non-physician practitioners will attempt to fill those roles. A robust primary care physician workforce is associated with improved population health.[504] Also, building a relationship with a physician over time provides continuity of care, something which has also been shown to lower mortality.[505]

Physicians should train physicians

Medical schools must focus on producing physicians. Many schools train nurse practitioners and physician assistants alongside medical students, which may be diluting education and impeding opportunities for medical students. In addition, while medical students can certainly learn from non-physician practitioners, only physicians should be tasked with training medical students. The unique aspects of physician training can only be truly provided by a physician mentor.

Train students to be leaders of the healthcare team

Increasingly, medical schools are indoctrinating students into a politically correct culture in which all medical professionals "the same." While physicians need to listen to other team members and practice humility in medicine, the shift has gone too far. Instead of training medical students to be a strong and humble team leader, these teacher centers are increasingly downplaying the role of the physician, instead reminding them that they are "just" a part of the healthcare team. *team leader, QB*

For example, a physician interviewer for medical school admissions at Stanford Medical School leaked one of the interview documents. The interviewer, who was instructed to introduce himself by his first name only, sans title, was to read this statement to prospective students: "Non-physician allied health professionals such as nurse practitioners, physician assistants and other advanced health professionals work both independently and alongside medical doctors in patient care. How would you respond to a patient who demands the service of a 'medical doctor' rather than an allied health professional in their healthcare?"

The correct answer included noting that "there continue to be power imbalances in healthcare teams as there has been a traditional hierarchy with physicians being on top."[506]

Patients benefit when medical care is coordinated by a team with an effective leader. According to Haig Aintablian, MD, the president of the American Academy of Emergency Medicine Resident and Student Association, that leader must be the physician. Aintablian calls on medical schools and residency programs to train future physicians to "accept, value, and embrace their role as the healthcare team leader."[507]

Make medical school affordable and incentivize primary care

Medical school must be made affordable so that students can choose medicine rather than entering a nurse practitioner or physician assistant program based on economic reasons. Financial incentives should be offered to those who choose primary care or work in an underserved area. Another alternative to lower cost would be to implement a more European-like model for medical education, which involves a 6-year training period and bypasses obtaining a four-year college degree.[508]

THE ROLE OF PHYSICIANS

Regain patient trust

Physicians need to regain patients' trust and reclaim the role of healer and provider of holistic care. To improve relationships with patients, physicians need to get back to direct patient care, improving our communication and better demonstrating our empathy.

In an article about nurse practitioner malpractice claims, medicalmalpractice.com makes an interesting observation. "The inquiries we receive regarding NP malpractice claims rarely involve a complaint regarding an aloof or arrogant NP who failed to listen to the patient or spend sufficient time with the patient, whereas such comments regarding medical doctors are not uncommon."[509] As physicians, we must take these concerns to heart. Physicians must learn to show patients that we are listening. We must insist that we have enough time with our patients. Above all, we must learn how to show empathy.

Physicians must do a better job at leadership and public relations, reminding our patients of their comprehensive education and training, and dedication to patient well-being. We need to speak out on social media about our role. We must lift each other up and publicize the good work that our colleagues are doing. We need to speak well of each other in front of our patients. We must remember that we are on the same team.

Properly supervise non-physicians

The non-physician practitioner model was developed by physicians, and many doctors have benefited from working with physician extenders. Indeed, working with carefully supervised non-physician practitioners using well-established protocols can be extremely beneficial to physicians, patients, and the healthcare system as a whole.

Physicians that choose to hire or supervise a non-physician practitioner must truly understand the responsibility. Physicians must not allow corporations to coerce them into supervising without a strong level of comfort with the non-physician practitioner and adequate time to provide guidance.

The substitution of the word collaboration for supervision has done a great disservice to the role of the physician in working with non-physician practitioners. In the end, physicians carry the ultimate responsibility for the patients receiving care from non-physician practitioners—even if they never laid eyes on the patient. This is a heavy load to bear and should not be taken lightly.

Train new physicians and support our colleagues

The Hippocratic Oath, written between the 5th and 3rd centuries BC, discusses the role of the physician as a teacher. "I will impart a knowledge of the art to my own sons, and those of my teachers, and to students bound by this contract and having sworn this Oath to the law of medicine, *but to no others.*" Medicine was considered a sacred calling and an art to be undertaken only by those with the utmost commitment. If we follow the Hippocratic Oath, we should be training physicians and not non-physician practitioners.

Physicians should consider a commitment to training those future physicians who will ultimately replace them. It is a sacred duty for physicians to mentor, support, and guide other physicians whenever possible. Doctors can do this by taking on medical students and residents, and even consider supervising an assistant physician while they await entry into a residency program. One physician put it this way: "Doctors are like sharks. We compete amongst ourselves from the womb to the grave. Nurses are like orcas. They hunt in packs. They support each other. We need to become more pack-like. We need to support each other instead of protecting our individual territories."[510]

Doctors must also support their fellow physicians by avoiding negative talk and by giving colleagues the benefit of the doubt whenever possible. When physicians see a colleague suffering from depression or burnout, they should offer support and help.

Get out of the corporate practice of medicine

Physicians must take back control of the practice of medicine by running their own practices whenever possible. This will ensure that physicians are not replaced by lesser trained practitioners on a whim from a corporate headquarter. Rather than taking early retirement because of the burnout caused by the healthcare system, physicians should consider transitioning to a direct care practice that removes the insurance headaches and Medicare bureaucracy that has made medicine so burdensome to many.

Physicians who remain in the employ of an organization, such as those in academia or whose specialties are tied to hospitals, must take steps to ensure that physicians are involved at the highest level of the organization. Doctors must become more engaged with credentialing and medical staff bylaws. Ensure that all employment agreements are reviewed by knowledgeable attorneys and refuse to sign contracts that create undue burdens on physicians, such as restrictive no-compete covenants or those that force physicians to supervise non-physicians improperly. To be effective in changing these organizations, physicians must band together and present a united front.

Get involved

The replacement of physicians by non-physician practitioners has led to discouragement and despair amongst many doctors. Some have given up on fighting, accepting the trend as a new normal in healthcare. Others sit back passively, arguing that pendulum will swing as patients realize the difference in quality and start to demand better care. While there may be truth to this thought, it is unfair to allow patients to be harmed by our silence. We must continue to speak the truth.

Finally, physicians need to get more politically involved, educate lawmakers on their unique role, and unite with other physicians to fight for common goals. Historically, physicians have focused exclusively on caring for patients or had their heads so buried in books that they have failed to act and allowed others to make the decisions about healthcare in America. Organized medicine can help by training physicians in leadership and encouraging doctors to participate on boards and local government. It's time that physicians take a leadership role in our country's future.

CONCLUSION

On Thursday, March 21, 2019, an Oklahoma jury returned a verdict for $6,190,000 against Mercy Health and other defendants for Alexus Ochoa's wrongful death. Following the verdict, Ochoa family attorney Glendell Nix said, "The family is hopeful that the lawsuit and verdict will lead to changes at Mercy to ensure there are appropriately qualified medical providers at all Oklahoma hospitals, so this kind of tragedy does not happen to another family." If only this were the case. At the time of the trial, there had been no changes to the credentialing requirements of advanced practice nurses at Mercy Health.

While Douglas Danker was no longer CEO of Mercy-El Reno at the time of the trial, he continued to work with Mercy Health in a leadership position as director of emergency medical services.[511] Dr. Jeffrey Reames, who was responsible for signing off on Thompson's hiring, had been promoted to the position of Vice President of Emergency Medicine, overseeing 34 emergency departments across a four-state area. In his deposition, he acknowledged that the practice of allowing family nurse practitioners to work solo in emergency settings at Mercy Hospital Oklahoma facilities—in direct violation of the Oklahoma Board of Nursing regulations—had continued. On Doximity, an online health professional networking site, Reames is listed as "Medical Director, Emergency Department Mercy Hospital OKC."[512]

In November 2018, due to declining patient volumes and steep financial losses, St. Louis-based Mercy Health Systems announced they would close the El Reno, Oklahoma hospital on April 30, 2019. Mercy reported they lost $2.9 million in 2018 on inpatient care and experienced a loss of more than $700,000 in the first quarter of 2019.

Following the trial, Antoinette Thompson, the nurse practitioner who provided Alexus Ochoa's medical care, quietly moved to Waukon, Iowa, where she began working at the Veterans Memorial Hospital.

At the time of this writing, Thompson is listed on the hospital's website as an emergency room provider. In addition to Thompson, the website lists five other nurse practitioners and three physician assistants on the emergency department staff, but no emergency physicians.[513] As both the Veterans Administration and the state of Iowa allow nurse practitioners full practice authority, it is likely that Thompson is treating veterans in the emergency department today without physician supervision.

In December 2019, Thompson completed an online Doctor of Nursing Practice (DNP) at the very same institution where she received her online master's degree, the University of South Alabama. Her Doximity profile, states, "Dr. Antoinette Thompson is a family nurse practitioner in Des Moines, IA and is affiliated with multiple hospitals in the area, including Mercy Medical Center-Des Moines and Veterans Memorial Hospital. She is experienced in emergency medicine, dermal fillers, botulinum toxin injeciton [sic] for cosmesis, and suturing."[514]

Notably, Thompson identifies herself with the prefix "Dr." on her Doximity profile. While it is unclear whether Thompson referred to herself as a doctor when she was treating Alexus Ochoa, family members were under the impression that Thompson was indeed a physician, rather than a nurse practitioner. According to Ochoa family attorney Travis Dunn, Alexus's boyfriend Cortez Wright "broke down" in tears during his deposition upon apparently learning for the first time that Thompson was a nurse practitioner and not a physician.[515]

No action was taken against nurse practitioner Thompson until nearly five years after the death of Alexus Ochoa. On July 22, 2020, the Oklahoma Nursing Board finally took official action against Nurse Antoinette Thompson. She was given a one-year suspension and a $1,000 fine, as well as substantial education requirements and a mandate to work under the direct supervision of another nurse practitioner for one year—if she wishes to practice in the State of Oklahoma.[516]

PARALLELS TO THE AVIATION INDUSTRY

On March 10, 2019, Ethiopian Airlines Flight 302 crashed shortly after take-off, killing all 157 passengers on board. While the ultimate cause of the crash seems to be flawed software and a faulty sensor, questions arose regarding insufficient training of one of the doomed flight's pilots. Captain Chelsey B. Sullenberger, Captain Sully of 'Miracle on the Hudson' fame pointed out that the co-pilot had only 200 hours of flight experience, "a small fraction of the minimum in the US, and an absurdly low amount for someone in the cockpit of a jet airliner."[517] Ethiopian Airlines denied improper training, reporting that pilots had been trained on "all appropriate simulators."[518]

John Warren, a professional pilot with a major US airline, who is using an alias as he is not authorized by his employer to speak publicly, notes that in aviation, nothing can replace actual flight time.[519] "Technology is not the answer. Experience cannot be replicated in any simulator or on an iPad. It can only come with time in the air." Warren, who sees many parallels between pilot and physician training, notes that a plane's first officer position is similar to the role of a resident physician. The Captain sits beside the less-experienced first officer, supervising and ready to act if necessary. To get to the Captain's seat, a pilot must advance through years of experience, starting with small operations and moving to cargo flights before being promoted to commercial flights. The airline industry faces some of the same challenges as healthcare, including a lack of trained personnel. With many trained pilots approaching mandatory retirement age, the industry is actively seeking ways to increase the pipeline of new pilots. "We are losing 400 pilots per year to retirement," says Warren. "This is unprecedented in the industry."

Although the Federal Aviation Administration extended the mandatory retirement age from 60 to 65, buying an additional five years to train new pilots, Warren notes that the 2008 recession required many airlines to furlough pilots, decreasing the opportunity for less experienced pilots to gain flight time and shutting off advancement. To increase the supply of pilots, some airlines have sought a decrease in flight hour requirements, which were raised in 2009 following the crash of Colgan Air Flight 3407. This crash, which killed 50 passengers, was the fourth fatal airline accident in 6 years in the US and resulted in changes in the airline industry, including an increase in the minimum training of pilots from 250 hours to 1500 hours. This mandate in increased training hours seems to have paid off. In the following ten years, there has only been one passenger fatality in US airline operations.

This hasn't stopped profiteers from seeking a reduction in pilot training hours in the name of a pilot shortage, arguing that pilots don't really need so much training and that allowing newer pilots to fly with less training will increase access to flights for smaller communities. This argument sounds awfully familiar. But unlike physicians, pilots have drawn a line in the sand. The Airline Pilots Association, made up of 100,000 pilots,

A 50 *experience*

has actively opposed legislation to reduce training hours.[520] It helps that the flying public is extremely supportive; no reasonable person is willing to stake his or her life on a poorly trained pilot.

It is ironic that the public is not as supportive when it comes to the topic of unsupervised non-physician practitioners. The parallels and controversies are nearly the same as those faced by the airline industry today. One of the differences may be that when a plane crashes, the media bombards the public with photos of the wreckage, biographies of the victims, and elaborate explanations of how the accident occurred for weeks after. When an incompletely trained clinician harms patients it rarely makes the news, let alone headlines.

KNOWLEDGE CAN CHANGE THE SYSTEM

Patients are constantly being told by hospitals, companies, and government agencies that non-physician professionals are 'just as good' as physicians, or not being informed about the actual credentials of the white-coat-clad practitioner they are in the room with at all. While non-physician advocates cite "five decades" of research supporting their public campaign, they almost always omit one essential detail, that studies on care provided by non-physicians have always included physician supervision to assist these practitioners in providing safe and effective care. There are simply no credible studies that demonstrate that independent non-physicians can provide the same care as physicians.

Why do healthcare systems, politicians, and hospital administrators willfully disregard this critical piece of information? That is perhaps the most important question of all.

While this book may have initially seemed like a tome against non-physician practitioners working in healthcare, it should now be quite clear that the issue is not at all about a turf war in medicine. Rather, it is about an entirely different battle against public misinformation, healthcare conglomerates, politicians, and corporate overlords that are doing little more than chasing profits. Nurses, doctors, non-physician practitioners, janitors, cooks, clerks, and every other essential worker in healthcare on the front lines are treated as expendable pawns in a system that lost its way a long time ago. There is no longer room for values like compassion, empathy, and safety.

If the COVID-19 pandemic has exposed any single thing, it has laid bare the fact that the American people are living in a time where hospitals, hedge funds, and large conglomerate organizations are making decisions without regard for the human beings laying on gurneys within their proverbial walls. Today, your healthcare and who will provide it is controlled not by a physician, but by a healthcare administrator. Doctors, nurses, and patients are just cogs in a seemingly unstoppable money-making healthcare machine.

If there are any lingering doubts about who is calling the shots in healthcare, one only has to look to Bellingham, Washington. In March 2020, Ming Lin, an emergency physician who had worked at PeaceHealth St. Joseph Medical Center for 17 years, was terminated by his employer TeamHealth, after publicly criticizing the hospital for not protecting its staff with adequate personal protective equipment.[521] TeamHealth, one of the largest employers of emergency physicians, is owned by private equity company Blackstone, a worldwide investment firm.[522]

At a time when more than 9,000 healthcare workers had contracted COVID-19, including 27 deaths, organizations like HCA Florida, the state's largest private hospital system, restricted the use of protective masks for healthcare workers. The system also prohibited staff members from bringing their own protective equipment from home.[523] Healthcare workers across the country who refused to comply with what they perceived as dangerous policies from administrators were fired. For example, in April 2020, nurses at Providence St. John's Health Center in Santa Monica, CA were suspended when they refused to treat patients with active COVID-19 infection without proper personal protective equipment.[524]

While healthcare workers in New York City begged for more protective masks and donned garbage bags due to insufficient hospital isolation gowns, Mount Sinai Health System care executives Kenneth Davis and Arthur Klein left the City to work remotely from their ocean-front Florida homes.[525] As these executives self-isolated in Florida, medical students and resident physicians were being graduated early to help out in the fight, losing educational opportunities and without hazard pay. Those who complained were harshly criticized by their administration and threatened with termination. New York authorities asked physicians to volunteer service without pay or even a stipend for housing or a guarantee of personal protective equipment. New York mayor Bill DeBlasio called on the federal government to institute a draft of physicians and nurses.[526]

At the same time that front-line workers were putting their lives at risk and the nation braced for an increase in numbers of COVID-19 patients, thousands of other healthcare workers were laid off, furloughed, and given pay cuts.[527] Meanwhile, many hospital executives failed to cut their own pay, with some, like Denver Health Center, even paying themselves performance bonuses. A local news agency reported that one week after announcing a hiring freeze and asking employees to take time off without pay, hospital leaders at Denver Health granted themselves sizeable performance bonuses "ranging from $50,000 up to $230,000."[528]

There is hope. While devastating, the COVID-19 pandemic has opened the eyes of healthcare workers, patients, and the public alike to the flaws inherent in our healthcare system. The media is beginning to report on the previously hidden injustices that healthcare workers face from administrators. Physicians and nurses are standing up to administrators to demand protection, support, and proper treatment on behalf of themselves and their patients. Patients are more appreciative than ever for the sacrifices front-line healthcare workers make every day and are supporting doctors and nurses in their efforts.

Systemic change is never easy. But when patients, physicians, and all healthcare professionals come together to demand the prioritization of high quality and safe care of patients, positive change can occur. All of our lives depend on it.

ACKNOWLEDGMENTS

The authors wish to thank the many contributors who made this book possible. This project was inspired by the group Physicians for Patient Protection, a grassroots physician organization with a mission to ensure physician-led care for all patients and to advocate for truth and transparency regarding healthcare practitioners. Physicians in this group provided true stories, interviews, analysis of research studies, and editorial support. We would like to specifically thank the board of directors (Carmen Kavali MD, Purvi Parikh MD, Ainel Sewell MD, Roy Stoller DO, Amy Townsend MD, and Chantel O'Shea MD).

Thank you to the many patients and parents for your willingness and courage to share your stories openly or anonymously. Thank you for having faith in us to tell your stories. Thank you to the physicians, nurse practitioners, nurses, physician assistants, and patients who shared their experiences with us. Thank you to the family of Alexus Ochoa for allowing us to tell her story and use her photograph.

We also thank Henry (Pete) Travers MD, J. Ann Lentini MD, Christin Giordano MD, and Brian Wilhelmi MD JD for providing essential feedback and editorial assistance. Thank you to attorneys Glendell Nix, JD and Travis Dunn, JD for their feedback and assistance, as well as Monica Stransky, JD for providing supporting legal research. We thank Matthew Sewell MD for graphic design assistance.

Thank you to Jenny Barchfield and Kimberly Clark, for early editing assistance, feedback, and pointing us in the right direction when we needed it most. Thank you to editor John Irvine at TheDeductible.com for providing feedback and re-direction and to Ron Reimer, MD for sharing your feedback over coffee. We sincerely thank our editor Barbara Dalberry for her skilled copy-editing work and thoughtful insights that helped us strengthen our arguments and remove bias.

We are deeply appreciative of our publisher, Jeff Young, PhD at Universal Publishing for giving us this opportunity and for working with us to refine the manuscript.

We thank our families for tolerating the many days and hours that we spent away from them while writing this book. Thank you for your love and support.

APPENDIX

Find a physician-led practice
Comparison of clinical hours
Nurse practitioner scope of practice by state
Clinician abbreviations
Informed consent for non-physician care
Patient directive declining non-physician care

FIND A PHYSICIAN-LED PRACTICE

https://www.physiciansforpatientprotection.org/patient-resources/
find-a-physician/
www.MyDoqter.com

COMPARISON OF CLINICAL HOURS

	Clinical Hours	Residency Hours	Total Clinical Hours
Nurse Practitioner (MSN, DNP)	500–1,500	None required	500–1,500
Physician Assistant	2,000	None required	2,000
Physician	6,000 (medical school)	9,000–10,000	15,000–16,000

NURSE PRACTITIONER SCOPE OF PRACTICE—2020

Independent Practice States (23)

Alaska
Arizona
Colorado
Connecticut
Hawaii
Idaho
Iowa
Maine
Maryland
Minnesota
Montana
Nebraska
Nevada
New Hampshire
New Mexico
North Dakota
Oregon
Rhode Island
South Dakota
Vermont
Washington
Washington DC
Wyoming

Partial Independence Practice States (17)

Alabama
Arkansas
Delaware
Florida
Indiana
Illinois
Kansas
Kentucky
Louisiana
Mississippi
New Jersey
New York
Ohio
Pennsylvania
Utah
West Virginia
Wisconsin

Full Supervision States (11)

California
Georgia
Massachusetts
Michigan
Missouri
North Carolina
Oklahoma
South Carolina
Tennessee
Texas
Virginia

ABBREVIATIONS

Physicians
MD – Medical Doctor
DO – Doctor of Osteopathic Medicine
MBBS – Bachelor of Medicine, Bachelor of Surgery (UK)

Nurse practitioners
ACNP – acute care nurse practitioner
AGACNP – adult gerontology acute care nurse practitioner
ANP – adult nurse practitioner
APHN – advanced public health nurse
APN – advanced practice nurse
APRN – advanced practice registered nurse
ARNP – advanced registered nurse practitioner

CMCN – certified managed care nurse
CNM – certified nurse midwife
CNP – certified nurse practitioner
CNS – clinical nurse specialist
CRNA – certified registered nurse anesthetist
CRNP – certified registered nurse practitioner
DNAP – doctor of nurse anesthesia practice
DNP – doctor of nursing practice
DNS – doctor or nursing science
DNSc – doctor of nursing science
DSc – doctor of science
DSN – doctor of science in nursing
EdD – doctor of education
ENP – emergency nurse practitioner
FNP – family nurse practitioner
GNP – gerontological nurse practitioner
MA – master of arts (with a major in nursing)
MN – master or nursing
MS – master of science (with a major in nursing)
MSA – master of science in anesthesia
MSNA – master of science in nurse anesthesia
MSN – master of science in nursing
NNP – neonatal nurse practitioner
NP – nurse practitioner
ONP – oncology nurse practitioner
PhD – doctor of philosophy in nursing
PMHNP – psychiatric & mental health nurse practitioner
PNP – pediatric nurse practitioner
PNP – AC – pediatric nurse practitioner-acute care
PNP-PC – pediatric nurse practitioner-primary care
PsyMHNP – psychiatric mental health nurse practitioner
PsyNP – psychiatric nurse practitioner
WHNP – women's health nurse practitioner

Physician assistants
APA – physician assistant
APA-C – physician assistant certified
MPAS – "master" of physician's assistant studies
PA – physician assistant
PA-C – physician assistant certified

PAC – physician assistant certified
RPA – registered physician assistant
RPA-C – registered physician's assistant certified

Naturopaths
DNM – doctor of naturopathic medicine
ND – naturopathic doctor
NMD – naturopathic medical doctor

Chiropractors
DC – doctor of chiropractic

SAMPLE LETTER DIRECTING CARE/INFORMED CONSENT

Sample Nurse Practitioner/Physician Assistant Consent for Treatment

_____ (name of company) utilizes nurse practitioners and physician assistants to assist in the delivery of medical care. A nurse practitioner is not a physician or medical doctor. A nurse practitioner (NP) is a registered nurse who has completed specific advanced nursing education (usually a master's degree or doctoral degree). A physician assistant is not a physician or medical doctor. A physician assistant (PA) is a healthcare professional trained and licensed to practice medicine with limited supervision of a physician.

I have read the above, and hereby consent to the services of a nurse practitioner or physician assistant for my healthcare needs. I understand that at any time I may refuse to see a nurse practitioner or physician assistant and request to see physician.

Patient Name	Date of Birth

Patient/Guardian signature	Date

Sample Directive Regarding Healthcare Choice

To the Healthcare Clinic, Hospital, Physician of the Undersigned:

RE: Request for MD or DO Care

I am requesting that this document be placed on file in my medical record at this practice, facility or hospital and stand as a directive until revoked by myself, or other power of healthcare appointed by myself. It has been signed by the witnesses below and dated.

I respect that nurse practitioners and physician assistants may be part of a supervised team and work to help my physician by taking notes, refilling routine medications, giving immunizations, taking a history, and consent ONLY to their use in my healthcare in those limited areas.

I do not consent to the use of either a nurse practitioner or physician assistant for any other areas of my healthcare to include but not limited to:

Diagnosis of diseases
Determination of which labs to be ordered, (other than yearly routine), x-rays or other studies.
Determination of and initiation of prescriptions and treatments plans, as well as any changes to those plans.
Referrals to specialists.
Evaluation of labs, x-rays, and studies.
Admission order to hospitals and rehabilitation centers

This directive includes states where there is allowed any type of independent practice as well as those that do not. I further do NOT expect that this directive should prejudice my healthcare by delaying any care I should receive in a timely manner. If you have any questions, please contact me or the person I may designate below. I look forward to continued quality care at your facility.

Respectfully,

Patient Signature: _____ Date: _____

Printed Name: _____ *Phone:* _____

Address: _____

Additional Contact Person If applicable: _____ *Phone:* _____

Witness Signature: _____ *Date:* _____

Witness Printed Name: _____

Witness Signature: _____ *Date:* _____

Witness Printed Name: _____

NOTES

INTRODUCTION

1. American Association of Nurse Practitioners. Nurse Practitioners to Lobby Federal Lawmakers in Record Numbers. PR Newswire: news distribution, targeting and monitoring. https://www.prnewswire.com/news-releases/nurse-practitioners-to-lobby-federal-lawmakers-in-record-numbers-300054546.html. Published March 24, 2015. Accessed June 9, 2020.
2. Quality of Nurse Practitioner Practice. American Association of Nurse Practitioners. https://www.aanp.org/advocacy/advocacy-resource/position-statements/quality-of-nurse-practitioner-practice. Accessed June 9, 2020.
3. Nurse Practitioner Cost Effectiveness. American Association of Nurse Practitioners. https://www.aanp.org/advocacy/advocacy-resource/position-statements/position-statements. Accessed June 9, 2020.
4. Primary Care Coalition. Practitioners Issue Brief: Collaboration between Physicians and Nurses Works. Compare the Education Gaps between Primary Care Physicians and Nurse Practitioners. [PDF File] Retrieved from https://www.tafp.org/Media/Default/Downloads/advocacy/scope-education.pdf. Accessed June 9, 2020.
5. Nursing Master's Programs with 100% Admit Rates. U.S. News & World Report. https://www.usnews.com/education/best-graduate-schools/the-short-list-grad-school/articles/nursing-masters-programs-with-the-highest-acceptance-rates. Accessed June 9, 2020.
6. How Much Can You Realistically Work During Your NP Program? Retrieved from https://thriveap.com/blog/how-much-can-you-realistically-work-during-your-np-program. Published May 20, 2015. Accessed March 26, 2020.
7. Staff Writers. Accelerated Online MSN-NP Programs for Registered Nurses. NursePractitionerSchools.com. https://www.nursepractitionerschools.com/online/msn/accelerated/. Published June 8, 2020. Accessed June 9, 2020.

8. Staff Writers. Are there NP Programs for Non-Nurses? (Direct Entry). Nurse-PractitionerSchools.com. https://www.nursepractitionerschools.com/faq/can-a-non-nurse-become-an-np/. Published May 21, 2020. Accessed June 9, 2020.

9. Frontier Nursing University. If you're a registered nurse and you'd like to take your nursing career to the next level, our Master of Science in Nursing (MSN) program offers you a flexible, convenient option to earn a graduate nursing degree almost entirely online. [Facebook post] Retrieved from https://www.facebook.com/search/top/?q=Frontier%20Nursing%20University%20%22online%22&epa=FILTERS&filters=eyJycF9hdXRob3IiOiJ7XCJuYW1lXCI6XCJhdXRob3JcIixcImFyZ3NcIjpcIjc0ODczMzU4MzkzXCJ9In0%3D. Accessed May 29, 2018.

10. Yale PA Online. We're excited to announce the first graduating class of the Yale PA Online Program! We're so proud of all their hard work and accomplishments. Congratulations to the Class of 2020! Go Bulldogs! #YalePAOnlineGrad [Facebook Status Update] Retrieved from https://www.facebook.com/YalePAonline/photos/a.1944492235793308/2596813657227826/?type=3&theater. Accessed May 18, 2020.

11. Press Release—FAA Boosts Aviation Safety with New Pilot Qualification. Retrieved from https://www.faa.gov/news/press_releases/news_story.cfm?newsId=14838. Published September 19, 2014. Accessed July 27, 2020.

12. FastStats–Physician office visits. (2017, January 19). Retrieved from https://www.cdc.gov/nchs/fastats/physician-visits.htm. Published January 19, 2017. Accessed July 27, 2020.

13. BeaumontEnterpirse.com. State suspends Nederland nurse practitioner's license. Retrieved from https://www.beaumontenterprise.com/news/article/State-suspends-Nederland-nurse-practitioner-s-12627383.php. Published February 20, 2018. Accessed September 19, 2019.

14. Texas Board of Nursing Charges. In the Matter of Permanent Advanced Practice Registered Nurse License Number AP 123323[PDF] Retrieved from https://drive.google.com/file/d/0ByNdLzZyUbqnUFlWYndhdVZaZEk. Published October 17, 2017. Accessed September 19, 2019.

15. Menchine, M. D., Wiechmann, W., & Rudkin, S. Trends in Midlevel Provider Utilization in Emergency Departments from 1997 to 2006. *Academic Emergency Medicine*. 2009. 16(10):963–969. doi: 10.1111/j.1553-2712.2009.00521.

16. Reno, J. Nurse Practitioner, No Doctor at Your Urgent Care Clinic. Retrieved from https://www.healthline.com/health-news/nurse-practitioner-no-doctor-urgent-care-center. Published November 4, 2019. Accessed November 10, 2019.

17. Andrus, L. H., O'Hara-Devereaux, M., Burr, B. D., & Mentink, J. L. A new teacher in medical education: the family nurse practitioner. *J Med Educ.* 1977;52(11):896–900. doi:10.1097/00001888-197711000-00004.

18. Goldberg, S. M.D. is no prescription for job security at hospital chains. Retrieved from https://www.chicagobusiness.com/health-care/md-no-prescription-job-security-hospital-chains. Published December 6, 2019. Accessed May 18, 2020.

19. Bernard, R. (2018, May 09). Physician replacements affecting vulnerable patient populations. Retrieved from https://www.medicaleconomics.com/med-ec-blog/physician-replacements-affecting-vulnerable-patient-popula-tions. Published May 9, 2018. Accessed May 19, 2020.

20. Maron, S. (2018, January 14). IN MY VIEW: Are NPs same as MDs? Retrieved August 07, 2020, from https://www.gvnews.com/opinion/in-my-view-are-nps-same-as-mds/article_f61574d2-f88e-11e7-912f-e75f6a0d0a49.html.

21. Bernard, R. Physicians face punishment for speaking out about non-physician care. Retrieved from https://www.medicaleconomics.com/med-ec-blog/physicians-face-punishment-speaking-out-about-non-physician-care. Published March 31, 2018. Accessed May 19, 2020.

22. United Community Health Center. Our Team. Retrieved August 7, 2020 from https://uchcaz.org/our-team/.

23. Sackett, D. L. The Burlington Randomized Trial of the Nurse Practitioner: Health Outcomes of Patients. *Annals of Internal Medicine.* 1974;80(2):137. doi: 10.7326/0003-4819-80-2-137.

24. Sharp, N. American College of Nurse Practitioners: experiment in democracy. *Nurs Manag.* 1995;26(1):22–23.

25. Wysocki, S. Nurse practitioners: experts in patient care, experts for health care policy. *Nurse Pract Forum.* 1990;1(1):6–8.

26. O'Brien, J. M. How nurse practitioners obtained provider status: lessons for pharmacists. *American Journal of Health-System Pharmacy.* 2003;60(22): 2301–2307. https://doi.org/10.1093/ajhp/60.22.2301.

27. Balanced Budget Act of 1997, Pub. L. No. 105–33. Retrieved from https://www.congress.gov/bill/105th-congress/house-bill/2015/text, Accessed July 27, 2020.

28. American College of Nurse Practitioners. Nurse practitioners victorious in budget bill; ACNP grassroots effort pays off. www.nurse.org/acnp/medicare/pr970813.shtml. Accessed July 2, 2001.

29. Wakefield, M. K. Nurses and the Affordable Care Act. *American Journal of Nursing.* 2010;10(9):11. doi: 10.1097/01.naj.0000388242.06365.4f.

30. Mena, F. N. Family Nurse Practitioner Kevin G. Morgan will be presented in the Worldwide Leaders of Healthcare. Retrieved from https://

menafn.com/qn_news_story_s.aspx?storyid=1096568223&title=Reputa-ble-Family-Nurse-Practitioner-Kevin-G-Morgan-FNPBC-will-be-Present-ed-in-the-Worldwide-Leaders-in-Healthcare Accessed September 19, 2019.

31. McNeese State University. Nursing, Family Nurse Practitioner Concentration, MSN. Retrieved from https://catalog.mcneese.edu/preview_program.php?catoid=47&poid=30189 Accessed June 18, 2020.

32. Bernard, R. Nursing Boards Failing at NP Oversight? Retrieved February 10, 2020 from https:/www.medpagetoday.com/blogs/rockstar/82253?vpass=1. Published December 11, 2019.

33. Guidelines for State Regulations of PAs, Adopted 1998, amended 1993, 1998, 2001, 2005, 2006, 2009, 2011, 2013, 2016, 2017 [PDF] Retrieved from https://www.aapa.org/download/35030/.

34. PAs across America celebrate First State with key components of optimal team practice following the legislative victory in North Dakota. AAPA. https://www.aapa.org/news-central/2019/04/pas-across-america-celebrate-first-state-with-key-components-of-optimal-team-practice-following-the-legisla-tive-victory-in-north-dakota/. Published April 9, 2019. Accessed July 23, 2019.

35. Kekevian, B. Expanding Scope of Practice: Lessons and Leverage. Retrieved July 15, 2020 from https://www.reviewofoptometry.com/article/expan ding-scope-of-practice-lessons-and-leverage. Published October 15, 2018.

36. Pharmacist Prescribing: Statewide Protocols and More. (2019, March 1). Retrieved from https://naspa.us/resource/swp/. Published March 1, 2019. Accessed June 18, 2020.

37. American Association of Naturopathic Physicians. Regulated States and Regulatory Authorities. Retrieved from https://naturopathic.org/page/RegulatedStates# f. Updated February 21, 2020, Accessed June 20, 2020.

38. Coulter, Ian D PhD, & Sandefuer, Ruth, D. C, PhD. Chiropractic in the United States: Licensure and Scope of Practice. Chirobase. Your Skeptical Guide to Chiropractic History, Theories and Practices. Retrieved from https://quack-watch.org/chiropractic/rb/ahcpr/5-2/. Accessed June 9, 2020.

39. Young, A., Chaudhry, H. J., Pei, X., Arnhart, K., Dugan, M., & Snyder, G. B. A Census of Actively Licensed Physicians in the United States, 2016. *Journal of Medical Regulation*. 2017;103(2):7–21. doi: 10.30770/2572-1852-103.2.7.

40. NP Fact Sheet. (n.d.). Retrieved from https://www.aanp.org/about/all-about-nps/np-fact-sheet, Accessed June 20, 2020.

41. National Commission on Certification of Physician Assistants. 2018 Statistical Profile of Certified Physician Assistants ANNUAL REPORT. [PDF]. Retrieved from https://prodcmsstoragesa.blob.core.windows.net/uploads/files/2018StatisticalProfileofCertifiedPhysicianAssistants.pdf, Accessed June 20, 2020.

42. National Commission on Certification of Physician Assistants. 2017 Statistical Profile of Certified Physician Assistants ANNUAL REPORT. [PDF]. Retrieved from http://prodcmsstoragesa.blob.core.windows.net/uploads/files/2017StatisticalProfileofCertifiedPhysicianAssistants%206.27.pdf, Accessed June 20, 2020.
43. Historical Timeline. (n.d.). Retrieved from https://www.aanp.org/about-aanp/historical-timeline#2010-s, Accessed June 20, 2020.
44. Young, A., Chaudhry, H. J., Pei, X., Arnhart, K., Dugan, M., & Snyder, G. B. A Census of Actively Licensed Physicians in the United States, 2016. *Journal of Medical Regulation.* 2017;103(2):7–21. doi: 10.30770/2572-1852-103.2.7

CHAPTER 1

45. Amelia Ochoa v. Mercy Health Oklahoma Communities, (2019), District Court Oklahoma County, Oklahoma. Court Records Provided by Plaintiff Attorney Glendall Nix.
46. NP Fact Sheet. (n.d.). Retrieved from https://www.aanp.org/about/all-about-nps/np-fact-sheet, Accessed June 20, 2020.
47. Casey, C. (n.d.). Ground-breaking Nurse Practitioner Program turns 50. Retrieved from https://www.cuanschutztoday.org/ground-breaking-nurse-practitioner-program-turns-50/, Accessed June 20, 2020.
48. Extending the Scope of Nursing Practice: A Report of the Secretary's Committee to Study Extended Roles for Nurses. *JAMA.* 1972;220(9):1231–1236. doi:10.1001/jama.1972.03200090053009.
49. Kohler, S. *Case 31: The Development of the Nurse Practitioner and Physician Assistant Professions.* The Commonwealth Fund, Robert Wood Johnson Foundation, and Carnegie Corporation of New York. 1965.
50. Brom, H. M., Salsberry, P. J., & Graham, M. C. Leveraging health care reform to accelerate nurse practitioner full practice authority. *Journal of the American Association of Nurse Practitioners.* 2018;30(3):120–130. https://doi.org/10.1097/JXX.0000000000000023.
51. Sharp, N. The power of nurse practitioners. *Nurse Pract.* 1997; 22(2):141–147.
52. Pearson, L. Survey shows NPs support unified umbrella organization. *Nurse Pract.* 1993;18(2):9–10.
53. O'Brien, J. How Nurse Practitioners Obtained Provider Status: Lessons for Pharmacists. *American Journal of Health-System Pharmacy.* 2003;60(22): 2301–2307. https://doi.org/10.1093/ajhp/60.22.2301.
54. D. Grieger. Personal communication October 2, 2018.

55. Future of Nursing: Campaign for Action. RWJF. https://www.rwjf.org/en/how-we-work/grants-explorer/featured-programs/future-of-nursing-campaign-for-action.html. Published August 14, 2018. Accessed June 10, 2020.

56. Grants Explorer. RWJF. https://www.rwjf.org/content/rwjf/en/how-we-work/grants-explorer.html#t=1928. Published May 27, 2020. Accessed June 10, 2020.

57. Robert Wood Johnson Foundation. Robert Wood Johnson Foundation Annual Report. (1997), [PDF] Retrieved from https://folio.iupui.edu/bitstream/handle/10244/444/AnnualReport1997.pdf?sequence=1, Accessed June 20, 2020.

58. SSA Commissioners: Shirley S. Chater". Social Security Administration. Retrieved February 13, 2014.

59. RWJ Health Policy Fellows. A National Program of the Robert Wood Johnson Foundation | RWJF Health Policy Fellows. https://www.healthpolicyfellows.org/.

60. RWJ Health Policy Fellows. RWJF Health Policy Fellows. https://www.healthpolicyfellows.org/eight-health-professionals-selected-for-rwjf-health-policy-fellows-program-at-the-national-academy-of-medicine/. Published May 23, 2016.

61. Bull, J., Sharp, N., & Wakefield, M. *The Nurses' Directory Of Capitol Connections*. 5th ed. Fairfax, VA; George Mason University Center for Health Policy, Research and Ethics; 2000.

62. Robert Wood Johnson Foundation. Robert Wood Johnson Executive Nurse Fellows Program Results Report Grant ID: ENL Originally Published: February 3, 2005 Last Updated: July 10, 2014, Accessed June 20, 2020.

63. United States. Physician Payment Review Commission. (1989–1997). Annual report to Congress. Washington, DC: The Commission.

64. Omnibus Budget Reconciliation Act of 1989, Pub. L. No. 101–239.

65. Sheila P. Burke. Bipartisan Policy Center. https://bipartisanpolicy.org/person/sheila-burke/.

66. A Goal and a Challenge: Putting 10,000 Nurses on Governing Boards by 2020. Retrieved June 12, 2020 from https://www.rwjf.org/en/library/articles-and-news/2014/12/a-goal-and-a-challenge--putting-10-000-nurses-on-governing-board.html?fbclid=IwAR2dV47Zgm4LYviYMgVr-Jb-j1xWfADVEL2i4H1P18NYYfP4_wNOAEXg-ZIg. Published September 17, 2019.

67. Robert Wood Johnson Foundation. Grant Number 65815. Grants Explorer. https://www.rwjf.org/content/rwjf/en/how-wework/grantsexplorer.

html#start=2007&end=2009&amt=1000001&t=1926 | 1928 | 1924 | 1923 | 1929&s=15&sortBy=organization&ascending=true. Accessed June 12, 2020.

68. RWJF and AARP. Campaign for Action. https://campaignforaction.org/about/leadership-staff/the-rwjf-and-aarp-partnership/. Accessed February 19, 2020.

69. National Academy of Sciences. Committee on the Robert Wood Johnson Foundation Initiative on the Future of Nursing at the Institute of Medicine. Published 2011. Retrieved from https://www.ncbi.nlm.nih.gov/books/NBK209889/ on June 12, 2020.

70. Institute of Medicine (US) Committee on the Robert Wood Johnson Foundation Initiative on the Future of Nursing, at the Institute of Medicine. The Future of Nursing: Leading Change, Advancing Health. Washington (DC): National Academies Press (US); 2011.

71. Robert Wood Johnson Foundation. Grant number: 67783. Grants Explorer. https://www.rwjf.org/en/how-we-work/grants-explorer.html. Accessed June 12, 2020.

72. Robert Wood Johnson Foundation. Grant numbers: 70501 (2013), 71600 (2014), 72464 (2015), 76049 (2019). Grants Explorer. https://www.rwjf.org/en/how-we-work/grants-explorer.html. Accessed June 12, 2020.

73. Campaign for Action. About. Retrieved August 9, 2020 from https://campaignforaction.org/about/our-story/.

74. Number of people receiving nursing doctoral degrees annually. Campaign for Action. https://campaignforaction.org/resource/number-people-receiving-nursing-doctoral-degrees-annually/. Published July 9, 2019, Accessed June 20, 2020.

75. Campaign for Action. Dashboard. 2020. Retrieved on August 9, 2020 from https://campaignforaction.org/wp-content/uploads/2019/07/r2_CCNA-0029_2019-Dashboard-Indicator-Updates_1-29-20.pdf.

76. Ibid.

77. Ellenbogen, M., & Segal, J. Differences in Opioid Prescribing Among Generalist Physicians, Nurse Practitioners, and Physician Assistants. *Pain Medicine.* 2020;21(1):76–83. https://doi.org/10.1093/pm/pnz005.

78. Drash W. Johnson & Johnson acted as opioid 'kingpin,' Oklahoma AG says. *CNN.* https://www.cnn.com/2019/03/12/health/oklahoma-opioid-trial-johnson-and-johnson-kingpin/index.html?fbclid=IwAR2Hxh-h_6mOP4uaQOu6syKTncSgeFMRU56iRw1fLt2j5CLKu5nndn59-7IM. Published March 12, 2019. Accessed June 10, 2020.

79. MinuteClinic. https://www.cvs.com/minuteclinic/visit/about-us/history. Accessed June 10, 2020.

80. Smart Retailing Rx. What's hot in the pharmacy front end? https://join. healthmart.com/clinical-performance/whats-hot-in-the-pharmacy-front-end/. Published December 8, 2015. Accessed August 9, 2020.

81. AARP is just a for-profit insurance company. *The Washington Times*. https:// www.washingtontimes.com/news/2019/dec/3/aarp-is-just-a-for-prof-it-insurance-company/?fbclid=IwAR1jB6_RBM9N92IBLEEVUsRqwez-rmRV1nR8JGgKSjDTWNq6pgaYb9ZvKg-I. Published December 3, 2019. Accessed June 10, 2020.

82. American Association of Nurse Practitioners. Issues at a Glance. https:// www.aanp.org/advocacy/advocacy-resource/policy-briefs/issues-full-practice-brief. Accessed August 9, 2020.

83. Morgan Assistant C. Nurse Practitioners Launch Unprecedented Lobbying Blitz to Build Public Support for VA Proposal Hurdle. *Daily Nurse*. https://dailynurse.com/nurse-practitioners-launch-unprecedented-lobbying-blitz-build-public-support-va-proposal-hurdle/. Published July 8, 2016. Accessed June 10, 2020.

84. Department of Veterans Affairs Health Services Research & Development Service. Evidence Brief: The Quality of Care Provided by Advanced Practice Nurses [PDF]. 2014. Retrieved from https://www.hsrd.research.va.gov/publications/esp/ap-nurses.pdf/. Accessed June 20, 2020.

85. Bernard, R. VA Goes Too Far on NP Independence. MedpageToday. www. medpagetoday.com/blogs/rockstar/84396. Published January 17, 2020. Accessed July 20, 2020.

86. Ibid.

87. H. Travers. Personal communication April 15, 2020.

88. Nurse practitioners outscore physicians in patient satisfaction survey. Clinical Advisor. https://www.clinicaladvisor.com/home/meeting-coverage/aanp-2011-conference/nurse-practitioners-outscore-physicians-in-patient-satisfaction-survey/. Published December 19, 2018. Accessed June 10, 2020.

89. We Choose NPs. https://www.wechoosenps.org/about. Accessed June 9, 2019.

90. Open Letter to the National Governors Association. American Association of Nurse Practitioners. https://www.aanp.org/news-feed/open-letter-to-the-national-governors-association.

91. N. Buckalew. Personal communication. April 26, 2020.

92. Five States Take Action to Expand Access to Care During COVID-19 Pandemic. American Association of Nurse Practitioners. https://www.aanp. org/news-feed/five-states-take-action-to-expand-access-to-care-during-covid-19-pandemic. Accessed June 10, 2020.

93. New York State Office of the Professions. COVID-19 Pandemic and Professional Practice. http://www.op.nysed.gov/COVID-19_EO.html#. Accessed June 15, 2020.

94. @ @pppforpatients. (2019, Aug 9). Photo of smiley face with a zippered mouth "And sometimes the strongest NP voice is silent…" How can #NPs-Lead by censoring their nurses for speaking up? Nurses want physician supervision and #physicianled care for all their patients? [Twitter post]. https://twitter.com/pppforpatients/status/1159660324229922816. Published August 9, 2019. Accessed June 12, 2020.

95. Conrad-Rendon, J. "The closing AANP conference ceremony speech was by the amazing Dr. Margaret A. Fitzgerald, and she brought up an important topic. If an APRN does not support FPA and vocalizes that … especially on social media … it actually can hurt our profession. I truly believe that any APRN who states that they are against FPA … it is usually due to a lack of understanding of FPA and it is our responsibility to explain it to them respectfully. So I encourage each of you … if you come across a post from an APRN who seems not to be in support of FPA … please send them a private message educating them about FPA in a respectful manner. If you do not feel comfortable doing that … please just send me a screenshot of their post and I will send them a message to address it." [Facebook post on group Professionals who support FPA for APRNs]. Screenshot. Posted 2019.

96. Report Now: Misrepresentation of NPs and the NP Role. American Association of Nurse Practitioners. https://www.aanp.org/about/about-the-american-association-of-nurse-practitioners-aanp/media/reportnow, Accessed June 20, 2020.

97. u/mursematthew. r/medicine - I'm about to graduate from NP school and I am utterly unprepared. Reddit. https://www.reddit.com/r/medicine/comments/abct1g/im_about_to_graduate_from_np_school_and_i_am/.

98. SublimeEMTP. Augmenting your education for bad NP programs. allnurses. https://allnurses.com/augmenting-education-bad-np-programs-t699754/?fbclid=IwAR2d7dvEoV2QxjAaxAnwratRl_8xsJFPRUqpJbb-j_6kS-2RZjDg2Ar6WIY8. Published May 11, 2019. Accessed June 10, 2020.

99. Sawyer Initiative. Open Letter to the CCNE. https://sawyerinitiative.com/news-and-development/open-letter-to-the-ccne/?fbclid=IwAR-1WXc7ctySj86cQQixu__egOjLlkIDJo6WKYzbn7vj0tczyVAu1uoh5fwk. Accessed February 20, 2020.

100. R. Thoman. Personal communication, August 7, 2020.

101. Aelnyk, B. M., Gallagher-Ford, L., & Zellefrow, C., et al. The First U.S. Study on Nurses' Evidence-Based Practice Competencies Indicates Major Deficits

That Threaten Healthcare Quality, Safety, and Patient Outcomes. *Worldviews Evid Based Nurs*. 2018;15(1):16–25. doi:10.1111/wvn.12269.

102. Thomas, S. Social media is not for clinical references. The Journal for Nurse Practitioners. 2019. Retrieved August 7, 2020 from https://www.npjournal.org/article/S1555-4155(19)30952-3/pdf.

103. C. Naslund. Personal communication. August 8, 2020.

CHAPTER 2

104. Staff Writers. Top Online RN-to-MSN Programs. Published May 11, 2020. Retrieved June 20, 2020 from https://nursejournal.org/msn-degree/7-best-online-rn-to-msn-programs/.

105. Planning Your Nurse Practitioner (NP) Education. (n.d.). Retrieved from https://www.aanp.org/student-resources/planning-your-np-education#:~:text=There are approximately 400 academic,adult, family or pediatrics).

106. A Map of All Medical Schools in the United States. Retrieved from https://shortwhitecoats.com/2015/a-map-of-all-medical-schools-in-the-united-states. Published May 5, 2011, Accessed June 20, 2020.

107. Nursing Master's Programs with 100% Admit Rates. (n.d.). Retrieved from https://www.usnews.com/education/best-graduate-schools/the-short-list-grad-school/articles/nursing-masters-programs-with-the-highest-acceptance-rates. Accessed June 20, 2020.

108. For-Profit NP admissions ... I thought they were joking! Allnurses. https://allnurses.com/for-profit-np-admissions-i-thought-t657202/?fb-clid=IwAR3ww5dA0DRDtUh5S_UfOz7qLtoewDAeE8iPXpbl6ElxM9LW-w75mae-fG1s. Published June 9, 2019. Accessed June 10, 2020.

109. P. Jenson. Facebook message [screenshot].

110. Staff Writers. Are there NP Programs for Non-Nurses? (Direct Entry). Retrieved from https://www.nursepractitionerschools.com/faq/can-a-non-nurse-become-an-np/. Accessed May 21, 2020.

111. CNL (Direct Entry) . University of Virginia School of Nursing. https://www.nursing.virginia.edu/academics/msn/cnl/. Accessed June 20, 2020.

112. Marquette University Nursing. Becoming a Nurse Practitioner with a Non-Nursing Bachelor's. Distance MSN Programs. https://mastersnursing.marquette.edu/blog/becoming-a-nurse-practitioner-with-a-non-nursing-bachelors-degree/. Published May 11, 2020. Accessed June 9, 2020.

113. D. Grieger. Personal communication. October 18, 2018.

114. Direct Entry MSN For Aspiring Nurses with a Non-Nursing Degree. (n.d.). Retrieved June 18, 2020, from https://www.rntomsnedu.org/direct-entry-msn/.

115. Staff Writers. Schools with Online Nurse Practitioner Programs. Retrieved from https://www.nursepractitionerschools.com/online/. Published November 18, 2019.

116. Family Nurse Practitioner Program. https://nursing.columbusstate.edu/fnp.php. Published March 12, 2020. Accessed June 20, 2020.

117. 10 Fastest Online MSN Degree Programs for 2020. (n.d.). Retrieved June 10, 2020, from https://www.besthealthdegrees.com/accelerated-msn-programs-online.

118. RN to MSN Bridge Program–Family Nurse Practitioner (FNP). (n.d.). Retrieved June 10, 2020, from https://www.mcphs.edu/academics/school-of-nursing/nursing/family-nurse-practioner-rn-to-msn.

119. Bray, C. O., & Olson, K. K. Family nurse practitioner clinical requirements: Is the best recommendation 500 hours? *Journal of the American Academy of Nurse Practitioners.* 2009;21(3):135–139. https://doi.org/10.1111/j.1745-7599.2008.00384.x.

120. Preceptor Matching Service for NP Students. (n.d.). Retrieved from https://www.preceptorlink.com/. Accessed June 11, 2020.

121. Staff Writers. (2020, June 8). How do nurse practitioners become certified? | NP board certification. NursePractitionerSchools.com. https://www.nursepractitionerschools.com/faq/how-to-earn-np-certification/. Accessed June 20, 2020.

122. BoardVitals ANCC vs AANP: which FNP exam should I take? https://www.boardvitals.com/blog/ancc-aanp-fnp-exam/#:~:text=ANCC%3A%20In%202015%2C%20the%20average,the%20FNP%20exam%20was%2081.4%25. Published February 10, 2020. Accessed June 12, 2020.

123. Frequently asked questions – Exam – AANPCB. (n.d.). The American Academy of Nurse Practitioners Certification Board. https://www.aanp-cert.org/faq-exam#:~:text=To%20retake%20the%20examination%2C%20you,you%20sat%20for%20your%20exam, Accessed June 12, 2020.

124. United States Medical Licensing Examination®. https://www.usmle.org/, Accessed June 10, 2020.

125. One-day family medicine certification examination. (n.d.). American Board of Family Medicine | ABFM | American Board of Family Medicine. https://www.theabfm.org/continue-certification/cognitive-expertise/one-day-fmc-exam, Accessed June 12, 2020.

126. Taking the internal medicine board exam. (n.d.). NEJM Knowledge+. https://knowledgeplus.nejm.org/products/internal-medicine-board

-exam/#:~:text=Internal%20Medicine%20Board%20Exam%20 Day,exams%20are%20approximately%2010%20hours.

127. When and how exams offered. Board Certification | Medical | Physician | Board Exam | Recertification. https://www.abpsus.org/when-how-exams-offered. Published January 11, 2013. Accessed June 10, 2020.

128. Frequently asked questions – Recertification – AANPCB. (n.d.). The American Academy of Nurse Practitioners Certification Board. https:// www.aanpcert.org/faq-recertification. Accessed June 10, 2020.

129. Complete list of common nursing certifications. (n.d.). Nurse.org. https:// nurse.org/articles/nursing-certifications-credentials-list/#:~:text=Nurse. org%20has%20compiled%20an,links%20to%20their%20certifying%20 organizations, Accessed February 10, 2020.

130. The consensus model for APRN regulation: Licensure, accreditation, certification, and education. *Journal of Nursing Regulation*. 2018;8(4):S48. https:// doi.org/10.1016/s2155-8256(18)30033-4.

131. Are you considering a career as a family nurse practitioner? American Association of Nurse Practitioners. Published July 3, 2019. https://www. aanp.org/news-feed/are-you-considering-a-career-as-a-family-nurse-practitioner. Accessed August 9, 2020.

132. Georgetown University School of Nursing and Health Studies. Retrieved August 9, 2020 from https://requestinfo.online.nursing.georgetown.edu/ fnp7-d.html?experimentid=18094470949&x=FNOF&s=search_nonbrand_ google&l=GGL_GU-Nursing_SEM_TIER2_ALL_NBD_Exact_OFL_STD_ AMB_Family&ef_id=c:340245084226_d:c_n:g_ti:kwd-108670316&ds_ rl=1283482&ds_rl=1283482&gclid=Cj0KCQjwvb75BRD1ARIsAP6Lcq-s9IqLjD3HL2YOu40fuXiZGR4Q53_l6gg-yJL5zfPS-gQMTvquxX5caAh-F1EALw_wcB&gclsrc=aw.ds.

133. Chamberlain University. Retrieved August 9, 2020 from https://go. chamberlain.edu/NP.html?vc=300460&ab.sc=iProspect-Non-Brand-Paid-Search-NP&ca.mp=GOOGLE&ca.kw=family%20nurse%20 practitioner&ca.target=aud-357304201667:kwd-108670316&ca. cr=447185400446&ca.mt=e&cb.device=c&ca.network=g&gclid=Cj0KCQ-jwvb75BRD1ARIsAP6LcquS9Ism0HfnA10QF4DaeOniOfCJJEGIrPmrC-no20-vW3cGasBlXxRwaAurXEALw_wcB&gclsrc=aw.ds.

134. Online MSN to DNP for Advanced Nursing Roles. University of Southern Alabama. Accessed August 9, 2020 from https://www.southalabama. edu/colleges/con/dnp/msn_dnp.html.

135. AACN. Exam Handbook. Adult-Gerontology Acute Care Nurse Practitioner Certification. Retrieved August 9, 2020 from https://www.aacn.

org/~/media/aacn-website/certification/get-certified/handbooks/acnp-cagexamhandbook.pdf.

136. Nurse Journal. FNP vs ACNP + Core Differences. https://nursejournal. org/family-practice/fnp-vs-acnp-core-differences/. Published June 3, 2020. Accessed August 9, 2020.

137. Martsolf, G., Gigli, K., Reynolds, B., & McCorkle, M. Misalignment of Specialty Nurse Practitioners and the Consensus Model: A Potentially Looming Crisis. *Nursing Outlook*. Published March 1, 2020. https://doi. org/10.1016/j.outlook.2020.03.001.

138. NP Fact Sheet. American Association of Nurse Practitioners. https://www. aanp.org/about/all-about-nps/np-fact-sheet. Accessed June 10, 2020.

139. U.S. Department of Health and Human Services, Health Resources and Services Administration, National Center for Health Workforce Analysis. Highlights From the 2012 National Sample Survey of Nurse Practitioners. Rockville, Maryland: U.S. Department of Health and Human Services, 2014 [PDF].Retrieved from https://bhw.hrsa.gov/sites/default/files/ bhw/nchwa/npsurveyhighlights.pdf. Accessed June 10, 2020.

140. Dorothy LaCombe MSN, ANP-BC Nurse Practitioner PLLC. (n.d.). Retrieved June 10, 2020, from https://dorothylacombenp.com/home/ staff/dorothy-lacombe-msn-anp-bc-nurse-practitioner-pllc/.

141. Staff writers. A Day in the Life of an Aesthetic Nurse Practitioner (Cosmetic NP). NursePractitionerSchools.com. https://web.archive.org/save/ https://www.nursepractitionerschools.com/blog/day-in-the-life-of-an-aesthetic-np/. Published June 8, 2020, Accessed June 10, 2020.

142. Anonymous. Personal communication. February 10, 2020.

143. Becher, K. I Referred My Patients to Subspecialists; So Why Did They See NPs? AAFP Home.https://www.aafp.org/news/blogs/freshperspec-tives/entry/i_referred_my_patients_to.html?fbclid=IwAR3Lkd2w1sa68t-JcWUh5UZpSNk_Emj9WB54mXeQbz0TKvn0h-jASq57bBDA. Published May 30, 2017. Accessed February 9, 2020.

144. Antineoplastic therapy ordering protocol allows APPs to 'expand their scope of practice'. Healio. https://www.healio.com/hematology-oncology/practice-management/news/print/hemonc-today/{2f2496dd-ef3f-46bf-b5d8-cd9d37efb412}/antineoplastic-therapy-ordering-protocol-al-lows-apps-to-expand-their-scope-of-practice?fbclid=IwAR3ZGkpNjIK4Y-wRLJ8QNYwK3ZckQsdh1JGg66hf7hXF72BWjeYWqTDXufg0. Accessed June 10, 2020.

145. Psychiatric-Mental Health Nurse Practitioner (Lifespan). Educational Formats | Psychiatric-Mental Health Nurse Practitioner (Lifespan)

(Lifespan)|MSN|School of Nursing|Vanderbilt University. https://web.archive.org/save/https://nursing.vanderbilt.edu/msn/pmhnp/pmhnp_format.php. Accessed June 20, 2020.

146. Become a Psychiatric Nurse Practitioner (PMHNP). Nursing License Map. https://nursinglicensemap.com/advanced-practice-nursing/nurse-practitioner/psychiatric-and-mental-health-nurse-practitioner-pmhnp/?fbclid=IwAR3Mk9jtPLDuF9MBdEHnDGGz1d_V42qK6r6AuHiHi-epJK5zXrU7hZWyP1WU. Accessed June 20, 2020.

147. Bernard, R. Physician replacements affecting vulnerable patient populations. Medical Economics. https://www.medicaleconomics.com/med-ec-blog/physician-replacements-affecting-vulnerable-patient-populations/page/0/2. Published May 9, 2018. Accessed February 10, 2020.

148. Ibid.

149. Thoman, R. Personal communication. August 6, 2020.

150. Duprey, R. Personal communication. June 20, 2019.

151. Hiring psychiatric nurse practitioner or psychiatrist – $180,000–200,000 per year [Screenshot]. Indeed.com. Accessed March 10, 2019.

152. Richards, E. P. The problems of certified registered nurse anesthetists. Law and the Physician Homepage. Retrieved from: https://biotech.law.lsu.edu/Books/lbb/x943.htm Published 1993. Accessed March 3, 2020.

153. Ibid.

154. American Association of Nurse Anesthetists. CRNAs: We are the Answer. [PDF] Retrieved June 10, 2020 from https://www.aana.com/docs/default-source/marketing-aana-com-web-documents-(all)/crnas-we-are-the-answer.pdf?sfvrsn=b310d913_4.

155. American Society of Anesthesiologists. Summary of research studies comparing anesthesia professionals [PDF]. Retrieved June 10, 2020 from file:///C:/Users/rebek/Downloads/researchcomparinganesthprofs-two-pages%20(1).pdf. Published 2016.

156. Silber, J. H., Kennedy, S. K., & Even-Shoshan, O., et al. Anesthesiologist direction and patient outcomes. *Anesthesiology*. 2000;93(1):152–163. doi:10.1097/00000542-200007000-00026.

157. Buschi, R. Co-Defendant CRNA denies responsibility for failed resuscitation. https://www.omic.com/co-defendant-crna-denies-responsibility-for-failed-resuscitation/. Published Summer 2012. Accessed August 10, 2020.

158. Egerton, B. No discipline. Big payout for girl's death, but state does nothing. Dallas News. http://interactives.dallasnews.com/2015/deadly-dentistry/part3.html. Published December 9, 2015. Accessed August 10, 2020.

159. Sexton, C. Nursing Board Signs Off On 'Anesthesiologist' Title. WGCU PBS & NPR for Southwest Florida. https://news.wgcu.org/post/nursing-board-signs-anesthesiologist-title. Published May 11, 2020. Accessed June 9, 2020.

160. Anesthesia Patient Safety Foundation. A Note from the APSF President about Support of APSF. Retrieved from https://www.apsf.org/news-updates/a-note-from-the-apsf-president-about-support-of-apsf/?fbclid=IwAR39hFedLyZmZtqmZQb_WCwKKsWNMRcqLLfkV7nCjRb-Vn.d.WjwG3a-ZINaw. Published March 24, 2019. Accessed June 9, 2020.

161. APRN Consensus Work Group. (n.d.) Retrieved fromhttps://www.midwife.org/ACNM/files/ccLibraryFiles/Filename/000000001766/APRN%20Consensus%20Model%20Final%20Report_july_7_2008.pdf. Accessed February 20, 2020.

162. Apply. (n.d.). Retrieved from https://frontier.edu/nurse-midwife/. Accessed June 20, 2020.

163. Nurse-Midwifery/Family Nurse Practitioner. (n.d.). Retrieved June 20, 2020 from https://nursing.vanderbilt.edu/msn/nmwfnp/nmwfnp_format.php.

164. CBS News. Physician exposes dangerous practice involving high-risk pregnancies at Indiana hospital Retrieved from https://stories.usatodaynetwork.com/failuretodeliver/#. Published June 14, 2019, Accessed January 10, 2020.

165. Physician exposes dangerous practice involving high-risk pregnancies at Indiana hospital. Retrieved from https://www.cbsnews.com/news/whistleblower-physician-exposes-dangerous-practice-involving-high-risk-pregnancies-at-indiana-hospital/?fbclid=IwAR3V1lqPxXu0wC_pUA9vrhgOEgPVqgbbXW3jzGfBRsBk1WpSuSxo52H6B5E. Published June 14, 2019. Accessed January 10, 2020.

166. DNP Fact Sheet. DNP Fact Sheet. Retrieved from https://www.aacnnursing.org/News-Information/Fact-Sheets/DNP-Fact-Sheet. Published 2019. Accessed June 20, 2020.

167. O. Weinhold. Personal communication. April 21, 2019.

168. Mundinger, M. O., & Carter, M. A. Potential Crisis in Nurse Practitioner Preparation in the United States. *Policy Polit Nurs Pract*. 2019;20(2):57–63. doi:10.1177/1527154419838630.

169. Curriculum & Course Faculty. (n.d.). Retrieved June 22, 2020, from https://dev.nursing.duke.edu/academic-programs/dnp-program-nursing/dnp-curriculum-course-faculty.

170. Chamberlain University. Doctor of Nursing Practice (DNP) Degree Program Healthcare Systems Leadership (HSL) Specialty Track. [PDF].

Retrieved from http://www.aspmn.org/Documents/Chamberlin_Univ/DNP%20Curriculum%201.2017.pdf. Accessed on June 22, 2020.

171. Doctor of Nursing Practice. (n.d.). Retrieved June 22, 2020, from https://www.aacnnursing.org/DNP/DNP-Essentials.

172. Staff writers. FAQ: How Long is a BSN to DNP Program? Retrieved June 22, 2020, from https://www.onlinefnpprograms.com/faqs/length-of-bsn-to-dnp-programs/. Published July 1, 2019.

173. Ibid.

174. Health eCareers. Doctor of Nursing Practice: An Origin Story. Retrieved June 22, 2020, from https://www.healthecareers.com/article/career/doctor-of-nursing-practice-an-origin-story. Published December 4, 2015.

175. DeCapua, M. Why pursue a DNP? NursePractitionerSchools.com. https://www.nursepractitionerschools.com/faq/why-pursue-a-dnp-degree/. Published May 8, 2020. Retrieved June 20, 2020.

176. Cassell, E. J. Historical Perspective of Medical Residency Training: 50 Years of Changes.*JAMA*.1999;281(13):1231.doi:10.1001/jama.281.13.1231-JMS0407-6-1.

177. Weiss, P., Kryger, M., & Knauert, M. Impact of extended duty hours on medical trainees. *Sleep health*. 2016;2(4):309–315. https://doi.org/10.1016/j.sleh.2016.08.003.

178. Accreditation. (n.d.). Retrieved June 22, 2020, from https://www.acgme.org/What-We-Do/Accreditation.

179. Nurse Practitioner Fellowship and Residency Programs. (n.d.). Retrieved June 22, 2020, from https://www.graduatenursingedu.org/nurse-practitioner-residency-programs/.

180. Ibid.

CHAPTER 3

181. US Physicians Hear About Warnings and Hopes. The Milwaukee Journal. June 23, 1972. Accessed June 20, 2020.

182. National Commission on Certification of Physician Assistants, Inc. 2018 Statistical Profile of Certified Physician Assistants: An Annual Report of the National Commission on Certification of Physician Assistants. Retrieved June 20, 2020, from http://www.nccpa.net/research. Published April 2019.

183. Is It Time to Ditch the Name 'Physician Assistant'? Advisory Board Daily Briefing, www.advisory.com/daily-briefing/2019/05/31/physician-assistant. Published May 31, 2019. Accessed June 20, 2020.

184. Ibid.

185. Lane, S. From Physician Assistant to PA. PA Professional. [PDF], Retrieved June 20, 2020 from https://www.chlm.org/wp-content/uploads/2017/10/Just_Say_PA.pdf. Published 2017.

186. Harris, G. When the Nurse Wants to Be Called Doctor. *The New York Times*. Retrieved September 15, 2019 from https://www.nytimes.com/2011/10/02/health/policy/02docs.html. Published October 1, 2011.

187. Truth in Advertising Campaign. Truth in Advertising Campaign. Retrieved June 20, 2020 from https://www.ama-assn.org/system/files/2018-10/truth-in-advertising-campaign-booklet.pdf. Published 2010.

188. Anderson, J. Navigating the waters of independently practicing physician assistants. Clinical Advisor. Published March 9, 2018. Accessed August 9, 2020 from https://www.clinicaladvisor.com/home/the-waiting-room/navigating-the-waters-of-independently-practicing-physician-assistants/.

189. Optimal Team Practice: Learn More About OTP. AAPA, www.aapa.org/advocacy-central/optimal-team-practice/. Accessed June 20, 2020.

190. Ibid.

191. Your PA Can Handle It. https://yourpacan.org/ Accessed June 13, 2020.

192. Pasquini, S. Direct Entry and Dual Degree BS/MS Pre-Physician Assistant Programs. The Physician Assistant Life. www.thepalife.com/direct-entry-and-dual-degree-bsms-physician-assistant-programs/. Published February 15, 2020.

193. Are PAs Part of the Solution to the Physician Shortage? WTOP. wtop.com/news/2018/12/are-pas-part-of-the-solution-to-the-physician-shortage/. Published January 4, 2019. Accessed June 20, 2020.

194. Ibid.

195. H. Travers. Personal communication. April 15, 2020.

196. Pasquini, Stephen, et al. Physician Assistant Programs Offering Part-Time Options. The Physician Assistant Life. www.thepalife.com/physician-assistant-programs-offering-part-time-options/. Published May 7, 2019. Accessed June 10, 2020.

197. Tuition and Fees. Tuition and Financial Aid | Yale School of Medicine, paonline.yale.edu/admissions/tuition-and-financial-aid/.

198. The 2020 Guide to Online Physician Assistant (PA) Programs. Teach, teach.com/online-ed/healthcare-degrees/online-pa-programs/. Accessed June 20, 2020.

199. MD vs. NP vs. PA: Here's How the Number of Clinical Hours Compare. ThriveAP, thriveap.com/blog/md-vs-np-vs-pa-heres-how-number-clinical-hours-compare. Published January 10, 2017. Accessed June 10, 2020.

200. Primary Care Coalition. Compare the Education Gaps between Primary Care Physicians and Nurse Practitioners. [PDF]. Retrieved from https://

www.tafp.org/Media/Default/Downloads/advocacy/scope-education. pdf on June 13, 2020. Accessed January 10, 2020.

201. Carder, Pam. Doctor of Medical Science. University of Lynchburg, www.lynchburg.edu/academics/college-of-health-sciences/physician-assistant-medicine/doctor-of-medical-science/?utm_source=-Google&utm_medium=Search&utm_campaign=DMSc&utm_content=-Davion&gclid=CjwKCAjw8pH3BRAXEiwA1pvMsWU9hOXVXdoFPD-KJP_ddPpqKhoNP5jn5zbfKeyykeYh_MliAcMEfpRoC3y8QAvD_BwE. Accessed June 20, 2020.

202. Champigney, D. Physician Assistant Doctorate. Medgeeks. medgeeks.co/articles/physician-assistant-doctorate. Published January 1, 2019. Accessed June 10, 2020.

203. Slaby, M. J. LMU Adds Doctor of Medical Science Program. archive.knoxnews.com/news/local/lmu-adds-doctor-of-medical-science-program-293b4a59-a666-473c-e053-0100007f6fc7-365346471.html/. Published January 14, 2016. Accessed June 20, 2020.

204. Louissaint, M. 'It totally prepared me for this': University of Lynchburg student skips graduation to treat COVID-19 patients in New York. Retrieved from https://www.wsls.com/news/local/2020/04/10/it-totally-prepared-me-for-this-university-of-lynchburg-medical-student-skips-graduation-to-treat-covid-19-patients-in-new-york/. Published April 13, 2020. Accessed April 20, 2020.

205. Tanner, B. How do Physician Assistants Specialize? Quora, Retrieved from https://www.quora.com/How-do-physician-assistants-specialize. Accessed June 14, 2020.

206. Physician Assistant subthread. Reddit. https://www.reddit.com/r/prephysicianassistant/. Accessed February 10, 2020.

207. Fishfader, Vicki, et al. Physician Assistant Student and Faculty Perceptions of Physician Assistant Residency Training Programs. *The Journal of Physician Assistant Education.* 2002;13(1)34–38. doi:10.1097/01367895-200213010-00006.

208. Necessary, J. How do Physician Assistants Specialize? Quora, Retrieved from https://www.quora.com/How-do-physician-assistants-specialize. Accessed June 14, 2020.

209. Saley, C. Explosive Growth for PAs Says the 2016 AAPA PA Salary Report. Retrieved from https://comphealth.com/resources/2016-pa-salary-report/. Published June 1, 2018. Accessed February 10, 2020.

210. Keith Chen, J. C. Is Medical School a Worthwhile Investment for Women? Retrieved from https://www.theatlantic.com/health/archive/2012/07/is-medical-school-a-worthwhile-investment-for-women/260051/. Published June 30, 2015. Accessed September 10, 2019.

211. Giordano, C. M. From PA to MD: An appreciation for physician education. Retrieved from https://www.kevinmd.com/blog/2014/10/pa-md-appreciation-physician-education.html. Published October 13, 2014. Accessed September 10, 2019.

212. PAs across America celebrate First State with key components of optimal team practice following the legislative victory in North Dakota. AAPA. https://www.aapa.org/news-central/2019/04/pas-across-america-celebrate-first-state-with-key-components-of-optimal-team-practice-following-the-legislative-victory-in-north-dakota/. Published July 23, 2019. Accessed June 20, 2020.

213. Big news for OTP in North Dakota. (n.d.). North Dakota Academy of Physician Assistants NDAPA | My PA Network. https://ndapa.mypanetwork.com/physician-assistant-news/425-big-news-for-otp-in-north-dakota. Accessed June 10, 2020.

214. @ChrissyPA_C,_ATC. #PAs have the unique ability to move and fill gaps in the healthcare teams. We are embracing our ability to "pivot" from one field to another to meet the demands of this healthcare crisis. #InItToPivot #Covid19 #PAsAreTheSolution #PAsNeedFullPracticeAuthority. Retrieved from https://twitter.com/chrissyPA_C_ATC/status/1246064312206180352 on June 14, 2020. Published April 3, 2020.

215. Maine legislature fast tracks PA legislation to help combat COVID-19. AAPA. https://www.aapa.org/news-central/2020/03/maine-legislature-fast-tracks-pa-legislation-to-help-combat-covid-19/. Published March 27, 2020. Accessed June 10, 2020.

216. Gov. Reynolds signs legislation expanding roles for physician assistants | Office of the governor of Iowa. https://governor.iowa.gov/press-release/gov-reynolds-signs-legislation-expanding-roles-for-physician-assistants#:~:text=Today%20Gov.,Reynolds. March 18, 2020. Accessed June 10, 2020.

217. Jones Day. (2020, March). States Relax Physician Assistant Supervision and Delegation Laws. https://www.jonesday.com/en/insights/2020/03/states-relax-physician-assistant-supervision-and-d. Accessed June 10, 2020.

218. @PA_C_Life. I had no idea how many PAs out there want full practice authority. Do they not realize that they can get it …. by going to med school? https://twitter.com/PA_C_Life/status/1248629279174176769. Published April 10, 2020. Accessed April 10, 2020.

219. American Psychological Association. Retrieved from https://www.apa.org/topics/about-psychologists. Published December 11, 2019. Accessed June 10, 2020.

220. American College of Neuropsychopharmacology. DoD Prescribing Psychologists: External Analysis, Monitoring, and Evaluation of the Program

and its Participants [PDF] Retrieved from February 10, 2020 https://www.esd.whs.mil/Portals/54/Documents/FOID/Reading%20Room/Personnel_Related/Prescribe_Psychologists.pdf. 1998.

221. Dittman, M. Psychology's first prescribers. Retrieved February 10, 2020 from https://www.apa.org/monitor/feb03/prescribers. Published February 2003.

222. Fox, R. E., DeLeon, P. H., Newman, R., Sammons, M. T., Dunivin, D. L., & Backer, D. C. Prescriptive authority and psychology: A status report. *American Psychologist*. 2009;64(4):257–268.

223. AMA Physician Masterfile, Center for Medicare and Medicaid Services. ama-assn.org/go/healthworkforcemapper. Accessed June 10, 2020.

224. Madara, J. Letter from the American Medical Association to Mr. Ron Biel Program Manager Division of Public Health, Licensure Unit Nebraska Department of Health and Human Services [PDF] Retrieved from https://drive.google.com/drive/u/0/search?q=psychology. Published April 7, 2017. Accessed June 11, 2020.

225. Psychologists Prescribing: Release of Data Reveal Facts on the Ground in Louisiana and New Mexico [PDF]. Retrieved from https://drive.google.com/drive/u/0/search?q=psychology. Accessed June 12, 2020.

226. Why do we oppose RxP? (n.d.). Retrieved February 10, 2020 from https://www.poppp.org/blank.

227. Golding, R. CDCR Mental System Report. [PDF] Retrieved June 10, 2020 from https://rbgg.com/wp-content/uploads/Dkt-5988-1-Redacted-REPORT-of-MICHAEL-GOLDING-OCR-10-31-2018-489-3.pdf. Published October 31, 2018.

228. T. Sepah. Personal communication. May 10, 2020.

229. National Alliance of State Pharmacy Associations. Retrieved June 10, 2020 from https://naspa.us/resource/swp/. Published November 9, 2018.

230. Sexton, C. Gov. DeSantis signs major bills on nurses, pharmacists. Retrieved June 20, 2020 from https://www.news4jax.com/news/local/2020/03/11/house-speakers-health-care-reform-bills-head-to-gov-desantis/. Published March 11, 2020.

231. Centers for Medicare and Medicaid Services. CMCS Informational Bulletin. January 17, 2017. Retrieved July 27, 2020 from https://www.medicaid.gov/sites/default/files/federal-policy-guidance/downloads/cib011717.pdf.

232. O'Brien, J. How nurse practitioners obtained provider status: lessons for pharmacists, *American Journal of Health-System Pharmacy*. 2003;60(22):2301–2307. https://doi.org/10.1093/ajhp/60.22.2301.

233. Gabler, E. How Chaos at Chain Pharmacies is Putting Patients at Risk. *New York Times.* Retrieved from https://www.nytimes.com/2020/01/31/health/pharmacists-medication-errors.html. Published January 31, 2020.

234. Requirements to Become a Pharmacy Technician. (n.d.). Retrieved February 10, 2020 from https://www.medicaltechnologyschools.com/pharmacy-technician/how-to-become-pharmacy-tech.

235. Benavides, S., & Rambaran, K. A. Pharmacy technicians: Expanding role with uniform expectations, education and limits in scope of practice. *J Res Pharm Pract.* 2013;2(4):135–137. doi:10.4103/2279-042X.128141.

236. Kekevian, B. Expanding Scope of Practice: Lessons and Leverage. Retrieved June 20, 2020 from https://www.reviewofoptometry.com/article/expanding-scope-of-practice-lessons-and-leverage. Published October 15, 2018.

237. Ocular Surgery News: Optometric integration and scope of practice still disputed. Retrieved June 20, 2020 from https://www.healio.com/news/ophthalmology/20190517/optometric-integration-and-scope-of-practice-still-disputed. Published 2019.

238. Coulter, I., & Sandefur, R. Chiropractic in the United States: Licensure and Scope of Practice. https://www.chirobase.org/05RB/AHCPR/05.html. Accessed June 13, 2020.

239. Lamm, L. C., Wegner, E., & Collord, D. Chiropractic scope of practice: what the law allows--update 1993. *J Manipulative Physiol Ther.* 1995;18(1):16–20.

240. Madden, M. Chiropractor brings brain-based therapy to Ringgold. Retrieved February 14, 2020 from https://web.archive.org/save/https://www.timesfreepress.com/news/community/story/2018/dec/26/chiropractor-brings-brabased-therapy-ringgold/485360/?fbclid=IwAR1-9xU-jZnUSjh2USsRLqYn2S8-zlVJdBUOw3QT-G_F1a2KMcikI7zRwe-g. Published December 26, 2018.

241. Gerry, A. Family gives warning about bats after man becomes Utah's first fatal rabies case in over 70 years. Retrieved February 14, 2020 from https://fox13now.com/2018/11/08/utah-man-dies-from-rabies-the-first-case-in-over-70-years/?fbclid=IwAR3RjRljMEWTJaeM8RE8bsNAuYqPCiy35ABD-M4wjPJ_X3fXhvCyhSo6tJmM. Published November 9, 2018.

242. Constantine, R. 7 Times 'Modern Alternative Mama' Was So Stupid She Was Dangerous. Retrieved February 15, 2020 from https://whatculture.com/offbeat/7-times-39-modern-alternative-mama-39-was-so-stupid-she-was-dangerous. Published October 5, 2016.

243. Chiropractor crackdown: College gives ultimatum on misleading health claims|CBC News. Retrieved February 15, 2020 from https://www.cbc.ca/news/canada/british-columbia/chiropractor-crackdown-college-

gives-ultimatum-on-misleading-health-claims-1.4861575?fbclid=IwAR02
gieq76WzooSLuengBLEGN13gZXYwO4Sdy9ncsA4Qkq1RLq3Q8Ld-
QOsA. Published October 15, 2018.

244. Atwood, K. Naturopathy: A Critical Appraisal. (2003, December 30).
Retrieved August 9, 2020, from https://www.medscape.com/view
article/465994.

245. Fleming, S. A., & Gutknecht, N. C. Naturopathy and the primary care
practice. *Primary Care*. 2010;37(1):119–136. https://doi.org/10.1016/j.pop.
2009.09.002.

246. LaCorte, R. State's Medicaid Program Now Covers Naturopaths. *The Seattle
Times*. Retrieved June 10, 2020 from https://www.seattletimes.com/seat-
tle-news/statersquos-medicaid-program-now-covers-naturopaths/#:~:-
text=Naturopathic%20doctors%20are%20licensed%20in,Washington%20
joined%20Vermont%20and%20Oregon. Published May 25, 2014.

247. Perry, N. 2 Naturopathic Physicians from Bastyr appointed to Medicare
Advisory Group. The Seattle Times. Retrieved June 20, 2020 from https://
archive.seattletimes.com/archive/?date=20030127&slug=bastyr27e. Published January 27, 2003.

248. Naturopaths can't suggest they're 'medically trained,' New Brunswick
judge rules|CBC News. Retrieved February 15, 2020 from https://
www.cbc.ca/news/canada/new-brunswick/naturopaths-naturopath-
ic-clinic-new-brunswick-saint-john-moncton-fredericton-1.4950901?fb-
clid=IwAR0-Rac59kry7HVZtBv_NmYTdwIILASHUxUd4EtLI2fvnDy-
Ga-ZP5NdS534. Published December 18, 2018.

249. What's the harm? What's the harm in naturopathy? http://whatstheharm.
net/naturopathy.html. Accessed June 13, 2020.

250. Naturopath guilty of manslaughter will get hearing at Supreme Court.
Retrieved February 15, 2020 from https://montreal.ctvnews.ca/natu-
ropath-guilty-of-manslaughter-will-get-hearing-at-supreme-court-
1.4207481. Published December 6, 2018.

251. Naturopathic Death from IV Turmeric. (n.d.). Retrieved February 20, 2020 from
https://sciencebasedmedicine.org/naturopathic-death-from-iv-turmeric/.

252. Alberta mom asked naturopath for help before toddler died of meningitis,
court hears|CBC News. Retrieved February 15, 2020 from https://www.
cbc.ca/news/canada/calgary/naturopath-says-collet-stephan-asked-for-
something-for-meningitis-1.3484501. Published March 15, 2016.

253. Rose, S. American missionary in 'unlawful medical practice' suit after
babies died in Uganda. Retrieved June 13, 2020 from https://www.cnn.
com/2019/07/03/africa/renee-bach-lawsuit-uganda-intl/index.html.
Published July 4, 2019.

254. Kruk, M. E., Gage, A. D., Joseph, N. T., Danaei, G., García-Saisó, S., & Salomonm, J. A. Mortality due to low-quality health systems in the universal health coverage era: a systematic analysis of amenable deaths in 137 countries [published correction appears in Lancet. 2018 Sep 20]. Lancet. 2018;392(10160):2203–2212. doi:10.1016/S0140-6736(18)31668-4.

255. Schreiber, M. What Kills 5 Million People A Year? It's Not Just Disease. Retrieved June 10, 2020 from https://www.npr.org/sections/goatsand-soda/2018/09/05/644928153/what-kills-5-million-people-a-year-its-not-just-disease. Published September 5, 2018.

CHAPTER 4

256. Kruger, J., & Dunning, D. Unskilled and unaware of it: How difficulties in recognizing one's own incompetence lead to inflated self-assessments. *Journal of Personality and Social Psychology*. 1999;77(6): 1121–1134. doi:10.1037/0022-3514.77.6.1121.

257. Dunning, D. We Are All Confident Idiots. Retrieved February 20, 2020 from https://psmag.com/social-justice/confident-idiots-92793. Published October 27, 2014.

258. Craig, P. Tragedy of girl, 10, who died hours after seeing nurse. Retrieved September 20, 2020 from https://www.grimsbytelegraph.co.uk/news/grimsby-news/tragedy-girl-10-who-died-1667924. Published June 13, 2018.

259. C. Majerus. Personal Communication. April 14, 2020.

260. Ericsson, K. A. *Toward a general theory of expertise: Prospects and limits*. Cambridge: Cambridge University Press; 2010.

261. Chase, W. G., & Simon, H. A. The mind's eye in chess. In W.G. Chase (Ed.) *Visual information processing*. San Diego, CA: Academic Press; 1973:215–281.

262. Raskin, E. Comparison of scientific and literary ability: A biographical study of eminent scientists and letters of the nineteenth century. *Journal of Abnormal and Social Psychology*. 1936;31:20–35.

263. Lesgold, A. M. Acquiring Expertise. In J. R. Anderson & S. M. Kosslyn (Eds.) *Tutorials in learning and memory: Essays in honor of Gordon Bower*. New York: Freeman; 1984:31–60.

264. Patel, V. L., & Groen, G. J. The general and specific nature of medical expertise: A critical look. In K. A. Ericsson & J. Smith (Eds.) *Toward a general theory of expertise*. Cambridge, England: Cambridge University Press; 1991:93–125.

265. D. Grieger. Personal communication. October 2, 2018.

266. H. Travers. Personal communication. April 15, 2020.

267. A quote by William Osler. (n.d.). Goodreads | Meet your next favorite-book. https://www.goodreads.com/quotes/3221915-listen-to-your-patient-he-is-telling-you-the-diagnosis. Accessed June 20, 2020.

268. Association of American Medical Colleges. Applicants, First-Time Applicants, Acceptees, and Matriculants to U.S. Medical Schools by Sex, 2007–2008 through 2016–2017 [Internet]Washington, DC: [cited 2017 Nov 05]. Available from:https://www.aamc.org/download/321470/data/factstablea7.pdf. [Ref list].

269. "2015 Performance Data". United States Medical Licensing Examination. 2016. Retrieved 16 April 2016.

270. American Board of Comprehensive Care. Exam Pass Rates. [Screenshots]. Retrieved from http://abcc.dnpcert.org/.

271. National Board of Medical Examiners Statement on Doctor of Nursing Practice (DNP) Certification [PDF]. Retrieved June 22, 2020 from http://www.studentdo.com/files/political_affairs/nbome_statement_dnp_cert.pdf.

272. Park, R. Why So Many Young Doctors Work Such Awful Hours. Retrieved September 10, 2019 from https://www.theatlantic.com/business/archive/2017/02/doctors-long-hours-schedules/516639/. Published March 16, 2017.

273. Landrigan, C. P., Barger, L. K., Cade, B. E., Ayas, N. T., & Czeisler, C. A. Interns' Compliance with Accreditation Council for Graduate Medical Education Work-Hour Limits. *JAMA*. 2006;296(9):1063–1070. doi:10.1001/jama.296.9.1063.

274. Rampell, C. Solving the Shortage in Primary Care Doctors. New York Times. Retrieved June 13, 2020 from https://www.nytimes.com/2013/12/15/business/solving-the-shortage-in-primary-care-doctors.html?_r=0. Published December 14, 2013.

275. Zavlin, D., Jubbal, K. T., Noé, J. G., & Gansbacher, B. A comparison of medical education in Germany and the United States: from applying to medical school to the beginnings of residency. *Ger Med Sci*. 2017;15:Doc15. doi:10.3205/000256.

276. Residencies for Sale. Retrieved June 10, 2020 from https://www.managedcaremag.com/archives/2019/11/residencies-sale. Published December 9, 2019.

277. Cooke, M., Irby, D. M., Sullivan, W., & Ludmerer, K. M. American medical education 100 years after the Flexner report. *N Engl J Med*. 2006;355(13):1339–1344. doi:10.1056/NEJMra055445.

278. Duffy, T. P. The Flexner Report—100 years later. *Yale J Biol Med*. 2011;84(3): 269–276.

279. Sawyer, B., & Daniel McDermott, K. F. F. (n.d.). How do mortality rates in the U.S. compare to other countries? Retrieved from https://www.healthsystemtracker.org/chart-collection/mortality-rates-u-s-compare-countries/?_sf_s=mortality#item-start.

280. Health Care Resources—Physicians Overall. Organization for Economic Cooperation. Retrieved June 10, 2020 from https://stats.oecd.org/Index.aspx?QueryId=74634.

281. Pereira Gray, D. J., Sidaway-Lee, K., & White, E., et al. Continuity of care with doctors—a matter of life and death? A systematic review of continuity of care and mortality. *BMJ Open*. 2018;8:e021161. doi: 10.1136/bmjopen-2017-021161.

282. Sanjay Basu et al. Association of Primary Care Physician Supply with Population Mortality in the United States, 2005–2015. *JAMA Intern Med*, 2019 DOI: 10.1001/jamainternmed.2018.7624.

283. Sawyer, B., & Daniel McDermott, K. F. F. (n.d.). How does the quality of the U.S. healthcare system compare to other countries? Retrieved from https://www.healthsystemtracker.org/chart-collection/quality-u-s-healthcare-system-compare-countries/#item-adults-comparable-countries-quicker-access-doctor-nurse-need-care.

284. Association of American Medical Colleges. US Medical School Enrollment up 25% since 2002. Retrieved June 20, 2020 from https://news.aamc.org/press-releases/article/enrollment-05252017/. Published May 26, 2018.

285. Organisation for Economic Co-operation and Development. Retrieved July 27, 2020 from https://stats.oecd.org/Index.aspx?QueryId=74639.

286. Wexler, R. The primary care shortage, nurse practitioners, and the patient-centered medical home. *Virtual Mentor*. 2010;12(1):36–40. doi:10.1001/virtualmentor.2010.12.1.pfor1-1001.

287. Centers for Medicare and Medicaid Services. The Graduate Nurse Education Demonstration Project: Final Evaluation Report. August 2019. Retrieved July 27, 2020 from https://innovation.cms.gov/files/reports/gne-final-eval-rpt.pdf.

288. Bowman, R. C. Measuring primary care: The standard primary care year. *Rural Remote Health*. 2008;8(3):1009. [Epub September 10, 2008.]

289. How to become a medical doctor in Germany. Retrieved February 20, 2020 from https://www.deutschland.de/en/topic/knowledge/how-to-become-a-medical-doctor-in-germany. Published March 12, 2019.

290. Meunier, Y. Retrieved February 20, 2020 from https://scopeblog.stanford.edu/2009/11/10/the_french_and/. Published November 10, 2009.

291. Medical school. Retrieved June 20, 2020 from https://en.wikipedia.org/wiki/Medical_school. Published June 8, 2020.

292. Maier, C. B., Barnes, H., Aiken, L. H., & Busse, R. Descriptive, cross-country analysis of the nurse practitioner workforce in six countries: size, growth, physician substitution potential. *BMJ Open.* 2016;6(9):e011901. doi:10.1136/bmjopen-2016-011901.

293. NCCPA. 2018 Statistical Profile of Physician Assistants. Retrieved August 10, 2020 from https://prodcmsstoragesa.blob.core.windows.net/uploads/files/2018StatisticalProfileofCertifiedPhysicianAssistants.pdf.

294. Canadian Association of Physician Assistants. PA Fact Sheet 2015. Retrieved July 27, 2020 from https://capa-acam.ca/wp-content/uploads/2014/08/PA-FACT-SHEET-2015_FINAL.pdf.

295. v Christine F. Legler, James F. Cawley & William H. Fenn. Physician assistants: education, practice and global interest, *Medical Teacher.* 2007;29(1): e22–e25, DOI: 10.1080/01421590601034696.

296. Lo, C. H. K. The development of physician assistant education in Taiwan. *Perspect Physic Assist Edu.* 2005;16:107–108.

297. The Role of GME Funding in Addressing the Physician Shortage. Retrieved June 10, 2020 from https://news.aamc.org/for-the-media/article/gme-funding-doctor-shortage//. Published May 9, 2019.

298. Weigley, S., Hess, A., & Sauter, M. B. Doctor Shortage Could Take Turn for the Worse. USA Today. Retrieved June 15, 2020 from https://www.usa-today.com/story/money/business/2012/10/20/doctors-shortage-least-most/1644837. Published October 20, 2012.

299. The Role of GME Funding in Addressing the Physician Shortage. Retrieved from June 15, 2020 https://news.aamc.org/for-the-media/article/gme-funding-doctor-shortage/. Published May 9, 2019.

300. Fagan, E. B., Gibbons, C., Finnegan, S. C., Petterson, S., Peterson, K. E., Phillips, R. L., & Bazemore, A. W. Family Medicine Graduate Proximity to Their Site of Training: Policy Options for Improving the Distribution of Primary Care Access. *Fam Med.* 2015;47(2):124–130.

301. Weigley, S., Hess, A., & Sauter, M. B. Doctor Shortage Could Take Turn for the Worse. USA Today. Retrieved from https://www.usatoday.com/story/money/business/2012/10/20/doctors-shortage-least-most/1644837. Published October 20, 2012.

302. Emanuel, E. J., & Fuchs, V. R. Shortening medical training by 30%. *JAMA.* 2012;307(11):1143–1144. doi:10.1001/jama.2012.292.

303. Giaritelli, A. Missouri Looks to Ease Doctor Shortage with 'Assistant Physicians'. *The Washington Examiner.* Retrieved July 10, 2020 from https://www.washingtonexaminer.com/missouri-looks-to-ease-doctor-shortage-with-assistant-physicians. Published June 5, 2017.

304. Mareck, D. G. Federal and state initiatives to recruit physicians to rural areas. *Virtual Mentor.* 2011;13(5):304–309. doi:10.1001/virtualmentor. 2011.13.5.pfor1-1105.

305. Green, L., Savin, S., & Lu, Y. Primary Care Physician Shortages Could Be Eliminated through Use of Teams, Nonphysicians, and Electronic Communication. *Health Affairs.* 2013;32(1):11–19.

306. Kelly, L. Doctor slams medical college group's prediction of massive doctor shortage by 2030. The Washington Examiner. Retrieved June 20, 2020 from https://www.washingtontimes.com/news/2017/mar/26/dr-ezekiel-emanuel-slams-association-of-american-m/. Published March 26, 2017.

307. Institute of Medicine. *Graduate Medical Education That Meets the Nation's Health Needs.* Washington, DC: The National Academies Press; 2014. https://doi.org/10.17226/18754.

308. Primary Care Coalition. Issue Brief: Collaboration between Physicians and Nurses Works. Retrieved July 27, 2020 from https://www.tafp.org/Media/Default/Downloads/advocacy/scope-distribution.pdf.

309. Haddad, L. M., Annamaraju, P., & Toney-Butler, T. J. Nursing Shortage. [Updated 2020 Mar 29]. In: StatPearls [Internet]. Treasure Island (FL): StatPearls Publishing; 2020 Jan-. Available from: https://www.ncbi.nlm.nih.gov/books/NBK493175/.

310. Ibid.

311. Auerbach, D. I., Buerhaus, P. I., & Staiger, D. O. Implications of The Rapid Growth of The Nurse Practitioner Workforce in the US. *Health Aff (Millwood).* 2020;39(2):273–279. doi:10.1377/hlthaff.2019.00686.

312. Institute of Medicine (US) Committee on the Robert Wood Johnson Foundation Initiative on the Future of Nursing, at the Institute of Medicine. *The Future of Nursing: Leading Change, Advancing Health.* Washington (DC): National Academies Press (US); 2011.

313. The College of the People. Retrieved June 20, 2020 from https://nightingale.edu/blog/adn-vs-bsn-differences/. Published January 31, 2017.

314. Anbari, Allison. The RN to BSN transition: A qualitative systematic review. *Global Qualitative Nursing Research.* 2015;2. Doi:10.1177/2333393615614306.

315. Nursing.org. The state of nursing 2016. Retrieved June 10, 2020 from https://www.nursing.org/wp-content/uploads/2015/10/Nursing.org_.State-ofNursing_2016.pdf.

316. Ibid.

317. American Association of Colleges of Nursing. Nursing Faculty Shortage. Retrieved July 27, 2020 from https://www.aacnnursing.org/news-information/fact-sheets/nursing-faculty-shortage.

318. Change.org. Allow LPNs to Challenge the Board of Medicine to Obtain RN Licensure. https://www.change.org/p/allow-lpns-to-challenge-the-board-of-nursing-to-obtain-rn-licensure?use_react=false. Accessed on June 14, 2020.

319. Rieger, S. Reccommendation to replace higher-educated nurses with cheaper staff could backfore, nurses warn. Retrieved June 20, 2020 from https://www.msn.com/en-ca/news/canada/recommendation-to-replace-higher-educated-nurses-with-cheaper-staff-could-backfire-nurses-warn/ar-BBZESjl?fbclid=IwAR1nD-FF6q_OwEopB1W9FRiaaQnHFyfuLZN-JVVVw9JM5nwt_ZUlmcWn8QXQ. Published February 5, 2020.

320. Ibid.

CHAPTER 5

321. Mercy El-Reno website. Evidence submitted in Amelia Ochoa v. Mercy Health Oklahoma Communities. District Court Oklahoma County, Oklahoma. 2019.

322. Mercy Health System Hospital Privileges Regulations. 2012.

323. Sinclair Affidavit, Paragraph 7, March 22, 2018.

324. Sinclair Affidavit, Paragraph 4–6, March 22, 2018.

325. Sinclair Affidavit, Paragraph 9–11, March 22, 2018.

326. Sinclair Affidavit, Paragraph 11–13, March 22, 2018.

327. Americans views on medical doctors. Retrieved June 22, 2020, from https://www.pewresearch.org/science/2019/08/02/findings-at-a-glance-medical-doctors/. Published May 30, 2020.

328. Merritt Hawkins. 2019 Physician Inpatient/ Outpatient Revenue Survey. Retrieved June 22, 2020 from https://www.merritthawkins.com/upload-edFiles/MerrittHawkins_RevenueSurvey_2019.pdf.

329. Meyersohn, N. This is the CVS of the Future. February 16, 2019. Retrieved July 27, 2020 from https://www.cnn.com/2019/02/16/business/cvs-health-healthhub-minuteclinic-aetna/index.html.

330. Trends in Primary Care Visits. (n.d.). Retrieved July 21, 2020 from https://healthcostinstitute.org/hcci-research/trends-in-primary-care-visits.

331. University of Wisconsin Madison. Department of Obstetrics and Gynecology. Faculty and Staff Directory. Retrieved June 22, 2020 from https://www.obgyn.wisc.edu/Directory/List/Division/Academic%20Specialists%20in%20Obstetrics%20and%20Gynecology.

332. Cedars-Sinai. Can I See a Nurse Practitioner Instead of a Doctor? (n.d.). Retrieved June 20, 2020 from https://www.cedars-sinai.org/blog/

difference-nurse-practitioner-vs-doctor.html?fbclid=IwAR0oHFzCHIDSP-JC5XcxcSbTKgncNZ2pm6dRiHP0oeU5fmCNcr_HceKssC40.

333. Dozens of Pediatricians Losing Jobs as Children's Health Clinics Close. (n.d.). Retrieved June 20, 2020 from https://dfw.cbslocal.com/video/3868944-dozens-of-pediatricians-losing-jobs-as-childrens-health-clinics-close/.

334. Shinneman, S. Children's Health To Sell 13 Clinical Sites, Take a Minority Stake In New Owner MD Medical Group. Retrieved June 20, 2020 from https://www.dmagazine.com/healthcare-business/2018/05/childrens-health-to-sell-13-clinical-sites-take-a-minority-stake-in-new-owner-md-medical-group/. Published May 23, 2018.

335. Amelia Ochoa v. Mercy Health Oklahoma Communities. District Court Oklahoma County, Oklahoma. 2019. Court documents provided by plaintiff attorney G. Nix.

336. Menchine, M. D., Wiechmann, W., & Rudkin, S. Trends in Midlevel Provider Utilization in Emergency Departments from 1997 to 2006. *Academic Emergency Medicine.* 2009;16:963–969. doi:10.1111/j.1553-2712.2009.00521.x.

337. Finnegan, J. Report: 8,000 medical practices acquired by hospitals in 18 months. Retrieved June 22, 2020, from https://www.fiercehealthcare.com/practices/consolidation-trend-continues-8-000-more-hospital-owned-practices-14-000-more-hospital. Published February 21, 2019.

338. Shinneman, S. Children's Health To Sell 13 Clinical Sites, Take a Minority Stake In New Owner MD Medical Group. Retrieved June 22, 2020 from https://www.dmagazine.com/healthcare-business/2018/05/childrens-health-to-sell-13-clinical-sites-take-a-minority-stake-in-new-owner-md-medical-group/. Published May 23, 2018.

339. Goldberg, S. M.D. is no prescription for job security at hospital chains. Retrieved June 20, 2020 from https://www.chicagobusiness.com/health-care/md-no-prescription-job-security-hospital-chains. Published December 6, 2019.

340. Court, E. Medical practices have become a hot investment – are profits being put ahead of patients? Retrieved June 20, 2020 from https://www.marketwatch.com/story/doctors-are-being-bought-up-by-private-equity-and-its-your-health-on-the-line-2018-06-08?fbclid=IwAR0Adcg_WmRmgT4R6rWgI-Mpf3Y7vzSU5jsWiiZRKJ9X_Ct1Ji-cYjA4MAkY. Published June 19, 2018.

341. Ibid.

342. Physician-Owned Hospitals. (n.d.). Retrieved June 22, 2020, from https://www.cms.gov/Medicare/Fraud-and-Abuse/PhysicianSelfReferral/Physician_Owned_Hospitals.

343. Carthon, J. M., Barnes, H., & Sarik, D. A. Federal Polices Influence Access to Primary Care and Nurse Practitioner Workforce. *The Journal for Nurse Practitioners: JNP.* 2015;11(5):526–530. https://doi.org/10.1016/j.nurpra.2015.01.028.

344. Hain, D., & Fleck, L., Barriers to Nurse Practitioner Practice that Impact Healthcare Redesign. *OJIN: The Online Journal of Issues in Nursing.* 2014;19(2). Manuscript 2.

345. Federation of State Medical Boards. Increasing Scope of Practice: Critical Questions in Assuring Public Access and Safety. Draft report presented at: Annual Meeting of FSMB; February 2004.

346. AMA. State Law Chart. Retrieved February 20, 2020 from https://www.ama-assn.org/sites/ama-assn.org/files/corp/media-browser/specialty%20group/arc/ama-chart-np-practice-authority.pdf. Published 2017.

347. Juan, A. S. TMB says doctor didn't properly supervise two nurse practitioners at Optimum clinic. Retrieved February 19, 2020 from https://kfdm.com/news/local/tmb-says-doctor-didnt-properly-supervise-two-nurse-practitioners-at-optimum-clinic. Published September 12, 2018.

348. Bernard, R. Physician replacements affecting vulnerable patient populations. Medical Economics. https://www.medicaleconomics.com/med-ec-blog/physician-replacements-affecting-vulnerable-patient-populations. Published 2018. Accessed February 20, 2020.

349. Ibid.

350. Leap, E. The risks of co-signing PA and NP charts. Retrieved June 20, 2020 from https://www.kevinmd.com/blog/2018/11/the-risks-of-co-signing-pa-and-np-charts.html. Published November 7, 2018.

351. Ibid.

352. Chaiyarat SERMCHIEF, et al., Appellants, v. Mario GONZALES, et al., Respondents, and State of Missouri, Intervenor-Respondent. No. 64692. Supreme Court of Missouri, En Banc. November 22, 1983.

353. Hsu, J. Artificial intelligence could globally revolutionize health care-unless it destroys it. Retrieved June 20, 2020 from https://qz.com/1680098/ai-could-dramatically-improve-health-care-unless-it-destroys-it/. Published August 1, 2019.

354. Edwards, C. Computer says no: when AI struggles to explain its answers. Retrieved June 22, 2020 from https://eandt.theiet.org/content/articles/2018/04/computer-says-no-when-ai-struggles-to-explain-its-answers/. Published April 17, 2018.

355. Hawkins, A. J. Pilots complained about autopilot issues with Boeing jets involved in two deadly crashes. Retrieved June 10, 2020 from https://

www.theverge.com/2019/3/13/18263751/boeing-737-max-8-pilot-complaint-autopilot-mcas. Published March 13, 2019.

356. Pasztor, A., & Tangel, A. Ethiopian Airlines Pilots Initially Followed Boeing's Required Emergency Steps to Disable 737 MAX System. Wall Street Journal. Retrieved June 20, 2020 from https://www.wsj.com/articles/ethiopian-airlines-pilots-initially-followed-boeings-required-emergency-steps-to-disable-737-max-system-11554263276. Published April 3, 2019.

357. Obermeyer, Z., Powers, B., Vogeli, C., & Mullainathan, S. Dissecting racial bias in an algorithm used to manage the health of populations. *Science.* 2019;366(6464):447–453. doi:10.1126/science.aax2342.

358. Gianfrancesco, M. A., Tamang, S., Yazdany, J., & Schmajuk, G. Potential Biases in Machine Learning Algorithms Using Electronic Health Record Data. *JAMA Intern Med.* 2018;178(11):1544–1547. doi:10.1001/jamainternmed.2018.3763.

359. Hoffman, K. M., Trawalter, S., Axt, J. R., & Oliver, M. N. Racial bias in pain assessment and treatment recommendations, and false beliefs about biological differences between blacks and whites. *Proc Natl Acad Sci USA.* 2016;113(16):4296–4301. doi:10.1073/pnas.1516047113.

360. Lekesha Benson. (n.d.). "My healthy 19-year-old son told me he thought he was having a heart attack. He looked fine-I thought he was joking, but he said he was serious & that he'd collapsed outside. Without another word, I grabbed my keys, said come on, & we went to the ER. They took him straight back & a doctor never came in to see him. As a woman who has sickle cell anemia, I have more experience than most with going to the hospital, and have NEVER only seen a nurse practitioner but I was told that was normal, so it may be." Facebook Post. June 4, 2020. https://www.facebook.com/lekeshasb/posts/10214281784318534. Accessed June 4, 2020.

361. Hoffman, K. M., Trawalter, S., Axt, J. R., & Oliver, M. N. Racial bias in pain assessment and treatment recommendations, and false beliefs about biological differences between blacks and whites. *Proc Natl Acad Sci USA.* 2016;113(16):4296–4301. doi:10.1073/pnas.1516047113.

CHAPTER 6

362. H. Travers. Personal communication. April 14, 2020.

363. Ibid.

364. Scope of Practice for Nurse Practitioners. (n.d.). Retrieved June 22, 2020, from https://www.aanp.org/advocacy/advocacy-resource/position-statements/scope-of-practice-for-nurse-practitioners.

365. AAPA. Articles and Reports on the PA Profession Selected Topics. [PDF]. Accessed on June 22, 2020 from https://www.aapa.org/download/39029/.

366. Flynn, B. C. The effectiveness of nurse clinicians' service delivery. *American Journal of Public Health.* 1974;64:604–61. https://doi.org/10.2105/AJPH.64.6.604.

367. Sackett, D. L. The Burlington Randomized Trial of the Nurse Practitioner: Health Outcomes of Patients. *Annals of Internal Medicine.* 1974;80(2):137. doi:10.7326/0003-4819-80-2-137.

368. Newhouse, R. P., Stanik-Hutt, J., & White, K. M., et al. Advanced practice nurse outcomes 1990–2008: a systematic review. *Nurse Econ.* 2011;29(5):230–251.

369. Mundinger, M. O., Kane, R. L., & Lenz, E. R., et al. Primary care outcomes in patients treated by nurse practitioners or physicians: a randomized trial. *JAMA.* 2000;283(1):59–68. doi:10.1001/jama.283.1.59.

370. Grimshaw, J. So what has the Cochrane Collaboration ever done for us? A report card on the first 10 years. *Canadian Medical Association Journal.* 2004;171(7):747–749. doi:10.1503/cmaj.1041255. PMC 517860. PMID 15 451837.

371. Lewis, C. E., & Resnik, B. A. Nurse clinics and progressive ambulatory patient care. *New England Journal of Medicine.* 1967;277:1236–41. [DOI: 10.1056/NEJM196712072772305].

372. Laurant, M., van der Biezen, M., Wijers, N., Watananirun, K., Kontopantelis, E., & van Vught A. J. A. H. Nurses as substitutes for doctors in primary care. *Cochrane Database of Systematic Reviews.* 2018;7(Art): CD001271. doi: 10.1002/14651858.CD001271.pub3.

373. Mundinger, M. O., Kane, R. l., Lenz, E. R., Totten, A. M., Tsji, W. Y., & Cleary P. D., et al. Primary care outcomes in patients treated by nurse practitioners or physicians. A randomized trial. *JAMA.* 2000;283(1):59–68. doi: 10.1001/jama.283.1.59.

374. Lewis, C. E., & Resnik, B. A. Nurse clinics and progressive ambulatory patient care. *New England Journal of Medicine.* 1967;277:1236–41. doi: 10.1056/NEJM196712072772305.

375. Hemani, A., Rastegar, D. A., Hill, C., & Al–Ibrahim, M. S. A comparison of resource utilization in nurse practitioners and physicians. *Effective Clinical Practice.* 1999;2(6):258–265. [PUBMED: 10788023].

376. Ibid.

377. Mundinger, M. O., Kane, R. l., Lenz, E. R., Totten, A. M., Tsji, W. Y., & Cleary, P. D., et al. Primary care outcomes in patients treated by nurse practitioners or physicians. A randomized trial. *JAMA.* 2000;283(1):59–68. doi: 10.1001/jama.283.1.59.

378. Sox, H. C. Independent primary care practice by nurse practitioners. *JAMA.* 2000;283(1):106–108.

379. Contributor, N. T. What are the differences in nurse practitioner training and scope of practice in the US and UK? Retrieved September 10, 2020 from https://www.nursingtimes.net/roles/district-and-community-nurses/what-are-the-differences-in-nurse-practitioner-training-and-scope-of-practice-in-the-us-and-uk-09-07-2010/. Published August 2, 2019.

380. Lattimer, V., Sassi, F., George, S., Moore, M., Turnbull, J., & Mullee, M. Cost analysis of nurse telephone consultation in out of hours primary care: evidence from a randomised controlled trial. *BMJ*. 2000;320:1053–1057. doi: 10.1136/bmj.320.7241.1053.

381. Campbell, J. L., Fletcher, E., Britten, N., Green, C., Holt, T. A., & Lattimer, V., et al. Telephone triage for management of same–day consultation requests in general practice (the ESTEEM trial): a cluster randomised controlled trial and cost–consequence analysis. *The Lancet*. 2014;384:1859–1868. doi: http://dx.doi.org/10.1016/S0140–6736(14)61058–8.

382. Shum, C., Humphreys, A., Wheeler, D., Cochrane, M. A., Skoda, S., & Clement, S. Nurse management of patients with minor illnesses in general practice: multicentre randomised controlled trial. *BMJ*. 2000;320:1038–1043. doi: 10.1136/bmj.320.7241.1038.

383. Venning, P., Durie, A., Roland, M., Roberts, C., & Leese, B. Randomised controlled trail comparing cost effectiveness of general practitioners and nurse practitioners in primary care. *BMJ*. 2000;320:1048–1053. doi: 10.1136/bmj.320.7241.1048.

384. Moher, M., Yudkin, P., Wright, L., Turner, R., Fuller, A., & Schofield, T., et al. for the Assessment of Implementation Strategies (ASSIST) Trial Collaborative Group. Cluster randomised controlled trial to compare three methods of promoting secondary prevention of coronary heart disease in primary care. *BMJ*. 2001;322:1338–1342. doi: 10.1136/bmj.322.7298.1338.

385. Larsson, I., Fridlund, B., Arvidsson, B., Teleman, A., & Bergman, S. Randomized controlled trial of a nurse–led rheumatology clinic for monitoring biological therapy. *Journal of Advanced Nursing*. 2013;70(1):164–175. doi: 10.1111/jan.12183.

386. Chan, D., Harris, S., Roderick, P., Brown, D., & Patel, P. A randomised controlled trial of structured nurse–led outpatient clinic follow–up for dyspeptic patients after direct access gastroscopy. *BMC Gastroenterology*. 2009;9:12. doi: 10.1186/1471–230X–9–12.

387. Dierick–van Daele, A. T., Metsemakers, J. F., Derckx, E. W., Spreeuwenberg, C., & Vrijhoef, H. J. Nurse practitioners substituting for general practitioners: randomized controlled trial. *Journal of Advanced Nursing*. 2009;65(2):391–401. doi: 10.1111/j.1365–2648.2008.04888.x.

388. Houweling, S. T., Kleefstra, N., Hateren, K. J. J., Groenier, K. H., Meyboomde Jong, B., & Bilo, H. J. G. Can diabetes management be safely transferred

to practice nurses in a primary care setting? A randomised controlled trial. *Journal of Clinical Nursing.* 2011;20:1264–1272. doi: 10.1111/jan.12120.

389. Voogdt–Pruis, H. R., Beusmans, G. H. , Gorgels, A. P., Kester, A. D., & Ree, J. W. Effectiveness of nurse–delivered cardiovascular risk management in primary care: a randomised trial. *British Journal of General Practice.* 2010;60(570):40–46. doi: 10.3399/bjgp10X482095.

390. Sackett, D. L., Spitzer, W. O., Gent, M., Roberts, R.S. (in collaboration with: Hay, W. I., Lefroy, G. M., Sweeny, G. P., Vandervlist, I., Sibley, J. C., Chambers, L. W., Goldsmith, C. H., Macpherson, A. S., & McAuley, R. G. The Burlington randomized trial of the nurse practitioner: health outcomes of patients. *Annals of Internal Medicine.* 1974;80:137–142. doi: 10.7326/0003–4819–80–2–137.

391. Chambers, L. W., & West, A. E. St John's randomized trial of the family practice nurse: health outcomes of patients. *International Journal of Epidemiology.* 1978;7(2):153–161. doi: 10.1093/ije/7.2.153.

392. Sanne, I., Orrell, C., Fox, M. P., Conradie, F., Ive, P., & Zeinecker, J., et al. CIPRA–SA Study Team. Nurse versus doctor management of HIV–infected patients receiving antiretroviral therapy (CIPRA–SA): a randomised non–inferiority trial. *The Lancet.* 2010;376(9734):33–40. doi: 10.1016/S0140–6736(10)60894–X.

393. Iglesias, B., Ramos, F., Serrano, B., Fàbregas, M., Sánchez, C., & Garcíam, J., et al. A randomized controlled trial of nurses vs. doctors in the resolution of acute disease of low complexity in primary care. *Journal of Advanced Nursing.* 2013;69(11):2446–2457. doi: 10.1111/jan.12120.

394. Larsson, I., Fridlund, B., Arvidsson, B., Teleman, A., & Bergman, S. Randomized controlled trial of a nurse–led rheumatology clinic for monitoring biological therapy. *Journal of Advanced Nursing.* 2013;70(1):164–175. doi: 10.1111/jan.12183.

395. Martsolf, G., Auerbach, D., & Arifkhanova, A. Front Matter. In *The Impact of Full Practice Authority for Nurse Practitioners and Other Advanced Practice Registered Nurses in Ohio* (pp. I–II). Santa Monica, Calif.: RAND Corporation; 2015. Retrieved June 13, 2020, from www.jstor.org/stable/10.7249/j.ctt14bs1z6.1.

396. Stange, K. "How Does Provider Supply and Regulation Influence Health Care Markets? Evidence from Nurse Practitioners and Physician Assistants," *Journal of Health Economics,* Vol. 33, January 2014, pp. 1–27.

397. McCleery, E., Christensen, V., & Peterson, K., et al. Evidence Brief: The Quality of Care Provided by Advanced Practice Nurses. 2014 Sep. In: VA Evidence Synthesis Program Evidence Briefs [Internet]. Washington (DC):

Department of Veterans Affairs (US). Retrieved May 20, 2019 from: https://www.ncbi.nlm.nih.gov/books/NBK384613/.

398. Ibid.

399. Silber, J. H., Kennedy, S. K., & Even-Shoshan, O., et al. Anesthesiologist direction and patient outcomes. *Anesthesiology.* 2000;93(1):152–163.

400. Spitzer, W. The Nurse Practitioner Revisited—Slow Death of a Good Idea. *N Engl J Med.* 1984;310:1049–1051. doi:10.1056/NEJM198404193101610.

401. AAPA Responds to AAEM Position Statement on Advanced Practice Providers. Retrieved June 20, 2020 from https://www.aapa.org/news-central/2019/02/aapa-responds-aaem-position-statement-ad-vanced-practice-providers/. Published February 12, 2019.

402. Gallego, B., Runciman, W.B., & Perez-Concha, O., et al. The management of severe hypertension in Australian general practice. *BMC Health Serv Res.* 2013;13:414. https://doi.org/10.1186/1472-6963-13-414.

403. Kleinpell, A. P. A., Ruth M. Ely, Wesley, E., & Grabenkort, Robert, P. A. Nurse practitioners and physician assistants in the intensive care unit: An evidence-based review. *Critical Care Medicine.* 2008;36(10):2888–2897. doi:10.1097/CCM.0b013e318186ba8c.

CHAPTER 7

404. O. Weinhold. Personal communication. April 21, 2019.

405. D. Grieger. Personal communication. October 18, 2018.

406. N. Chesnavich. Personal communication. January 1, 2019.

407. Shoemaker, J. K. Characteristics of a nursing diagnosis. *Occupational Health Nursing.* 1985;33(8):387–389. https://doi.org/10.1177/216507998503300803.

408. J. D'Aprile. Personal communication. April 10, 2020.

409. C. Ferguson. Personal communication. April 10, 2020.

410. H. Travers. Personal communication. April 16, 2020.

411. O. Weinhold.; Personal communication. April 21, 2019.

412. Epstein, Ronald. *Attending: Medicine, Mindfulness, and Humanity.* Scribner, an Imprint of Simon & Schuster, Inc.; 2018.

413. D. Grieger. Personal communication. October 18, 2018.

414. Judge-Ellis, T., Wilson, T. Time and NP Practice: Naming, Claiming, and Explaining the Role of Nurse Practitioners. *The Journal for Nurse Practitioners.* 2017;13(9):583–589.

415. What's a Nurse Practitioner (NP)? (n.d.). AANP. Retrieved June 20, 2020 from https://www.aanp.org/all-about-nps/what-is-an-np/.

416. Role Definition of Family Medicine. American Academy of Family Physicians. Retrieved June 20, 2020 from https://www.aafp.org/about/policies/all/family-medicine-roledefinition.html. Published October 7, 2019.

417. About Internal Medicine. (n.d.). ACP Online. Retrieved June 20, 2020 from https://www.acponline.org/about-acp/about-internal-medicine.

418. Hemani, A., Rastegar, D. A., Hill, C., & al-Ibrahim, M. S. A comparison of resource utilization in nurse practitioners and physicians. *Eff Clin Pract.* 1999;2(6):258–265.

419. Subramanian, U., Kerr, E. A., Klamerus, M. L., Zikmund-Fisher, B. J., Holleman, R. G., & Hofer, T. P. Treatment decisions for complex patients: differences between primary care physicians and midlevel providers. *Am J Manag Care.* 2009;15(6):373–380.

420. Corinthia [name withheld for privacy]. Personal interview. April 20, 2019.

421. Goldberg, G. A., Jolly, D. M., Hosek, S., & Chu, D. S. Physician's extenders' performance in Air Force clinics. *Med Care.* 1981;19(9):951–965. doi:10.1097/00005650-198109000-00007.

422. Morrison, F., Shubina, M., Goldberg, S. I., & Turchin, A. Performance of primary care physicians and other providers on key process measures in the treatment of diabetes. *Diabetes Care.* 2013;36(5):1147–1152. doi:10.2337/dc12-1382.

423. Kurtzman, E. T., Barnow, B. S. A Comparison of Nurse Practitioners, Physician Assistants, and Primary Care Physicians' Patterns of Practice and Quality of Care in Health Centers. *Med Care.* 2017;55(6):615–622. doi:10.1097/MLR. 0000000000000689.

424. Flynn, B. C. The effectiveness of nurse clinicians' service delivery. *American Journal of Public Health.* 1974;64(6):604–611. doi: 10.2105/ajph.64.6.604.

425. Mizrahi, D. J., Parker, L., Zoga, A. M., Levin, D. C. National Trends in the Utilization of Skeletal Radiography from 2003 to 2015. *J Am Coll Radiol.* 2018;15(10):1408–1414. doi:10.1016/j.jacr.2017.10.007.

426. N. Al-Agba. Personal medical records.

427. APA Rosenberg, Karen NPs and Physician Assistants Order more Imaging Tests than Primary Care Physicians, *AJN The American Journal of Nursing.* March 2015;115(3):63. doi: 10.1097/01.NAJ.0000461827.78558.29.

428. Goldberg, G. A., Jolly, D. M., Hosek, S., Chu, D. S. Physician's extenders' performance in Air Force clinics. *Med Care.* 1981;19(9):951–965. doi:10.1097/00005650-198109000-00007.

429. Hemani, A., Rastegar, D.A., Hill, C., & Al-Ibrahim, M. (1999). A comparison of resource utilization in nurse practitioners and physicians. *Effective Clinical Practice: ECP.* 1999;2(6): 258–65.f.

430. Hughes, D. R., Jiang, M., & Duszak, R. A Comparison of Diagnostic Imaging Ordering Patterns Between Advanced Practice Clinicians and

Primary Care Physicians Following Office-Based Evaluation and Management Visits. *JAMA Intern Med.* 2015;175(1):101–107. doi:10.1001/jamainternmed.2014.6349.

431. Hughes, D. R., Jiang, M., & Duszak, R. A Comparison of Diagnostic Imaging Ordering Patterns Between Advanced Practice Clinicians and Primary Care Physicians Following Office-Based Evaluation and Management Visits. *JAMA Intern Med.* 2015;175(1):101–107. doi:10.1001/jamainternmed.2014.6349.

432. Jalian, H. R., & Avram, M. M. Mid-Level Practitioners in Dermatology: A Need for Further Study and Oversight. *JAMA Dermatol.* 2014;150(11):1149–1151. doi:10.1001/jamadermatol.2014.1922.

433. Nault, A., Zhang, C., Kim, K., Saha, S., Bennett, D. D., & Xu, Y. G. Biopsy Use in Skin Cancer Diagnosis: Comparing Dermatology Physicians and Advanced Practice Professionals. *JAMA Dermatol.* 2015;151(8):899–902. doi:10.1001/jamadermatol.2015.0173.

434. Coldiron, B., & Ratnarathorn, M. Scope of Physician Procedures Independently Billed by Mid-Level Providers in the Office Setting. *JAMA Dermatol.* 2014;150(11):1153–1159. doi:10.1001/jamadermatol.2014.1773.

435. Hafner, K. (n.d.). Skin Cancers Rise, Along with Questionable Treatments. *New York Times.* Retrieved from https://www.nytimes.com/2017/11/20/health/dermatology-skin-cancer.html.

436. Confidential patient. Personal communication. March 10, 2019.

437. Smith, M. D. Best care at lower cost: the path to continuously learning health care in America. Washington, D.C.: National Academies Press; 2013.

438. Lohr, R. H., West, C. P., & Beliveau, M, et al. Comparison of the quality of patient referrals from physicians, physician assistants, and nurse practitioners. *Mayo Clin Proc.* 2013;88(11):1266–1271. doi:10.1016/j.mayocp.2013.08.013.

439. R. McPherson. Personal communication, April 20, 2020.

440. Muench, U., Perloff, J., Thomas, C., & Buerhaus, P. Prescribing Practices by Nurse Practitioners and Primary Care Physicians: A Descriptive Analysis of Medicare Beneficiaries. *Journal of Nursing Regulation.* 2017;8(1):21–30. doi:https://doi.org/10.1016/S2155-8256(17)30071-6.

441. Cipher, D. J., Hooker, R. S., & Guerra P. Prescribing trends by nurse practitioners and physician assistants in the United States. *J Am Acad Nurse Pract.* 2006;18(6):291–296. doi:10.1111/j.1745-7599.2006.00133.x.

442. Yang, B. K., Burcu, M., Safer, D. J., Trinkoff, A. M., & Zito, J. M. Comparing Nurse Practitioner and Physician Prescribing of Psychotropic Medications for Medicaid-Insured Youths. *J Child Adolesc Psychopharmacol.* 2018;28(3):166–172. doi:10.1089/cap.2017.0112.

443. Dvorin, E. L., Lamb, M. C., Monlezun, D. J., Boese, A. C., Bazzano, L.A., & Price-Haywood, E. G. High Frequency of Systemic Corticosteroid Use for Acute Respiratory Tract Illnesses in Ambulatory Settings. *JAMA Intern Med*. 2018;178(6):852–854. doi:10.1001/jamainternmed.2018.0103.

444. Roumie, C., & Halasa, N. Differences in antibiotic prescribing among residents, physicians, and non-physician clinicians. *American Journal of Medicine*. June 2005;118(6):641–648.

445. Mafi, J. N., Wee, C. C, Davis, R. B., & Landon, B. E. Comparing Use of Low-Value Health Care Services Among U.S. Advanced Practice Clinicians and Physicians. *Ann Intern Med*. 2016;165(4):237–244. doi:10.7326/M15-2152.

446. Schmidt, M., Spencer, M., & Davidson, L. (2018). Patient, Provider, and Practice Characteristics Associated with Inappropriate Antimicrobial Prescribing in Ambulatory Practices. *Infection Control & Hospital Epidemiology*. 2017;39(3):307–315. doi:10.1017/ice.2017.263.

447. N. Al-Agba, personal patient case.

448. Hollinghurst, S., Horrocks, S., Anderson, E., & Salisbury, C., Comparing the cost of nurse practitioners and GPs in primary care: modelling economic data from randomised trials. *British Journal of General Practice*. 2006; 56 (528): 530–535.

449. Allen, J. K., Dennison Himmelfarb, C. R., Szanton, S. L., & Frick, K. D. Cost-effectiveness of nurse practitioner/community health worker care to reduce cardiovascular health disparities. *The Journal of Cardiovascular Nursing*. 2014;29(4):308–314. doi: 10.1097/jcn.0b013e3182945243.

450. American Association of Nurse Practitioners. Strategic Plan Accordion [Screenshot].

451. Spitzer, W. The Nurse Practitioner Revisited—Slow Death of a Good Idea. *N Engl J Med*. 1984; 310:1049–1051 doi: 10.1056/NEJM198404193101610.

452. NP Payment Parity Bill Signed into Law, Oregon Nurses Association Newsletter 2016, page 670. Retrieved June 20, 2020 from https://www.oregonrn.org/page/670.

453. Altimari, D. Nurse-midwives seek pay parity with OB-GYNs. Retrieved June 20, 2020 from https://www.courant.com/politics/capitol-watch/hc-pol-nurse-midwives-pay-equity-20190228-ojopek4yd5ah5kvifqshhs-dej4-. story.html?fbclid=IwAR3S07T7uNmGnltgAYRhrFL0WwyxG0WefrB-f_3GPzx02KXlY4yVymJEC30M. Published February 28, 2019.

454. Executive Order on Protecting and Improving Medicare for Our Nation's Seniors. (n.d.). Retrieved June 20, 2020 from https://www.whitehouse.gov/presidential-actions/executive-order-protecting-improving-medicare-nations-seniors/.

455. Admin. MSSNY Statement in Response to President's Executive Order on Medicare. Retrieved February 20, 2020 from http://www.mssnyenews. org/press-releases/mssny-statement-in-response-to-presidents-executive-order-on-medicare/?fbclid=IwAR3EZOohVsY2a4IXc76eTPK_7EqirO-0zUNbLBvVyqQvvt4osQPtBXTy6-78. Published February 10, 2020.

456. CMA responds to Trump order: Protecting and Improving Medicare for our Nation's Seniors. (n.d.). Retrieved February 20, 2020 from https://www.cmadocs.org/newsroom/news/view/ArticleId/28181/CMA-President-Responds-to-Trump-Administration-s-Executive-Order-on-Protecting-and-Improving-Medicare-for-our-Nation-s-Seniors?fbclid=IwAR396l-jSw77Z9m12wfph_gWAR3ubNKF-rTeKNjhBMGMxhI6-E-kRpeQKYp8.

457. TMA Says "No" to Federal Scope Expansion Under President's Medicare Executive Order. (n.d.). Retrieved February 25, 2020 from https://www.texmed.org/TexasMedicineDetail.aspx?id=51707&utm_source=Informz&utm_medium=Email&utm_campaign=TMT&fbclid=IwAR3lpSE-FOiMAK2xxSfnkSO5OHWMd46lAghD0Ju5T3cZG6g_NV3nUrDGU834.

458. How Much Should NPs Expect to Pay a Collaborating Physician? Retrieved June 22, 2020, from https://thriveap.com/blog/how-much-should-nps-expect-pay-collaborating-physician. Published April 27, 2017.

459. How Much Should a Collaborating Physician Be Paid? Retrieved June 10, 2020 from https://www.medscape.com/viewarticle/908194. Published January 29, 2019.

460. Ruggiero v Miles. (n.d.). Retrieved June 20, 2020 from https://law.justia.com/cases/new-york/appellate-division-third-department/2015/518595.html.

461. Oliva health care priorities passes house. Retrieved June 10, 2020 from https://www.nwfdailynews.com/news/20200308/oliva-health-care-priorities-passes-house. Published March 8, 2020.

CHAPTER 8

462. Pellegrino, E. D., & Pellegrino, A. A. Humanism and Ethics in Roman Medicine: Translation and Commentary on a Text of Scribonius Largus. *Literature and Medicine*. 1988;7(1):22–38. doi: 10.1353/lm.2011.0164.

463. Federation of State Medical Boards, Assessing the Scope of Practice in Health Care Delivery: Critical Questions in Assuring Public Access and Safety. Retrieved June 20, 2020 from http://www.fsmb.org/pdf/2005-gr-pol-scope-oftpractice.pdf. Published 2005.

464. Painter, R. What you should know about certified registered nurse anesthetists (CRNA) and anesthesia medical malpractice. https://www.painterfirm.com/a/707/What-you-should-know-about-certified-registered-nurse-anesthetists-CRNA-and-anesthesia-medical-malpractice. Published January 22, 2019. Accessed August 10, 2020.

465. Ducey, J., & Williams, M. Fake Urgent Care centers popping up across Arizona. Retrieved June 10, 2020 from https://www.abc15.com/news/let-joe-know/fake-urgent-care-centers-popping-up-across-arizona?fbclid=IwAR0OhJvO5T8ysdYMdgfU5Eo8-unxksQr006Vam0CP_kCP-CNYk5IH5AlgKg. Published February 24, 2020.

466. Hadley, E. H. Nurses and prescriptive authority: a legal and economic analysis. *Am J Law Med.* 1989;15(2–3):245–299. (citing Hurdis Griffith, Nursing Practice: Substitute or Complement According to Economic Theory, *Nursing Econ.* Mar- Apr 1984: 105, 108).

467. Does The Increasing Prevalence Of Nurse Practitioners (NP) Providing Primary Care Affect Patient Safety? Retrieved June 10, 2020 from https://www.medicalmalpracticelawyers.com/nurse-practitioner-malpractice/increasing-use-nurse-practitioners-np-affect-patient-safety/. Published June 27, 2017.

468. Fein v. Permanente Medical Group S.F. No. 24336. Retrieved June 10, 2020 from https://law.justia.com/cases/california/supreme-court/3d/38/137.html. 1985.

469. *Simonson v. Keppard*, 225 S.W.3d 868 (Tex. App. 2007).

470. Lattimore vs Dickey. Retrieved June 10, 2020 from https://law.justia.com/cases/california/court-of-appeal/2015/h040126.html. 2015.

471. CPH and Associates. Who can testify as to the standard of care of a nurse practitioner? Accessed May 28, 2019 at https://www.cphins.com/who-can-testify-as-to-the-standard-of-care-of-a-nurse-practitioner/.

472. Tammelleo, A. David. Nurse practitioner not liable for failure to diagnose. The Free Library. https://www.thefreelibrary.com/Nurse practitioner not liable for failure to diagnose.-a0167508128. Published July, 1, 2007. Accessed June 9, 2020.

473. Does The Increasing Prevalence Of Nurse Practitioners (NP) Providing Primary Care Affect Patient Safety? Medical Malpractice Lawyers. Retrieved February 20, 2020 from www.medicalmalpracticelawyers.com/nurse-practitioner-malpractice/increasing-use-nurse-practitioners-np-affect-patient-safety/. Published June 27, 2017.

474. Federal Trade Commission. Truth in Advertising. Retrieved July 27, 2020 from https://www.ftc.gov/news-events/media-resources/truth-advertising.

475. Ideal Medical Care. I'm a doctor. I'm on Medicaid. I work as a waitress. Retrieved from http://www.idealmedicalcare.org/im-a-doctor-im-on-medicaid-i-work-as-a-waitress/. Published September 9, 2016.

476. Physician Workforce Trends to Watch in 2020. Retrieved from https://www.jacksonphysiciansearch.com/physician-workforce-2020/?fbclid=I-wAR2XWjuc2cJFHko9DrbIuN7RXA0ybul-Vp60WZZd7RRbdLnXyze0wt-ME9yQ. Published February 18, 2020.

477. National Resident Matching Program. The Match. [PDF] Retrieved June 20, 2020 from http://www.nrmp.org/wp-content/uploads/2015/03/ADT2015_final.pdf. Published 2015.

478. Primary Care Pathway Program (MD to RN to NP). (n.d.). Retrieved June 20, 2020 from http://www.clinicalclerkship.org/md-to-np-program/?f-bclid=IwAR3yXx6bTvZGNLM90wDe4GQYZFHCsgNZZM_JZCvhmX-2Qz7w1jUZ2bvNwofY.

479. Resident Physician Shortage Reduction Act of 2019. SB 348, 116th Congress. February 6, 2019.

480. Fagan, E. B., Gibbons, C., Finnegan, S. C., Petterson, S., Peterson, K. E., Phillips, R.L., & Bazemore, A. W. Family Medicine Graduate Proximity to Their Site of Training: Policy Options for Improving the Distribution of Primary Care Access. *Fam Med.* 2015;47(2):124–130.

481. Weigley, S., Hess, A. E. M., & Sauter, M. B. Doctor shortage could take turn for the worse. Retrieved June 20, 2020 from https://www.usatoday.com/story/money/business/2012/10/20/doctors-shortage-least-most/1644837/. Published October 20, 2012.

482. Missouri Division of Professional Registration. Assistant Physicians. (n.d.). Retrieved July 27, 2020 from https://pr.mo.gov/assistantphysicians.asp Assistant Physician Association. Association of Medical Doctor Assistant Physicians. (n.d.). Retrieved June 10, 2020 from https://assistantphysicianassociation.com/.

483. Ibid.

484. Staff Reports. Bill's aim is more rural doctors. PaulsValleyDemocrat.com. Retrieved June 10, 2020 from https://www.paulsvalleydailydemocrat.com/news/local_news/bill-s-aim-is-more-rural-doctors/article_6045b343-6ee1-55aa-8cc4-847b1fea4169.html?fbclid=IwAR2rPm-mK66zlFHC3-zToz99hrlmXe0Q2mhPmbQXqA9dkC-rT3PT8CPLPFCI. Published February 13, 2020.

485. Davidson, J. Perspective: VA doctor shortage fueled by management issues, poor pay. Retrieved February 19, 2020 from https://www.washingtonpost.com/news/powerpost/wp/2018/07/16/va-doctor-shortage-fueled-by-management-issues-poor-pay/?noredirect=on&utm_term=.31d38927acf1. Published July 16, 2018.

486. The Physicians Foundation 2016 Physician Survey. Retrieved June 10, 2020 from https://physiciansfoundation.org/research-insights/physician-survey/. Published January 30, 2018.

487. Shute, D. Is it time to lift the ban on physician-owned hospitals? Retrieved June 10, 2020 from https://www.medicaleconomics.com/business/it-time-lift-ban-physician-owned-hospitals. Published May 16, 2018.

488. CBS Sacramento. (2020, June 30). Audit: California Nursing Board Faked Docs On Investigations. Retrieved August 07, 2020, from https://sacramento.cbslocal.com/2020/06/30/audit-california-nursing-board-faked-docs-on-investigations/.

489. Coldiron, B., Ratnarathorn M. Scope of Physician Procedures Independently Billed by Mid-Level Providers in the Office Setting. *JAMA Dermatol.* 2014;150(11):1153–1159. doi:10.1001/jamadermatol.2014.1773.

490. Ibid.

491. Bertness, Janette A. Rhode Island Nurse Practitioners: Are They Legally Practicing Medicine Without a License? *Roger Williams University Law Review.* 2009;14(2): 2. Available at: http://docs.rwu.edu/rwu_LR/vol14/iss2/2.

492. Truth in Healthcare Marketing Act of 2017. HR 3928, 115th Congress, October 3, 2017.

493. New Bill Would Expand the Sunshine Act to Cover Physician Assistants and Advance Practice Nurses. (n.d.). Retrieved from https://www.natlawreview.com/article/new-bill-would-expand-sunshine-act-to-cover-physician-assistants-and-advance?fbclid=IwAR2sk-l6OZQb_t_vVRBkcVRNyEAHFTTPs2kY9aZwa3L9bVOZ6kMXjth-DtWc.

494. Bertness, Janette A. Rhode Island Nurse Practitioners: Are They Legally Practicing Medicine Without a License? *Roger Williams University Law Review.* 2009;14(2): 2. Available at: http://docs.rwu.edu/rwu_LR/vol14/iss2/2.

495. Brous, E. A. The Nurse Practitioner. *The Nurse Practitioner.* 2017;42(3): 8–11. Brous, Edith Ann BSN, MS, MPH, JD, RN.

496. CRICO. Medical Malpractice Frequency Decreased Over 10-year Period. Published February 12, 2019. Retrieved July 27, 2020 from https://www.rmf.harvard.edu/About-CRICO/Media/Press-Releases/News/2019/February/Medical-Malpractice-Case-Frequency-Decreased-over-10-year-Period#:~:text=A%20new%20report%20issued%20by%20CRICO%20Strategies%2C%20Medical,frequency%2C%20payment%2C%20and%20root%20causes%20of%20preventable%20harm.

497. Troxel, D. B. (n.d.). Nurse Practitioner Closed Claims Study. Retrieved June 10, 2020 from https://www.thedoctors.com/the-doctors-advocate/first-quarter-2018/nurse-practitioner-closed-claims-study/.

498. Richards, E., & Rathbun, K. Law and the Physician: A Practical Guide. Little, Brown and Company; 1993.

499. Goldacre, M. J., Evans, J., & Lambert, T. W. Media criticism of doctors: review of UK junior doctors' concerns raised in surveys. *BMJ*. 2003;326(7390):629–630. doi:10.1136/bmj.326.7390.629.

500. Robert Wood Johnson Foundation. Grant Number 75928. Grants Explorer https://www.rwjf.org/en/how-we-work/grants-explorer.html. Accessed June 12, 2020.

501. Jensen, E. Call The Midwives, But Ring The Doctors, Too. Retrieved February 20, 2020 from https://www.npr.org/sections/publiceditor/2018/09/27/650057708/call-the-midwives-but-ring-the-doctors-too?fbclid=IwAR2sgpV-AeVNZQzk4-UxQXo4uKjlP4w3r32SN_2I4X-TyJLg4MvPYmM66Yc4. Published September 27, 2018.

502. Appleton, A. (n.d.). This Fresno State nursing program was never accredited. Now alumni credentials are at risk. Retrieved May 28, 2020 from https://www.fresnobee.com/news/local/education/article227671044.html?fbclid=IwAR0V-olzLhjZOf3i08zevN5CI56Fff341D5FO2siV8EeS-6GX7V_L73910dc.

503. HR Goals Healthcare Recruiting Executive Search. (n.d.). Retrieved June 10, 2020 from https://www.apnandpsychrecruiting.com/.

504. Starfield, B., Shi, L., & Macinko, J. Contribution of primary care to health systems and health. *Milbank Q*. 2005;83(3):457–502. doi:10.1111/j.1468-0009.2005.00409.x.

505. Pereira Gray, D. J., Sidaway-Lee, K., & White, E., et al. Continuity of care with doctors—a matter of life and death? A systematic review of continuity of care and mortality. *BMJ Open*. 2018;8:e021161. doi: 10.1136/bmjopen-2017-021161.

506. Anonymous. Personal communication. April 1, 2020.

507. Aintablian,H.It'stimewetaughtLeadershipinMedicalSchoolCommonSense. https://www.aaemrsa.org/UserFiles/file/RSAPresident.pdf?fbclid=IwAR0vI6SQlkRs0cA0VnOgdf2RM09wsq_m3VKTHYsT8B8BtBu_QFYpfyzWvEw. Published 2020. Accessed June 22, 2020.

508. Emanuel, E. J., & Fuchs, V. R. Shortening Medical Training by 30%. *JAMA*. 2012;307(11):1143. doi: 10.1001/jama.2012.292.

509. Does the Increasing Prevalence Of Nurse Practitioners (NP) Providing Primary Care Affect Patient Safety? Medical Malpractice Lawyers.com. Retrieved June 10, 2020 from www.medicalmalpracticelawyers.com/nurse-practitioner-malpractice/increasing-use-nurse-practitioners-np-affect-patient-safety/. Published June 27, 2017.

510. Anonymous. Personal communication. June 1, 2019.

CONCLUSION

511. Admin.MercyAnnouncesNewLeaderinElReno.RetrievedMay30,2019from https://oknursingtimes.com/031215/mercy-announces-new-leader-in-el-reno/. Published September 10, 2017.

512. J. Reames Doximity Profile. Retrieved at https://www.doximity.com/profiles/6ed7596b-fed0-4b6b-aa47-e9f680285495. Accessed on June 13, 2020.

513. Providers. Veterans Memorial Hospital. Retrieved August 2, 2020 from https://www.veteransmemorialhospital.com/category/providers/.

514. A. Thompson Doximity Profile. Retrieved at https://www.doximity.com/profiles/584e6a0f-24d8-43c1-94f0-a1d7200624cf. Accessed on August 2, 2020.

515. T. Dunn. Personal communication, July 29, 2020.

516. T. Dunn. Personal communication, July 29, 2020.

517. Joyce, K. Hero 'Miracle on the Hudson' pilot blasts 'absurd' lack of training in wake of fatal Ethiopian Airlines crash. Retrieved June 20, 2020 from https://www.foxnews.com/us/hero-pilot-who-landed-plane-in-hudson-river-blasts-pilot-training-in-wake-of-ethiopian-airlines-crash. Published March 30, 2019.

518. Meseret, E. Ethiopian Airlines says pilots got appropriate training. Retrieved June 20, 2020 from https://phys.org/news/2019-03-ethiopian-airlines.html. Published March 25, 2019.

519. Anonymous. Personal communication. April 3, 2019.

520. Advancing Aviation Safety and Security since 1931. (n.d.). Retrieved June 20, 2020 from http://www.alpa.org/news-and-events/air-line-pilot-magazine/colgan-3407-10-years-later.

521. Doctor fired after criticizing his hospital for coronavirus response. *LA Times*. Retrieved June 20, 2020 from https://www.latimes.com/world-nation/story/2020-04-03/fired-coronavirus-doctor. Published April 4, 2020.

522. Completes Previously Announced Transaction with Blackstone. (n.d.). TeamHealth.com. Retrieved June 20, 2020 from https://www.teamhealth.com/news-and-resources/press-release/blackstone/.

523. Chang, D. (2020, April 17). HCA hospitals restrict use of N95 masks for healthcare workers. Retrieved September 27, 2020, from https://www.miamiherald.com/news/coronavirus/article242084781.html.

524. Associated Press. Nurses suspended for refusing to treat coronavirus patients without N95 masks. Retrieved June 20, 2020 from https://nypost.com/2020/04/16/nurses-suspended-for-refusing-to-treat-patients-wit

hout-n95-masks/?fbclid=IwAR0p76zPTiwaj2BE5FFb7sdnvBfeWivSN-me1ogKHlh2evDJJ63j-fdlIcWk. Published April 16, 2020.

525. Klein, M., & Landman, B. Mount Sinai hospital leaders holed up in Florida vacation homes during coronavirus crisis. Retrieved June 10, 2020 from https://nypost.com/2020/03/28/mount-sinai-hospital-leaders-holed-up-in-florida-vacation-homes-during-coronavirus-crisis/. Published March 28, 2020.

526. Press, A. NYC mayor urges national enlistment program for doctors. PBS.org. Retrieved June 10, 2020 from https://www.pbs.org/newshour/health/nyc-mayor-urges-national-enlistment-program-for-doctors. Published April 3, 2020.

527. Norvell, K., & O'Donnell, J. Thousands of US medical workers furloughed, laid off as routine patient visits drop during coronavirus pandemic. *USA Today*. Retrieved June 10, 2020 from https://www.usatoday.com/story/news/health/2020/04/02/coronavirus-pandemic-jobs-us-health-care-workers-furloughed-laid-off/5102320002/. Published April 2, 2020.

528. Maass, B. Denver Health Executives Get Bonuses 1 Week After Workers Asked To Take Cuts. Retrieved June 10, 2020 from https://denver.cbslocal.com/2020/04/24/coronavirus-denver-health-bonus-ceo-pay-cuts/?fbclid=IwAR3I85c2vleOEXk5eqIQjY85V_6cbMiE1CrJz3UNDWyQDHRG-Vd-oZWtsF9M. Published April 24, 2020.

CPSIA information can be obtained
at www.ICGtesting.com
Printed in the USA
LVHW052214251120
672641LV00007B/358

9 781627 343169